The Diffusion of Western Loanwords
in Contemporary Japanese

Hituzi Linguistics in English

No. 5 *Communicating Skills of Intention*   Tsutomu Sakamoto
No. 6 *A Pragmatic Approach to the Generation and Gender Gap*
       in Japanese Politeness Strategies   Toshihiko Suzuki
No. 7 *Japanese Women's Listening Behavior in Face-to-face Conversation*
                                                                Sachie Miyazaki
No. 8 *An Enterprise in the Cognitive Science of Language*   Tetsuya Sano et al.
No. 9 *Syntactic Structure and Silence*   Hisao Tokizaki
No. 10 *The Development of the Nominal Plural Forms in Early Middle English*
                                                                Ryuichi Hotta
No. 11 *Chunking and Instruction*   Takayuki Nakamori
No. 12 *Detecting and Sharing Perspectives Using Causals in Japanese*   Ryoko Uno
No. 13 *Discourse Representation of Temporal Relations in the So-Called*
        Head-Internal Relatives   Kuniyoshi Ishikawa
No. 14 *Features and Roles of Filled Pauses in Speech Communication*   Michiko Watanabe
No. 15 *Japanese Loanword Phonology*   Masahiko Mutsukawa
No. 16 *Derivational Linearization at the Syntax-Prosody Interface*   Kayono Shiobara
No. 17 *Polysemy and Compositionality*   Tatsuya Isono
No. 18 *fMRI Study of Japanese Phrasal Segmentation*   Hideki Oshima
No. 19 *Typological Studies on Languages in Thailand and Japan*   Tadao Miyamoto et al.
No. 20 *Repetition, Regularity, Redundancy*   Yasuyo Moriya
No. 21 *A Cognitive Pragmatic Analysis of Nominal Tautologies*   Naoko Yamamoto
No. 22 *A Contrastive Study of Responsibility for Understanding Utterances*
        between Japanese and Korean   Sumi Yoon
No. 23 *On Peripheries*   Anna Cardinaletti et al.
No. 24 *Metaphor of Emotions in English*   Ayako Omori
No. 25 *A Comparative Study of Compound Words*   Makiko Mukai
No. 26 *Grammatical Variation of Pronouns in Nineteenth-Century English Novels*
                                                                Masami Nakayama
No. 27 *I mean as a Marker of Intersubjective Adjustment*   Takashi Kobayashi
No. 28 *Lexical Pragmatics*   Akihiko Kawamura
No. 30 *The Diffusion of Western Loanwords in Contemporary Japanese*   Aimi Kuya

Hituzi Linguistics in English
30

Aimi Kuya

—

The Diffusion of Western Loanwords in Contemporary Japanese

—

A Variationist Approach

松山大学研究叢書 第97巻

HITUZI
SYOBO

Copyright © Aimi Kuya 2019
First published 2019

Author: AIMI KUYA

All rights reserved. Except for the quotation
of short passages for the purposes of criticism
and review, no part of this publication may be
reproduced, stored in a retrieval system,
or transmitted in any form or by any means,
electronic, mechanical, photocopying, recording
or otherwise, without the written prior
permission of the publisher.

In case of photocopying and electronic
copying and retrieval from network personally,
permission will be given on receipts of payment
and making inquiries. For details please
contact us through e-mail. Our e-mail address is
given below.

Hituzi Syobo Publishing

Yamato bldg. 2f, 2-1-2 Sengoku
   Bunkyo-ku Tokyo, Japan 112-0011
Telephone: +81-3-5319-4916
Facsimile: +81-3-5319-4917
e-mail: toiawase@hituzi.co.jp
http://www.hituzi.co.jp/
postal transfer: 00120-8-142852

ISBN978-4-89476-949-6
Printed in Japan

For Takao and Asako

Acknowledgements

This book is based on the Ph.D. thesis I submitted to the University of Oxford in 2016, with the degree conferred in 2017. Chapters 4 and 7 of this volume include some revisions of my original journal papers: Kuya (2016b) and Kuya (2016a), respectively. Chapter 6 was largely revised from Kuya (2013b).

I owe my deepest gratitude to my supervisor, Bjarke Frellesvig; my university college advisor, Rosalind Temple; and also to the thesis examiners, Jieun Kiaer and Kenjiro Matsuda, for their plentiful suggestions and feedback in the course of developing the thesis.

I would like to express my deepest appreciation to Makiro Tanaka, Toshinobu Ogiso, Fumio Inoue, Masao Aizawa, Shoichi Yokoyama, Makoto Yamazaki, Eran Kim and Satoshi Nambu for providing me with invaluable scholarly guidance while I was conducting research in the National Institute for Japanese Language and Linguistics (NINJAL), Japan. I thank NINJAL for permission to use additional data from their corpora and opinion surveys. I owe special thanks to Takenori Nakamura for his technical support with data collection from the corpora. Special thanks also go to Anna Rayner-Grignon and Paul Anthony Marshall for proofreading my English. I would also like to express thanks to anyone I have forgotten to mention who supported me in so many ways on various occasions both in the UK and Japan. Any errors remaining are the responsibility of the author.

Finally, I would not have been able to complete this work without receiving constant support and tireless encouragement from my family.

The publication of this book was supported by funding from the Grant for the Publication of Research from Matsuyama University, Japan. The support of Hituzi Syobo Publishing is gratefully acknowledged.

Matsuyama, June 2018

Contents

Acknowledgements	VII
List of Tables	XIII
List of Figures	XV
List of Abbreviations	XVII

CHAPTER 1
Borrowing with Interest

1.1	Western loanwords as new alternatives to existing lexical items	1
1.2	Purpose and structure of this study	3

CHAPTER 2
Loanwords in Contemporary Japanese

2.1	Lexical strata in Japanese	9
2.2	History of loanwords in Japanese	11
2.3	Types of loanwords in focus	14
2.4	Previous approaches to loanwords, and their limitations	16
2.4.1	Quantitative lexicology	17
2.4.2	Corpus linguistics	18
2.4.3	Sociolinguistics	19

CHAPTER 3
Data and Analytical Method: Analyzing Lexical Variation

3.1	Nationwide opinion surveys on loanwords	23
3.2	BCCWJ: a written corpus	24
3.3	CSJ: a spoken corpus	25
3.4	Complementary use of different sources of data	26
3.5	S-curve model of language change	28

| 3.6 | Issues of extending variationist methodology to lexical variation | 31 |

CHAPTER 4

Age as an External Factor

4.1	Apparent-time approach to language change	35
4.2	Opinion surveys	36
4.3	Distribution according to gender	39
4.4	Distribution according to age	40
4.5	Delay in loanword diffusion among the youngest age group(s)	43
4.6	Developing an s-curve model	46
4.7	Predicting change based on apparent-time distributions	49
4.8	Patterns of loanword diffusion in apparent time	53

CHAPTER 5

Other External Factors: Gender, Education, Register, and Style

5.1	Establishing trends in loanword distribution according to social and stylistic factors	55
5.2	Using BCCWJ and CSJ as synchronic corpora	55
5.3	Selecting potential lexical variables	60
5.4	Analysis of the written corpus (BCCWJ)	64
5.5	Analysis of the spoken corpus (CSJ)	72
5.6	Summary of the factor-by-factor analyses	80

CHAPTER 6

Incorporating Internal and External Factors into Analysis:
A Case Study of *Keesu* (< *Case*)

6.1	Towards a more fine-grained analysis of lexical variation	85
6.2	Identifying envelope of variation	86
6.3	*Keesu* in BCCWJ	92
6.3.1	Internal factors: syntactic structure and co-occurring predicate	92

6.3.2	External factors: year of birth, gender, education, register,	
	and genre	96
6.3.3	Multivariate analysis	100
6.4	Additional analysis: *keesu* in CSJ	102
6.5	Sociolinguistically asymmetric distributions of *keesu*	108

CHAPTER 7

Stylistic Constraints on Lexical Choice:
A Case Study of *Sapooto* (< *Support*)

7.1	Elucidating the impact of style on lexical choice	113
7.2	Previous studies on style	114
7.3	*The National Survey on Attitudes to Loanwords II*	
	(NINJAL 2005a)	115
7.4	Effect of age, education, gender, and style	118
7.5	Predicting the diffusion of *sapooto* in a multi-dimensional	
	space	122
7.6	Motivations for switching *from* or *to* the loanword	127
7.7	Elaborate process of loanword diffusion across different	
	styles	133

CHAPTER 8

Loanword Diffusion in Real Time

8.1	The apparent-time hypothesis revisited	137
8.2	Using interview- and corpus-based data in diachronic	
	analyses	139
8.3	Examining the variability of the community overall	143
8.4	Examining the variability of the individual speakers	148
8.5	Patterns of loanword diffusion in real time	150
8.5.1	Change with no acceleration/deceleration	150
8.5.2	Accelerated change	151
8.5.3	Decelerated change	153
8.5.4	Reversed change	153
8.6	Towards more precise predictions of change	154

CHAPTER 9
General Summary and Discussion

9.1	Identyfying variation on a lexical level	157
9.2	Socially structured nature of lexical variation	158
9.3	Language attitudes and linguistic behavior	159
9.4	Demonstration of change in real time	160
9.5	Actuation problem of loanword diffusion	161
9.6	Prospects for further research	162

Appendices	169
References	203
Dictionaries & Corpora	213
Summary in Japanese	215
Index	227

List of Tables

Table 1.1: Outline of the main analyses   5

Table 2.1: Orthographical distinctions among the three lexical strata   10

Table 2.2: Examples of loanwords by period of borrowing   13

Table 2.3: Classification of loanwords   16

Table 2.4: Diachronic distribution of lexical strata in *Chuuookooron* (magazine)   17

Table 2.5: Preference *for* or *against* the present use of loanwords by age   20

Table 3.1: Examples of questions used in the opinion surveys   24

Table 4.1: Nationwide opinion surveys on loanwords   36

Table 4.2: The 17 selected LW variants and their native equivalents   37

Table 4.3: Diffusion (%) of loanwords by gender   40

Table 4.4: Data coding for *niizu* (< *needs*)   47

Table 4.5: Results of the regression analyses of the 17 variables: Model A   47

Table 4.6: Comparison of Model A and Model B (*with/without* the inclusion of the variable Acquisition)   48

Table 5.1: Distribution of lexical strata by year of birth of the authors (BCCWJ)   58

Table 5.2: Distribution of lexical strata by year of birth of the speakers (CSJ)   59

Table 5.3: Lexical strata by part of speech (type, BCCWJ)   60

Table 5.4: Criteria for making frequency lists of loanwords   62

Table 5.5: The 25 selected lexical variables   64

Table 5.6: Distribution of LW and non-LW variants (BCCWJ)   66

Table 5.7: Correlation matrix for the independent variables (BCCWJ)   71

Table 5.8: Distribution of LW and non-LW variants (CSJ)   73

Table 5.9: Correlation matrix for the independent variables (CSJ)   79

Table 5.10: Summary of the factor-by-factor analyses   81

Table 6.1: Type of predicate that co-occurs with *keesu*   90

Table 6.2: Tokens of *keesu* and its native variants (BCCWJ)   92

Table 6.3: Diachronic distribution of *keesu* by usage (%)   94

Table 6.4: Effect of structure on the occurrence of *keesu* (BCCWJ)   95

Table 6.5: Effect of co-occurring predicate on the occurrence of *keesu* (BCCWJ)   96

Table 6.6: Effect of year of birth on the occurrence of *keesu* (BCCWJ)   97

Table 6.7: Effect of gender on the occurrence of *keesu* (BCCWJ)   98

Table 6.8: Effect of education on the occurrence of *keesu* (BCCWJ)   98

Table 6.9: Effect of register (type of medium) on the occurrence of *keesu* (BCCWJ)   99

Table 6.10: Effect of genre on the occurrence of *keesu* (BCCWJ, PB only)   100

Table 6.11: Correlation matrix for the independent variables: *keesu* in BCCWJ   101

Table 6.12: Result of the logistic regression analysis: *keesu* in BCCWJ   102

Table 6.13: Tokens of *keesu* and its native variants (CSJ)   103

Table 6.14: Effect of structure on the occurrence of *keesu* (CSJ) 103

Table 6.15: Effect of co-occurring predicate on the occurrence of *keesu* (CSJ) 103

Table 6.16: Effect of year of birth on the occurrence of *keesu* (CSJ) 104

Table 6.17: Effect of gender on the occurrence of *keesu* (CSJ) 104

Table 6.18: Effect of education on the occurrence of *keesu* (CSJ) 104

Table 6.19: Effect of register (type of speech) on the occurrence of *keesu* (CSJ) 105

Table 6.20: Effect of spontaneity on the occurrence of *keesu* (CSJ) 105

Table 6.21: Effect of formality on the occurrence of *keesu* (CSJ) 105

Table 6.22: Effect of audience size on the occurrence of *keesu* (CSJ) 105

Table 6.23: Correlation matrix for the independent variables: *keesu* in CSJ 106

Table 6.24: Result of the logistic regression analysis: *keesu* in CSJ 107

Table 6.25: Semantic features of co-occurring predicates 109

Table 7.1: Lexical choice across different settings: Friends, Public, and Elders 117

Table 7.2: Effect of age on the use/non-use of *sapooto* 119

Table 7.3: Effect of education on the use/non-use of *sapooto* 120

Table 7.4: Proportion (%) of LW to non-LW by education and age 120

Table 7.5: Effect of gender on the use/non-use of *sapooto* 121

Table 7.6: Effect of style on the use/non-use of *sapooto* 121

Table 7.7: Example of data coding (Samples of those in their 20s) 123

Table 7.8: Result of the logistic regression analysis: *sapooto* 124

Table 7.9: Patterns of word-switching 128

Table 7.10: Patterns of word-switching by education (%) 129

Table 7.11: Reasons for word choice in Public: those choosing LW in Friends (1) 130

Table 7.12: Reasons for word choice in Public: those choosing LW in Friends (2) 131

Table 7.13: Reasons for word choice in Public: those choosing SJ in Friends 132

Table 7.14: Reasons for word choice in Public: those choosing NJ in Friends 132

Table 8.1: Types of language change defined by (i) Age differentiation, (ii) Variability of the individuals, and (iii) Variability of the community 139

Table 8.2: Surveys on individual lexical items: *wain* and *oopun-suru* 140

Table 8.3: Surveys on preference *for* or *against* the present loanword use 141

Table 8.4: Surveys on preference *for* or *against* a further expansion of loanwords 141

Table 8.5: Distribution of *keesu, sapooto, shinpuru,* and the LW stratum in LB, BCCWJ (1986–2005) 143

Table 8.6: Regression coefficients of (i) Year of Survey and (ii) Age 147

Table 8.7: Regression coefficients of (i) Year of Survey and (ii) Year of Birth 150

Table 8.8: Types of language change (Revised from Table 8.1) 155

Table 9.1: Average number of loanwords in the context surrounding each variant 164

List of Figures

Figure 4.1: Lexical choice by the speaker's age in Canadian English   35

Figure 4.2: The LW *suutsu* (< *suit*) and *sebiro* by age   41

Figure 4.3: The LW *wain* (< *wine*) and *budooshu* by age   41

Figure 4.4: The LW *risuku* (< *risk*) and *kikensei* by age   42

Figure 4.5: The LW *niizu* (< *needs*) and *hitsuyoosei* by age   42

Figure 4.6: Process of language standardization over time   43

Figure 4.7: Diffusion (%) of *niizu* (< *needs*) over time   44

Figure 4.8: Distribution (%) of *niizu* (< *needs*) by age and year of survey   45

Figure 4.9: Distribution (%) of *niizu* (< *needs*) by year of birth and year of survey   45

Figure 4.10: Adopter categorization on the basis of innovativeness   49

Figure 4.11: Predicted diffusion of *getto-suru* (< *get*)   50

Figure 4.12: Comparing the goodness of fit of the models for *niizu* (< *needs*)   51

Figure 4.13: Predicted diffusion of *niizu* (< *needs*)   51

Figure 4.14: Predicted diffusion of *bijon* (< *vision*): males ahead of females   52

Figure 4.15: Predicted diffusion of *oopun-suru* (< *open*): females ahead of males   52

Figure 5.1: The LW stratum by year of birth of the authors (BCCWJ)   58

Figure 5.2: The LW stratum by year of birth of the speakers (CSJ)   59

Figure 5.3: Effect of year of birth on the occurrence of LWs (BCCWJ)   67

Figure 5.4: Regression analysis of *keesu* (< *case*)   68

Figure 5.5: Regression analysis of *shinpuru* (< *simple*)   68

Figure 5.6: Effect of gender on the occurrence of LWs (BCCWJ)   69

Figure 5.7: Effect of education on the occurrence of LWs (BCCWJ)   70

Figure 5.8: Effect of register on the occurrence of LWs (BCCWJ)   70

Figure 5.9: Phonologically contracted forms by register (BCCWJ)   72

Figure 5.10: Effect of year of birth on the occurrence of LWs (CSJ)   74

Figure 5.11: Effect of gender on the occurrence of LWs (CSJ)   75

Figure 5.12: Effect of education on the occurrence of LWs (CSJ)   75

Figure 5.13: Effect of register on the occurrence of LWs (CSJ)   76

Figure 5.14: Effect of spontaneity on the occurrence of LWs (CSJ)   77

Figure 5.15: Effect of formality on the occurrence of LWs (CSJ)   77

Figure 5.16: Effect of audience size on the occurrence of LWs (CSJ)   78

Figure 6.1: Diachronic distribution of *keesu*, *baai*, *rei*, and *jirei* (newspapers)   86

Figure 6.2: *Keesu* and its native variants by structure (BCCWJ)   95

Figure 6.3: *Keesu* and its native variants by co-occurring predicate (BCCWJ)   96

Figure 6.4: *Keesu* and its native variants by year of birth (BCCWJ)   97

Figure 6.5: *Keesu* and its native variants by gender (BCCWJ)   97

Figure 6.6: *Keesu* and its native variants by education (BCCWJ)   98

Figure 6.7: *Keesu* and its native variants by register (type of medium) (BCCWJ)   99

Figure 6.8: Interaction between Register and Spontaneity
(Those co-occurring with Predicate [Many/Few])   108
Figure 7.1: Variable /ng/ in Norwich by class and style   115
Figure 7.2: Diffusion of *sapooto* across different settings and age groups 117
Figure 7.3: Lexical choice by age   118
Figure 7.4: Lexical choice by education   120
Figure 7.5: Lexical choice by gender   121
Figure 7.6: Distribution of *sapooto* by age and style   122
Figure 7.7: Distribution of *sapooto* by education and style   122
Figure 7.8: Predicted diffusion of *sapooto* defined by (i) Education, (ii) Style, and
(iii) Year of Birth   125
Figure 7.9: Interaction between Education and Style (Those in their 30s)   126
Figure 7.10: Diffusion of *sapooto* in three dimensions (Those born in 1987) 127
Figure 7.11: Patterns of word-switching by education (Simplified)   129
Figure 8.1: Standardization of the variable /u/ in Tsuruoka, Japan   138
Figure 8.2: Variability of the community: *wain* (< *wine*)   144
Figure 8.3: Variability of the community: *oopun-suru* (< *open*)   144
Figure 8.4: Variability of the community: the present use of LWs   145
Figure 8.5: Variability of the community: a further expansion of LWs in future 145
Figure 8.6: Variability of the community: *keesu* (< *case*)   146
Figure 8.7: Variability of the community: the LW stratum   146
Figure 8.8: Variability of the individuals: *keesu* (< *case*)   148
Figure 8.9: Variability of the individuals: *wain* (< *wine*)   149
Figure 8.10: Variability of the individuals: the present use of LWs   149
Figure 8.11: Change with no acceleration/deceleration: *oopun-suru* (< *open*) 151
Figure 8.12: Change with no acceleration/deceleration: the LW stratum   151
Figure 8.13: Accelerated change: *wain* (< *wine*)   152
Figure 8.14: Accelerated change: *sapooto-suru* (< *support*)   152
Figure 8.15: Decelerated change: the present use of LWs   153
Figure 8.16: Reversed change: a further expansion of LWs in future   154

List of Abbreviations

A: adjectival usage
ACC: accusative
APS: Academic Presentation Speech (in CSJ)
BBK: *Bunkachoo Bunkabu Kokugoka* (part of the Agency for Cultural Affairs, Japan)
BCCWJ: Balanced Corpus of Contemporary Written Japanese
COMP: complementizer
COP: copula
CSJ: Corpus of Spontaneous Japanese
DAT: dative
GEN: genitive
HB: hybrid (words)
intr.: intransitive
ISM: Institute of Statistical Mathematics
LB: Library (Library Book) sub-corpus (in BCCWJ)
lit.: literal translation
LW: loanwords
N: nominal usage
NEG: negative
NHK: *Nippon Hoso Kyokai* (Japan Broadcasting Corporation)
NICT: National Institute of Information and Communications Technology

NINJAL: National Institute for Japanese Language and Linguistics (formerly NLRI: National Language Research Institute)
NJ: native Japanese (words)
NOM: nominative
Non-LW: non-loanwords, including Sino-Japanese (SJ) and native-Japanese (NJ) words
NSDKK: *Naikaku Soori Daijin Kanboo Koohooshitsu* (Public Relations Office, Cabinet Secretariat)
PASS: passive
PAST: past tense
PB: Books in the Publication sub-corpus (in BCCWJ)
PM: Magazines in the Publication sub-corpus (in BCCWJ)
PN: Newspapers in the Publication sub-corpus (in BCCWJ)
POL: polite form
PROG: progressive
SJ: Sino-Japanese (words)
SPS: Simulated Public Speech (in CSJ)
TOP: topic marker
tr.: transitive
V: verbal usage

CHAPTER I

Borrowing with Interest

1.1 Western loanwords as new alternatives to existing lexical items

This study is, to my knowledge, the first attempt to examine the diffusion of Western loanwords, called *gairaigo* (or *katakanago*), in contemporary Japanese within the variationist framework. A large influx of lexical borrowings from Western languages, mostly from English, is one of the most noticeable linguistic changes in contemporary Japanese.

In the very early stage of studies of lexical borrowings, as Mougeon & Beniak (1991) implies, the most universal reason for lexical borrowing has been attributed to its linguistic ("gap filling") function. This type of borrowing, according to Myers-Scotton's definition (1993: 169, 2006: 212–213), is called *cultural borrowing*. Cultural borrowing occurs when a recipient language needs to fill gaps of its lexicon in order to refer to things or concepts new to the language. Such examples are often found in the fields of science, state-of-the-art technology and other fields of advanced cultural development. One of the most common examples would be computer-related terms such as *computer, email, software, website*, and so on (Myers-Scotton 2006: 213), all of which have also entered into Japanese as *konpyuutaa, iimeeru, sofutoueaa, uebusaito*, respectively.[1]

Myers-Scotton (2006: 213) proposes the existence of another type of borrowing, i.e., *core borrowing*, which occurs even when a recipient language already has equivalent native expressions in its lexicon. Hashimoto (2010) and Kim (2011) report that there has been an increasing use of loanwords[2] in Japanese over the 20th century, many of which are abstract words that have existing native equivalents. Compare the following examples taken from the Balanced Corpus of Contemporary Written Japanese (BCCWJ) (NINJAL[3] 2011a):

(1.1) a. 持ち家＝"家を所有"することのメリットとは、   (PB13_00092)
   Mochi-ie = "ie-o shoyuu"-suru koto-no meritto-towa,
   One's.own-house = house-ACC possess-do thing-GEN merit-TOP
   'The advantage of "having your own home" is,'

   b. このプログラミングモデルの利点は、   (PB13_00440)
   kono puroguramingu moderu-no riten-wa,
   this programing model-GEN merit-TOP
   'The advantage of this programing model is,'

In the above examples, the loanword *meritto* (< *merit*) in (1.1.a) and the existing word *riten* in (1.1.b) share the same general area of meaning ('advantage') and they are interchangeable without largely changing the meaning of the whole sentence.[4] Few studies, however, have shed light on the phenomenon where lexical alternation occurs between core lexical borrowings and existing lexical items.

While cultural borrowing is considered to be necessary to meet the lexical needs of a language, core borrowing is characterized as unnecessary or "gratuitous" (Myers-Scotton 2006: 215, Mougeon & Beniak 1991: 199). A very simple question then arises as to why "borrowing always goes well beyond the actual 'needs' of a language" (Haugen 1953: 373).

Corpus linguists may point out that there is a semantic division of labor between borrowed items (as core borrowings) and their existing near-synonyms. This is true in the sense that in principle none of loanwords has exactly the same meaning as its native equivalents do and that many of established loanwords had experienced diachronic semantic and structural developments to a certain degree after entering Japanese. It is, however, also true that these near-synonyms always share the same general area of meaning and that alternations between near-synonyms in such semantically overlapped areas cannot be fully accounted for only by linguistic factors.

Language-external reasons, then, need to be considered in the investigation of why people use such "gratuitous" foreign words as opposed to existing native words. Weinreich (1968) points out the possibility that bilingual speakers use core borrowing to display positive social values that the foreign words symbolize:

"Why use the word *belt* when the [Irish] word *crios* exists? Surely here the feeling that English is a superior language, and that an English word confers distinction upon an Irish sentence, plays an important part." Those American immigrants who borrow as "heavily" as possible to show their advanced state of acculturation, act upon a similar motive.

(Weinreich 1968: 60)

On the one hand, in the context of English as a world language, the recent influx of (core) borrowings mainly from English into Japanese demonstrates the prestigious nature of English over Japanese. Some Japanese people may be happy to use borrowed Western words for this reason. On the other hand, Japanese is not completely non-resistant to the spread of Western loanwords as the history of these loanwords is not so long as that of existing vocabulary such as *wago* ('native Japanese words') and *kango* ('Sino-Japanese words'). Some people criticize the recent "over-use" of lexical borrowings mostly from English for fear that the purity of the Japanese language is being compromised. Considering this historical and social context, it is presumed that loanwords have a particular social value and occupy a particular position in the Japanese lexical strata, functioning as more than mere near-synonyms of native equivalents.

The importance of the concept of core borrowing is that it enables us to treat loanwords as competing lexical *variants* of their native equivalents within the variationist framework. Many variationist studies have put emphasis on the importance of integrating language-external dimensions into description of variation, in addition to language-internal ones (Labov 1972, among others). A correlation between linguistic variation and social contexts was also repeatedly reported in the study of phonological, syntactic, lexical, and pragmatic variation in Japanese (Hibiya 1988a, Matsuda 1995, Sano 2009, Nambu 2014, Inoue 2000, Yokoyama, Asahi & Sanada 2008, among others). It is expected that the linguistic heterogeneity as shown in (1.1) exhibits systematic structure of lexical variation in terms not only of language-internal factors but also of language-external ones including social attributes and speech style. These two dimensions will have to be taken into account for a more comprehensive description of the phenomenon.

1.2 Purpose and structure of this study

Weinreich, Labov & Herzog (1968: 101–102, 183–187) raises the following five problems to be solved for the theory of language change: (i) constraints, (ii) transition, (iii) embedding, (iv) evaluation and (v) actuation.[5] Possible solutions

4

to these problems will be explored through discussions on the following four research questions.

QUESTIONS
I. Where does lexical alternation occur between a loanword and non-loanword(s)?
II. Is lexical variation socially structured? If so, which language-external factors affect lexical choice in favor of loanwords?
III. Is there a contrast between people's stated attitudes towards loanwords and their actual behavior?
IV. How does the diffusion of loanwords proceed in real time?

QUESTION I explores a theoretical and methodological argument over how to identify the environments in which a given linguistic variable could possibly occur, i.e., the *envelope of variation*. This includes the process of identifying competing lexical variants (near-synonyms) (Section 5.3) and also locating linguistic contexts where two or more variants can be used for the "same meaning" (Section 6.2). Although this procedure is essential for the study of linguistic variation, determining linguistic equivalence on a lexical level is not straightforward in practice because words are often polysemous and their meanings entail delicate nuances on a discourse level. In this study, the notion of linguistic equivalence is applied after some modification of the original definition of a linguistic variable in Labov (1972) (Section 3.6).

QUESTION II concerns the problem of the social and stylistic dimension of loanword distribution. The social aspects of loanword diffusion are studied by NINJAL (2004, 2005a, 2007b), Jinnouchi (2007), NHK[6] (1980, 1996) and BBK[7] (1995, 1999, 2000, 2003, 2008, 2013, among others). Their investigations, however, mainly focused on age differentiations, in which younger speakers show a more positive attitude towards the use of loanwords.[8] Given that age differentiation is an indication of an ongoing change towards the growing use of loanwords, we need to capture a more elaborate process of the change by investigating effects of a wider range of social variables. Although this book will explore age differentiation in depth (Chapters 4 and 8) (*Transition Problem*), the investigation into the effect of other *language-external* factors on the ongoing change (Chapters 5–7) will tell us how the change in question is embedded in a larger social context of the speech community (*Embedding Problem*).

QUESTION III deals with the relationship between social awareness and the process of change in behavior (*Evaluation Problem*). This is to inquire whether a particular pattern observed in interview-based data (Chapters 4 and 7) is attested to by evidence from corpus-based data (Chapters 5, 6 and 8). The comparison of people's stated language *attitude*[9] and observed actual linguistic *behavior* will provide a useful insight into the validity of arguments made in earlier sociolinguistic investigations, which have relied heavily on language attitude. We will come back to this point in Section 2.4.3 and Section 3.4.

QUESTION IV requires a shift of methodological paradigm from *apparent time* to *real time*. Despite the power of the concept in locating the presence of change, the apparent-time approaches often underestimate the rate of change (Sankoff, G. 2006: 115). It will be shown that a closer examination of the variability of individuals in real time, which the apparent-time approach does not presuppose, allows a more accurate prediction of change on a long-term basis (Chapter 8). (*Transition Problem*)

This book is organized as follows. Chapter 2 provides a review of the previous approaches to loanwords in Japanese, with introductions to the structure of the Japanese lexicon, a history of Western loanwords in Japanese and classification of loanwords from a variationist point of view. There are three major perspectives on the study of Western loanwords: (i) quantitative lexicology, (ii) corpus linguistics and (iii) sociolinguistics. Important discoveries made in each field of loanword study will be reviewed, to evaluate advantages and disadvantages of each approach and thereby to search for the methodology necessary for integrating these different approaches into one in order to lead to a comprehensive understanding of the phenomenon.

Chapter 3 outlines the methodological details of the study. First, I will give brief introductions to data sources. Two major data sources, interview-based and corpus-based, are examined in this project. As a single database is not sufficient for eliciting all of the independent variables of interest, I will make use of various databases in a complementary manner. Second, an introduction to an analytical model, the logistic regression model, is provided. I will show the set of independent variables under consideration: three social and one stylistic ones. Third, a brief description is given of the research framework, the variationist approach to lexical alternation. It includes discussion on the theoretical issue of how to identify the envelope of variation for lexical alternation.

Chapters 4–8 constitute the main body of this book, providing five analyses (I–V) as outlined in Table 1.1. These chapters are designed to investigate the phenomenon from two different dimensions: *attitude* vs. *behavior* and *apparent time* vs. *real time*.

	Attitude (interview-based)	Behavior (corpus-based)
Apparent time	Ch4 Analysis I (17 variables) Ch7 Analysis IV (case study)	Ch5 Analysis II (25 variables) Ch6 Analysis III (case study)
Real time	Ch8 Analysis V (8 variables)	

Table 1.1: Outline of the main analyses

Chapters 4 and 7 examine people's *attitudes* towards loanwords synchronically based on the data collected from several existing nationwide interviews (opinion polls) conducted between 1999 and the early 2000s. The aims of these chapters are to answer the question of which language-external factors are the leading causes of the diffusion of loanwords and in what manner they brings about the diffusion. Chapters 5 and 6 investigate the other dimension, people's actual linguistic *behavior*, based on the data collected from written and spoken corpora. Since these corpora, as with the above-mentioned interviews, concern language produced between 1999 and the early 2000s, it is reasonable to contrast the interview-based data with the corpus-based data.

Chapter 8, as opposed to Chapters 4–7, uses a longitudinal approach to the diffusion of loanwords by means of observing both interview- and corpus-based data. Although not much data is currently available for systematic *real-time* analyses, I will attempt several case studies on whether or not people's attitudes and behaviors change over their lifetime.

Chapter 9 summarizes and integrates all the findings made in this book. Based on the sociolinguistic findings from the earlier chapters, I will discuss what kind of social values loanwords are given in the Japanese vocabulary. I will also raise some points that remain uncovered, which should be addressed in future research.

Notes

1 Throughout this book Japanese forms are transliterated based on the modified Hepburn System in *Kenkyuusha's New Japanese-English Dictionary*, 4th Edition (1974: xiii), except (i) proper nouns and (ii) the representation of long vowels. Proper nouns are transliterated according to their official name in the origin language where available. Long vowels, which are sometimes indicated with a colon as [aː/iː/uː/eː/oː], are spelled as *aa/ii/uu/ee/oo*. A long vowel [eː] for Sino-Japanese words is however spelled exceptionally as *ei*, following the convention of this dictionary.

2 Throughout this volume, the term "loanwords" refers to lexical borrowings from Western languages and does not include borrowings from Chinese unless otherwise stated (see also Section 2.1).

3 The National Institute for Japanese Language and Linguistics, formerly NLRI: National Language Research Institute

4 One might point out that there is a slight difference in nuance or connotation of a phrase. This is similar to the discussion in Weiner & Labov (1983), as to whether the existence/absence of a passive structure triggers a change in meaning. We will come back to this point in Chapter 3.

5 First, the *constraints problem* looks at possible constraints on the form, direction, or structural character of linguistic changes (Labov 1994: 115). These points have been partly mentioned in Section 1.1 and will also be outlined in Section 2.4.3 and Section 3.5. Second, the *transition problem* questions how a linguistic change is "transmitted across successive generation" (Labov 2001a: 78). Third, the *embedding problem* is how to observe how a linguistic change is embedded in linguistic and social structures. Fourth, the *evaluation problem* is to understand the ways in which social awareness is imposed upon the process of change (Weinreich et al. 1968: 186). Fifth, the *actuation problem* is the question of why a certain change occurred here and now (Labov 2001a: 466). The answer to this question will be discussed at the end of the book (Chapter 9), based on all of the findings made in the current research.

6 *Nippon Hoso Kyokai* (Japan Broadcasting Corporation)

7 *Bunkachoo Bunkabu Kokugoka* (part of the Agency for Cultural Affairs)

8 There are only a few studies on social factors other than age, e.g., education (Ishiwata 1965), occupation (NINJAL 2004) and register (NINJAL 2005a).

9 Henceforth, the term "attitude" includes not only people's feelings about their use of loanwords in general, but also people's self-reports (or "reported behavior") on what they *think* of their use of particular loanwords.

CHAPTER 2

Loanwords in Contemporary Japanese

2.1 Lexical strata in Japanese

Lexicon of Japanese is roughly divided into three strata depending on its origin: *wago* (lit. 'Japanese indigenous words,' henceforth native Japanese words or NJ words), *kango* (lit. 'Chinese words,' henceforth Sino-Japanese words or SJ words) and *gairaigo* (lit. 'alien words, words coming from abroad,' henceforth loanwords or LWs).[1] These strata are differentiated in terms of their (i) history, (ii) orthography and (iii) sociolinguistic values in the language.

The history of the three lexical strata summarized in Kageyama & Saito (2016: 15, Figure 1[2]) is as follows. Native Japanese (NJ) words originate in the ancient Japanese and constitute an integral part of the Japanese lexicon. This is the only stratum that contains all parts of speech including the lexical and functional categories (Kageyama & Saito 2016: 17, see also Table 5.3 in Section 5.3). Sino-Japanese (SJ) words started to enter into Japanese from Chinese in the middle of the 8th century, while loanwords (LWs) started to enter in the 16th century. These two lexical strata are similar in a grammatical sense in that they were brought into the language as nouns without containing conjugable predicates (Kageyama & Saito 2016: 21, 26). They can also function as (i) verbs when verbalized with the NJ light verb *-suru* ('do') or (ii) adjectives when followed by the copula *-da* ('be'), as shown in Table 2.1 (see also Section 5.3 for more detailed examples).

With respect to orthography, NJ words are typically written in *hiragana*, *kanji* (lit. 'Chinese characters') or the blend of *kanji* and *hiragana* syllabaries, whereas SJ words and LWs are in principle written in *kanji* and *katakana*, respectively, as shown in Table 2.1. Therefore, LWs are sometimes referred to as *katakanago*.

	Writing	Examples		Meaning
Native Japanese (NJ)	*hiragana*	が	*ga*	particle.NOM
		これ	*kore*	this
	kanji	場合	*baai*	case
	blend	支える	*sasaeru*	to support
		新しい	*atarashii*	new
Sino-Japanese (SJ)	*kanji*	事例	*jirei*	case
		支援（する）	*shien(-suru)*	(to) support
		単純（だ）	*tanjun(-da)*	simple
Loanwords (LW)	*katakana*	ケース	*keesu*	case
		サポート（する）	*sapooto(-suru)*	(to) support
		シンプル(だ)	*shinpuru(-da)*	simple

Table 2.1: Orthographical distinctions among the three lexical strata

These strata are also differentiated with regard to sociolinguistic connotations. NJ words are more closely associated with the vernacular, everyday and colloquial style. SJ words, in contrast, are associated with more formal and prestigious settings such as public, ceremonial and academic writings. The contrast between NJ words and SJ words in Japanese seems to correspond with that between the Germanic stratum and the French/Latinate stratum in English. The latter stratum is generally considered more sophisticated in both languages as their donor languages used to be recognized as languages with a more advanced culture. For example, in Japanese, the SJ word *shien* ('support') has a formal connotation whereas the NJ equivalent *sasaeru* has a softer and colloquial connotation (Table 2.1). This is just as, for instance, the Germanic vocabulary *buy* sounds more colloquial than its French/Latin donor equivalent *purchase* (Kageyama & Saito 2016: 20).[3]

Loanwords, in contrast with SJ words, have been imported relatively recently (this history is further reviewed in Section 2.2). The majority of them are from Western languages including English, French, German, and Dutch (NINJAL 1987: 65, Hashimoto 2010). According to NINJAL (2004: 17, Figure 1-3-1), loanwords are often recognized as giving stylistic—(i) novel, (ii) stylish and (iii) intelligent—nuances to one's speech.[4]

Both LWs and SJ words, as opposed to NJ words, are classified as borrowings from a historical point of view. However, Japanese speakers in general recognize LWs and SJ words as distinct vocabulary types for various reasons. Ishiwata (2001: 9) states that SJ vocabulary does not generally fall into the LW stratum in contemporary Japanese for the following reasons: (i) SJ words entered into Japanese much earlier than Western loanwords; (ii) SJ words have developed as a writing system/script for NJ words rather than merely as a class of vocabulary in Japanese, which had not invented its own writing system yet[5]

CHAPTER 2 LOANWORDS IN CONTEMPORARY JAPANESE

and (iii) Chinese characters are well integrated into the Japanese vocabulary system because of their high productivity. The SJ stratum has thus acquired a special (prestigious) status in Japanese as opposed to that of the LW stratum. In these respects, it would not be an exaggeration to say that SJ words tend to be considered part of "native words" by Japanese speakers. As Haspelmath (2009: 38) says, "the status of native words is always relative to what we know about the history of language." Accordingly, SJ words, as with NJ words, are henceforth referred to as "native words" or "non-loanwords" (non-LWs) as opposed to LWs throughout this book.

2.2 History of loanwords in Japanese

The influx of Western loanwords into Japanese occurred in the following three phases: (i) Iberian period, (ii) Dutch-learning period and (iii) Western period (Irwin 2011: 23). Table 2.2 shows several examples of loanwords borrowed in each phase.[6]

The first phase that started from the mid-16th century witnessed the influx of lexical borrowings mainly from Portuguese (Po), along with a small number of Latin, Spanish and Dutch words, initiated by Jesuits. These borrowings are divided into two groups: those associated with Christianity and those associated with trade (Ishiwata 2001: 191). The former includes *kirishitan* (< *cristão* (Po) 'Christian') and *misa* (< *missa* (Po) 'mass') (Irwin 2011: 29, 32) and the latter includes *kasute(e)ra* (< *Castela* (Po) 'type of sponge cake'), *tabako* (< *tabaco* (Po) 'tobacco, cigarette') and so on (Irwin 2011: 33–34, see also Ishiwata 2001: 193–226).

Japanese entered the second phase in the mid-17th century (after *Sakoku* 'the Edicts of Seclusion' or 'Isolation policy'), where only the Dutch were permitted to trade with Japan. During this time, a number of Dutch (Du) words were borrowed by Japanese highbrows learning European science. This political background promoted lexical borrowings that are associated not only with trading but also with the fields of medicine and science. The former involves *koohii* (< *koffie* (Du) 'coffee'), *garasu* (< *glas* (Du) '(pane of) glass'), and so on. The latter involves *korera* (< *cholera* (Du) 'cholera'), *pesuto* (< *pest* (Du) 'plague, Black Death'), and so on, which were only fully understood by a few in the upper class (Irwin 2011: 38–40, see also Ishiwata 2001: 243–245).

The last phase started with the beginning of Meiji Restoration in 1868 (Irwin 2011: Section 2.4). Lexical borrowings in this period were motivated by eagerness to stand as equals with Western countries by means of modernization. These include those borrowed from Russian (Ru), French (Fr), German (Ge) and English. Lexical borrowing became especially oriented to English after

WWII with the rise of the economic and political power of the US. Examples from languages other than English include *sobieto* (< совет (Ru) 'soviet'), *ara-karuto* (< *à la carte* (Fr) 'à la carte'), *bakansu* (< *vacances* (Fr) 'holiday, vaca-tion'), *meetoru* (< *mètre* (Fr) 'meter'), *kapuseru* (< *Kapsel* (Ge) 'capsule'), *arubaito* (< *Arbeit* (Ge) 'part-time job'), *teeze* (< *These* (Ge) 'thesis'), and so on (Irwin 2011: 46, 49–50, 52–53).

Borrowings from English before WWII include those associated with seman-tic fields of sports, e.g., *riigu* (< *league*); music, e.g., *jazu* (< *jazz*); politics, e.g., *suroogan* (< *slogan*); fashion, e.g., *suutsu* (< *suit*) (Irwin 2011: 56). Despite the government campaign to ban the use of English donor loanwords during WWII,[7] the influx of loanwords from English continued after the war due to the re-rise of Anglicism. This includes *sekushii* (< *sexy*), *sutoresu* (< *stress*), *insu-tanto* (< *instant*), *niizu* (< *needs*), *ruutsu* (< *roots*), and so on (Irwin 2011: 57).

CHAPTER 2 LOANWORDS IN CONTEMPORARY JAPANESE   13

IBERIAN PERIOD: Mid-16th century to mid-17th century
  Christianity
    kirishitan 'early Japanese Catholic' [1587]
    pan 'holy wafer > bread' [1591]
    misa 'mass' [1591]
  Trade
    1) **Foodstuffs**: *kasute(e)ra* 'type of sponge cake' [1625]
    2) **Cloth & clothing**: *kappa* 'raincoat' [1608]
    3) **Drugs & medical goods**: *miira* 'mummy' [1610], *tabako* 'tobacco > cigarette' [1607]
    4) **Tools & appliances**: *furasuko* 'decanter' [1625], *karuta* 'traditional playing card' [1596]
    5) **Place names**: *igirisu* 'England > UK' [1613]

DUTCH-LEARNING PERIOD: Mid-17th century to mid-19th century
  Medicine & science—only understood by a few in the upper class
    korera 'cholera' [1793]
    pesuto 'plague, Black Death' [1829]
    morumotto 'guinea pig' [1872]
  Trade—penetrated the daily lives
    1) **Food & drink**: *koohii* 'coffee' [1615], *biiru* 'beer' [1724]
    2) **Materials**: *garasu* 'pane of glass' [1763], *gomu* 'rubber, gum' [1822]
    3) **Leisure**: *orugooru* 'music box' [1803], *dansu* 'dance' [1831]
    4) **Maritime terminology**: *dekki* 'deck' [1857]
    5) **Foreign currencies**: *pondo* 'pound sterling' [1822]
    6) **Place names**: *doitsu* 'Germany' [1725]

WESTERN PERIOD: 19th century to present
  BEFORE WWII (Rise of Anglicism)
    hoteru 'hotel' [1850], *hausu* 'house' [1864]
    1) **Student slangs**: *goorudo* 'gold', *mazaa* 'mother', *getto* 'get', *puree* 'play'
    2) **Baseball**: *beesubooru* 'baseball' [1889], *auto* 'out' [1896], *seefu* 'safe' [1906]
    3) **Sports**: *riigu* 'league' [1907], *fan* 'fan' [1920]
    4) **Music**: *jazu* 'jazz' [1924]
    5) **Politics**: *suroogan* 'slogan' [1924]
    6) **Fashion**: *burausu* 'blouse' [1925], *suutsu* 'suit' [1935]
  DURING WWII (De-Anglicization)
    nyuusu 'news' > *hoodoo* (報道) 'report'
    anaunsaa 'announcer' > *hoosooin* (放送員) 'broadcaster'
    sutoraiku 'strike (baseball)' > *yoshi* (よし) 'good'
  AFTER WWII (Re-rise of Anglicism)
    sekushii 'sexy' [1956]
    sutoresu 'stress' [1957]
    insutanto 'instant' [1960]
    niizu 'needs' [1975]
    ruutsu 'roots' [1977]

[ ] indicates first written attestation.

Table 2.2: Examples of loanwords by period of borrowing
(Summarized from Irwin 2011: Sections 2.2–2.4, modified by the author)

Lexical borrowings after the Meiji Restoration in the late 19th century also include loan translations (calques), where many abstract words, mainly academic and technical terms, were translated into SJ words or morphemes. Examples of loan translations involve (i) 社会 (*shakai* 'society'), (ii) 個人 (*kojin* 'individual'), (iii) 哲学 (*tetsugaku* 'philosophy') (Ishino 1983: 30, Ishiwata

2001: 11, Irwin 2011: 44), (iv) 電子計算機 (*denshi-keisanki* '(*electronic*) *computer*'), (v) 写真機 (*shashinki* '*camera*'), (vi) 葡萄酒 (*budooshu* '*wine*'), and so on. The first three examples (i)–(iii) are now well integrated into Japanese. As these examples are written in *kanji* (Chinese characters) and do not maintain their donor language pronunciations, ordinary Japanese speakers may use them without being aware that they are borrowed terms. In contrast, the latter three examples (iv)–(vi) failed to obtain established status in contemporary Japanese, having been almost completely replaced by their homophonic translations (i.e., their *katakana* equivalents) such as コンピュータ(ー) (*conpyuuta(a)* < *computer*), カメラ (*kamera* < *camera*) and ワイン (*wain* < *wine*).

2.3 Types of loanwords in focus

One may notice that early borrowings in Table 2.2 (e.g., those borrowed during the Iberian period), except for Christian terminologies, are primarily related to things (foods, clothes, medical goods, tools, place names, materials, foreign currencies, and so on) that were new to Japanese people. It should be noted that there are no native equivalents in the Japanese lexicon to rephrase them. In contrast, many recent loanwords, particularly abstract words such as *reberu* (< *level*), *ruuru* (< *rule*) and *keesu* (< *case*), are coexistent with existing native equivalents (Hashimoto 2010: 115). For example, *keesu* (< *case*) is considered equivalent to native words such as *jirei*, *baai* and *rei* (Kim 2011, see also Chapter 6).

This indicates that loanwords in contemporary Japanese are roughly divided into three groups based on their coexistence with equivalent native words as shown in Table 2.3. First, the examples in (I) have no established native equivalents. The first two examples *terebi* (< *television*) and *botan* (< *button*) are those that were borrowed into Japanese to introduce new things to the language at a very early phase of Japan's language contact history. More recent loanwords such as *deeta* (< *data*), *kurikku* (< *click*) and *intaanetto* (< *internet*) are also examples of lexical borrowings that introduce new things to the language.

In contrast, loanwords listed in (II) have native equivalents. First, loanwords such as *keesu* (< *case*), *sapooto* (< *support*), *shinpuru* (< *simple*) and *charenji* (< *challenge*) have well-attested native equivalents, which are frequently used and are in competition with loanword equivalents. Second, loanwords such as *konpyuuta(a)* (< *computer*), *kamera* (< *camera*), *wain* (< *wine*) and *basu* (< *bus*) also have native equivalents via loan translations such as *denshi-keisanki* ('*computer*'), *shashinki* ('*camera*'), *budooshu* ('*wine*') and *noriai-jidoosha* ('*bus*'), respectively. These calques were once in use but have been made obsolete, so they are no longer in active competition with their loanword (*katakana*)

CHAPTER 2 LOANWORDS IN CONTEMPORARY JAPANESE 15

equivalents. Third, loanwords such as *aakaibu* (< *archive*) and *aidentiti* (< *identity*) are the most recent examples of lexical borrowings from English. Words such as *hozon-kiroku* ('*archive*') and *dokuji-sei* ('*identity*') were recently calqued as the native equivalents of these loanwords (NINJAL 2007b). One of the aims of these calques is to avoid communicational difficulties caused by the "over-use" of loanwords, by helping loanword illiterate people, including the elderly and non-professionals, to understand the meaning of unpopular loanwords (Aizawa 2012: 141–143).[8] The use of these calques, however, does not seem to be gaining in popularity at this point.

Examples in (III) include in-betweens, which have native equivalent words but may not be as freely inter-exchangeable with native words as those in (II). In this category, there appears to be a relatively clear division of labor among loanwords and their native equivalents. For example, the loanword *supuun* (< *spoon*) is differentiated from its NJ near-synonym *saji* ('a Japanese traditional spoon') in terms of material or use (Jinnouchi 1993). The former typically refers to utensils made of metal and used for eating Western dishes, whereas the latter is generally associated with those made of wood and used for eating Japanese dishes. Jinnouchi reports that such semantic differentiation between the two lexical items has been gradually disappearing in apparent time. In other words, *supuun*, as opposed to *saji*, is obtaining an "unmarked" status among younger generations as a result of semantic broadening of the loanword.

	Loanwords (homophonic translation)	Native equivalents (incl. loan translation)
I	**Attested early**	
	terebi テレビ (< *television*)	?
	botan ボタン (< *button*)	?
	Attested recently	
	deeta データ (< *data*)	?
	kurikku クリック (< *click*)	?
	intaanetto インターネット (< *internet*)	?
II		**Well-established**
	sapooto サポート (< *support*)	*shien* 支援, *tedasuke* 手助け
	keesu ケース (< *case*)	*baai* 場合, *jirei* 事例, *rei* 例
	shinpuru シンプル (< *simple*)	*tanjun* 単純, *kanso* 簡素
	charenji チャレンジ (< *challenge*)	*choosen* 挑戦
		Obsoleted
	konpyuuta(a) コンピュータ(ー) (< *computer*)	*denshi-keisanki* 電子計算機
	kamera カメラ (< *camera*)	*shashinki* 写真機
	wain ワイン (< *wine*)	*budooshu* 葡萄酒
	basu バス (< *bus*)	*noriai-jidoosha* 乗合自動車
		Not in common use
	aakaibu アーカイブ (< *archive*)	*hozon-kiroku* 保存記録, etc.
	aidentiti アイデンティティ (< *identity*)	*dokuji-sei* 独自性, *jiko-ninshiki* 自己認識
III		**Distinguished clearly from loanwords in meaning**
	supuun スプーン (< *spoon*)	*saji* さじ ('Japanese traditional spoon')
	hoteru ホテル (< *hotel*)	*ryokan* 旅館 ('Japanese traditional hotel')

Table 2.3: Classification of loanwords

The focus of the present research is on those loanwords in (II) in Table 2.3; that is, those that coexist with native equivalents. It is worth pointing out that the distinction between (I) and (II), i.e., the presence/absence of native equivalents, does not necessarily correspond to the dividing line between cultural borrowing and core borrowing, because the introduction of new things or concepts occasionally leads to the adoption of loan translations that may later function as "native equivalents" of their homophonic translations (recall the example of *shashinki* vs. *kamera* (< *camera*)).

2.4 Previous approaches to loanwords, and their limitations

This section outlines three recent approaches to loanwords: (i) quantitative lexicology, (ii) corpus linguistics and (iii) sociolinguistics.

2.4.1 Quantitative lexicology

Investigating the frequency of vocabulary in print media is one way of grasping the proportion of the LW stratum out of the whole vocabulary of Japanese. Large-scale investigations started in Japan after WWII, initiated by NINJAL. These investigations aim to capture and describe the whole picture of the Japanese lexicon. It is usually done by means of counting the number of word entries (type) and the frequency of each entry (token) in a corpus. The previous surveys by NINJAL include investigations of texts from magazines, newspapers, textbooks, and TV broadcasting.

Although most of them are one-off surveys, there are a few longitudinal observations. One of the oldest surveys on a corpus of magazines conducted between 1956 and 1957 by NINJAL (NINJAL 1962, 1963, 1964) was followed up approximately 40 years later in 1994 (NINJAL 2005b), confirming that the proportion of the LW stratum as opposed to that of NJ, SJ and HB strata is on the increase. NINJAL (1987) also reported a gradual increase of the LW stratum in the magazine *Chuuookooron* (*Chūo-Kōron*) between 1906 and 1976. Several follow-up surveys of the same magazine confirmed that there was a further increase in the proportion of loanwords in the following decades: Ishii (1990) for the year 1986; Irie (2010) for the years 1996 and 2006. Table 2.4 summarizes a diachronic distribution of each lexical stratum by type and token over a century from 1906 to 2006. It shows a relatively consistent increase of the LW stratum in the Japanese vocabulary over the last century.

	1906	1916	1926	1936	1946	1956	1966	1976	1986	1996	2006
Token (%)											
NJ	58.0	60.5	60.7	57.7	53.5	57.5	53.9	54.8	51.8	53.0	50.4
SJ	32.6	30.1	29.1	31.4	34.5	30.9	34.1	30.9	33.8	32.4	33.3
LW	0.9	0.9	1.1	1.5	1.5	2.4	2.4	3.7	3.5	4.3	4.0
HB	8.5	8.5	9.1	9.4	10.5	9.2	9.6	10.6	10.9	10.3	12.3
Total	100.0	100.0	100.0	100.0	100.0	100.0	100.0	100.0	100.0	100.0	100.0
Type (%)											
NJ	35.6	36.3	37.7	34.2	29.7	32.8	28.7	30.8	27.0	28.9	27.8
SJ	48.8	47.4	45.1	47.2	50.6	47.0	50.4	45.4	48.7	46.5	46.0
LW	1.6	1.6	1.9	2.3	2.5	3.7	4.1	5.7	5.9	7.0	6.1
HB	14.0	14.8	15.3	16.4	17.1	16.5	16.8	18.1	18.5	17.6	20.1
Total	100.0	100.0	100.0	100.0	100.0	100.0	100.0	100.0	100.0	100.0	100.0

Table 2.4: Diachronic distribution of lexical strata in *Chuuookooron* (magazine)
(Adapted from NINJAL 1987: 54; Ishii 1990: 4; Irie 2010: 13)

Hashimoto (2010) and Kim (2011: 14) also reported an increase in the use of loanwords in newspapers during the 20th century, especially in the latter half of the century. A report in Hashimoto also includes the growing use of loanwords in addresses in the Minutes of the Diet after WWII. Although the scope is limited to a relatively formal register of spoken Japanese, this is one of the few recent investigations of loanwords in a spoken corpus.[9]

The contribution of quantitative lexicology is that it provides empirical evidence for a diachronic increase of the LW stratum as a whole in the lexicon of Japanese. In other words, it has been confirmed that there is an ongoing increase in the adoption of loanwords as opposed to NJ or SJ words. Another contribution of quantitative lexicology is that it describes the manner in which loanwords spread over time. Hashimoto (2010: 247) points out that the diffusion of loanwords in the 20th century follows an s-shaped curve with a gradual acceleration of increase at the start, the most rapid increase in the middle, and a gradual deceleration at the end (Hashimoto 2010: 244, Figure 10.11).

In this macro perspective, however, little attention is paid to the difference between loanwords that do not have native equivalents and those that coexist with their native equivalents, even though the mechanism of diffusion is quite different between the two groups. In the former case, as discussed in Section 1.1, borrowing usually occurs for a language-internal reason. In the latter group, in contrast, borrowing is motivated by language-external factors too, in which there should be various competitions—not only semantic, but also social and stylistic—among the loanwords and the existing native vocabulary. These aspects are captured only when we conduct a study from a micro perspective.

2.4.2 Corpus linguistics

Corpus linguistics views loanwords from a different perspective, focusing on the use of individual loanwords in context. Their main goal is to provide a detailed description of the meaning and usage of individual loanwords in an empirical manner for the purpose of lexicography, language education, and so on. Such an approach has been attempted by, among others, Mogi (2011, *katto-suru* 'to cut'; 2015, *maaku-suru* 'to mark') and Kim (2013, *chekku-suru* 'to check'). Semantics of loanwords is sometimes contrasted with that of existing native near-synonyms, e.g., Kim (2011, *keesu* 'case' and *toraburu* 'trouble'), Miyata & Tanaka (2006, *risuku* 'risk'), Miyata (2007, *meritto* 'merit') and Shimooka (2013, *rirakkusu-suru* 'to relax').[10] Among these studies Kim (2011) attempts diachronic investigations to describe the semantic development of loanwords in relation to their near-synonyms.

One of their contributions is that they revealed the division of labor in semantics between a particular loanword and its near-synonyms. They repeatedly reported that there is always difference in meaning or in collocational patterns between loanwords and their near-synonyms. In some cases of

CHAPTER 2 LOANWORDS IN CONTEMPORARY JAPANESE

well-attested loanwords, their meaning or usage tends to be more varied than that of existing words. For example, the loanword *meritto* (< *merit* 'merit') can take on more collocational patterns than its equivalent SJ word *riten* (Miyata 2007). Kim (2011) also pointed out that the loan noun *toraburu* (< *trouble* 'trouble') plays an active function as a general term or hypernym of its near-synonyms in newspapers. According to Miyata (2007: 408), loanwords generally have not been well established in their meanings or in their collocational pattern compared with existing native lexical items, and that is the reason why they are widely used or tolerant of various collocational patterns.

There is nevertheless a limitation to corpus linguistic approaches. Collocational pattern is only a tendency and not something that constrains the occurrence of a particular lexical item categorically. In other words, such linguistic factors cannot fully explain the reasons why a particular lexical item is chosen over the others that share the same or similar meaning. To make a comprehensive explanation of word choice, language-external factors, such as social and stylistic ones, will have to be explored.

2.4.3 Sociolinguistics

The arguments against the "flood of Western loanwords" that began to appear in the media in the 1980s (Ishiwata 2001: 27) have been drawing public attention to the use of loanwords in contemporary Japanese. BBK has been conducting annual opinion polls on public attitudes towards language and language use since 1995, and loanwords have been one of the main topics in the surveys. NHK (1980, 1986, 1996) and NINJAL (2004, 2005a, 2007b) also conducted sampling surveys on loanwords for their own purposes. Some surveys were designed to capture the level of recognition, comprehension and use of selected loanwords (BBK 2003, 2008, 2009; NINJAL 2007b). In a more general context, people were also asked whether they have a positive attitude towards the present use of loanwords (NSDKK[11] 1977; BBK 2000, 2003, 2008, 2013) or a further increase of them (NHK 1991, BBK 1995, NINJAL 2004). There are some surveys and analyses from a variationist point of view, in which the focus was on the choice between selected loanwords and their native equivalents (NHK 1980, 1996; BBK 1999, 2000; NINJAL 2004, 2005a; Jinnouchi 1993, 2007; Tanaka 2007).

One of the important findings from the previous sociolinguistic studies is the existence of age differentiation in attitude towards loanwords, with a younger generation more tolerant of the use or increase of loanwords in general than elder one. For example, in a recent survey conducted by BBK (2013), subjects were examined on their receptiveness to the fact that loanwords are in general use in their everyday lives. The result shows a striking tendency for younger generations to be more open to the use of loanwords than the older ones (Table 2.5). Furthermore, it is reported that younger speakers show a higher level of explosure to, understanding of, familiarity with, and use of particular individual loanwords (BBK 1999, 2000; NINJAL 2007b). These surveys indicate that change in favor of loanwords is in progress in apparent time.

Year of Survey	Age Range	No.of Informants	Like (%)	Neither (%)	Dislike(%)
2013	16–19	74	16.2	75.7	6.8
2013	20–29	175	13.1	70.3	16.6
2013	30–39	291	12.4	66.7	20.6
2013	40–49	327	8.6	60.2	31.2
2013	50–59	323	9.6	52.9	36.8
2013	60–69	446	7.0	46.6	45.1
2013	70+	517	7.5	41.4	47.2

Table 2.5: Preference *for* or *against* the present use of loanwords by age[12]

(Adapted from BBK 2013: 92)

It has also been reported that there appears to be gender and educational/occupational differentiations, although these tendencies are not as coherent across surveys as age differentiation. Loveday (1996: Ch6) points out that gender does not appear to be a significant variable on the social reception of contemporary contact with English. However, on the level of the use of individual loanwords, some loanwords are preferred by female speakers, whereas some are preferred by male speakers (BBK 1999, 2000). With respect to educational/occupational factors, there seems to be a bit clearer tendency: Those with higher educational/occupational backgrounds have a more positive attitude towards the use of loanwords in general (NINJAL 2004: 14, 31), or show a stronger tendency to accept or adopt English-based innovations (Loveday 1996: 187, see also Kuya 2013a). Ishiwata (1965) and Loveday (1996: 181–182) also point out that more educated people in general recognize the meaning of loanwords at higher rates.

There are also reports on stylistic differentiation, in which a loanword is selectively chosen from among near-synonyms depending on to whom one is talking or in what setting the utterance is taking place (NINJAL 2004: 32, NINJAL 2005a: 18–33, Jinnouchi 1993: 6). Such stylistic differentiation may be partly induced by the particular social connotations (functions) of that loanword. On the one hand, major advantages of using loanwords include sounding novel or adding a stylish nuance to one's speech (NINJAL 2004: 17). On the other hand, people are concerned that use of, particularly a heavy use of, loanwords may increase the risk of miscommunication, the devolution of traditional Japanese language, the chance of sounding snobby, and so on (NINJAL 2004: 20).

The earlier sociolinguistic studies have confirmed that there are social differentiations in the adoption and use of loanwords, but several points are still overlooked. First, statistical technique has not yet been employed in the sociolinguistic study of loanwords in earnest. In the earlier sociolinguistic approaches, the effect of language-external factors is often discussed univariately by means of cross tabulation. As language-external factors are often interrelated with each other (Labov 1982: 52), a *multivariate* analysis will be essential. In addition, we have seen that a statistical model can be a powerful tool in predicting the change (Hashimoto 2010). Now a sociolinguistic investigation will have to make use of such a statistical model in order to predict the diffusion of loanwords from multiple factors.

Second, sociolinguistic studies of loanwords in spontaneous speech have not yet been well investigated. In the previous sociolinguistic studies on loanwords, questionnaires have often been the main means of collecting empirical data and they have put little effort into the *corpus-based* approach. One of the reasons seems to be the absence of corpora suitable for the study of lexical variation, in terms of both size and quality. Investigation into an individual set of open-class lexical variants such as *keesu*, *jirei*, *baai* and *rei* ('case') requires a large collection of spontaneous utterance, because the probability for particular content words to occur is apparently lower than that for functional or grammatical ones (e.g., the nominal particle *ga/no*). To overcome such a difficulty, two large-scale corpora, written and spoken, will be investigated in this book.

Last, but not least, although a longitudinal approach has been often taken in quantitative lexicology (e.g., NINJAL 1987) and corpus linguistics (e.g., Hashimoto 2010, Kim 2011), sociolinguistic studies have often failed to capture changes in *real time*. Of course, considering the diachronic increase of the whole loanword stratum in corpora (NINJAL 1987, Hashimoto 2010, Kim 2011), it may not be unreasonable to interpret age gradient as change in progress, although no sufficient attempt has ever been made to confirm this in real time. Analysts should also pay attention to the possibility that the variability of speakers over their lifetime poses a problem in making a prediction of a given change. In order to provide a more accurate prediction of the linguistic phenomenon in question, a real-time approach will have to be used where possible.

To tackle the above problems, it is essential to introduce advanced techniques employed in quantitative and corpus linguistics to a sociolinguistic approach to loanwords. Further details about the methodology of the current research will be described in the following chapter.

Notes

1 There is another stratum called in Japanese as *konshugo/konseigo* (lit. 'mixed words,' henceforth hybrid or HB), where a word is formed by the combination of words or morphemes from different strata.

2 They include mimetic words as an independent stratum in their figure since the lexical items in this category often behave differently from those in the other three strata in terms of phonology, morphology and syntax. However, they attract our attention to the fact that most mimetics are considered to have as long history as NJ words do (Kageyama & Saito 2016: 14).

3 Trudgill (2000: 82–83) introduces several cases where formality (or style) in English are "for the most part characterized by vocabulary differences" as follows (emphasis added):

> Father was somewhat *fatigued* after his lengthy *journey*.
> Dad was pretty *tired* after his long *trip*.

We notice the pairs of words he compares in terms of formality (*tired* vs. *fatigued*; *trip* vs. *journey*) also exhibit the contrast between the Germanic vs. French/Latin donor vocabulary, although a speaker/writer may not necessarily be aware of the differences in lexical strata in the language in the same way that Japanese people are aware (due to the above-mentioned orthographical distinctions among the strata).

4 These three evaluations of loanwords are associated with the functions of *core borrowings*. In contrast, other evaluations including "expresses a new concept or thing," "reduces negative nuances of existing words" and "rephrases an indecent expression" seem to describe the functions of *cultural borrowings*, in which a word is borrowed primarily for language-internal reasons. Moreover, an evaluation such as "boosts communicative effectiveness" seems to be associated with the function of technical terms (as part of cultural borrowings).

5 The *hiragana* and *katakana* syllabaries were created after the adoption of Chinese characters.

6 For the visualization of the level/volume of borrowing in each phase, see Figure 2.1 in Irwin (2011: 25).

7 During the war, the government restricted the use of loanwords. Many of these were replaced with native words including SJ words. For example, *nyuusu* (< *news*), *anaunsaa* (< *announcer*) and *sutoraiku* (< *strike* (baseball)) were rephrased as *hoodoo* (報道 'report'), *hoosooin* (放送員 'broadcaster') and *yoshi* (よし 'good'), respectively (Irwin 2011: 57).

8 This movement is not a case of language purification like those that took place in France or South Korea. The public pressure for purification of language in Japan is not as strong as in these countries (Kajiki et al. 1995, Yang 2005).

9 Other investigations include the study of the language in TV broadcasting in 1989 conducted by NINJAL (1995, 1997, 1999).

10 Corpus linguistic approaches to loanwords were accelerated especially after the release of BCCWJ (Balanced Corpus of Contemporary Written Japanese). The studies that use BCCWJ include Mogi (2011, 2015); Miyata & Tanaka (2006); and Miyata (2007).

11 *Naikaku Soori Daijin Kanboo Koohooshitsu* (Public Relations Office of Cabinet Secretariat)

12 The proportions of those choosing "Not sure" are not shown in the table.

CHAPTER 3

Data and Analytical Method: Analyzing Lexical Variation

3.1 Nationwide opinion surveys on loanwords

Interview-based data is gathered mostly from several previous nationwide opinion surveys on language and language use in Japan conducted by various institutes including BBK, NINJAL and NHK between 1999 and 2005. Approximately 2,000–3,000 people aged 15–20 and above were randomly selected from the population of Japan in each survey. The interviewer(s) asked prepared questions to the selected informants in a face-to-face manner. The present study focuses on questions that are related to people's language attitudes towards loanwords and their use of loanwords. As shown in Table 3.1, questions concern the public attitude to (i) the use of specific loanwords as opposed to their native equivalents (Chapter 4), (ii) the alternation between a loan and non-loan variants across different settings or registers (Chapter 7) and (iii) the present use or a further expansion of loanwords in contemporary Japanese (Chapter 8). Some questions have been repeatedly asked with intervals of 5 to 20 years. For example, the third question in Table 3.1 has been asked in surveys conducted by NSDKK (1977) and BBK (2000, 2003, 2008 and 2013). Such data is studied diachronically to capture a change in the adoption of loanwords in real time (Chapter 8).

	Question	Choices
(i)	Among a loanword and its native equivalent, which lexical item do you usually use? (BBK 1999: 174–177)	(a) メリット (*meritto < merit*) (b) 利点 (*riten*) (c) Neither (a) nor (b)
(ii)	Among the following loanword and its native equivalents, which lexical item do you use when: a) talking to friends? b) talking in public? c) talking to elderly people? (NINJAL 2005a: 19)	(a) サポート (*sapooto < support*) (b) 支援 (*shien*) (c) 手助け (*tedasuke*)
(iii)	What do you feel about the present use of loanwords in our daily lives? (BBK 2013: 92)	(a) Like (b) Neither like nor dislike (c) Dislike

Table 3.1: Examples of questions used in the opinion surveys

3.2 BCCWJ: a written corpus

The Balanced Corpus of Contemporary Witten Japanese (BCCWJ) is a written corpus of a hundred million words[1] compiled and released by NINJAL in 2011 (Maekawa et al. 2014). It consists of three sub-corpora, called (i) the Publication sub-corpus (35 million words), (ii) the Library (Library Book) sub-corpus (30 million words) and (iii) the Special-purpose sub-corpus (35 million words).

Data in the first two sub-corpora was compiled with a random sampling technique (NINJAL 2011b: Ch 3). The population[2] of the Publication sub-corpus is complete written texts from books (PB), magazines (PM) and newspapers (PN) that were published in Japan between 2001 and 2005, so the selected sample is a representative of written texts published (or produced) in these media in this specific period of time. The population of the Library Book sub-corpus (LB), in contrast, is complete written texts from books that satisfy the following two criteria: (i) They were published during the period 1986–2005 and (ii) were stocked in the collections of public libraries in 13 or more administrative districts in Tokyo as of 2007 (NINJAL 2011b: 28). The selected sample is therefore considered to be a representative of written texts that have good exposure with the public, i.e., relatively popular texts. The Special-purpose sub-corpus, although it was not based on random sampling, consists of a wide range of written texts, including governmental text from White Papers and Minutes of the Diet, textbooks, online text from *Yahoo! Answers* and *Yahoo! Blog*, and so on.

The first two sub-corpora, the Publication and Library Book sub-corpora, are selected for the purpose of the present sociolinguistic investigation. First,

CHAPTER 3 DATA AND ANALYTICAL METHOD

both of them are good representatives of a given population of written language. Second, they are large enough to collect tokens of particular lexical items. Third, roughly half of the samples contain sociolinguistically useful information on the author, including year of birth, gender and educational background.[3] Such information is not usually available in other corpora of written Japanese, including the Special-purpose sub-corpus, which does not include such information about the authors.

These two sub-corpora are used differently in the current study: The Publication sub-corpus is used as a synchronic corpus to observe language change in apparent time at a certain point of time: the beginning of the 21st century (2001–2005) (Chapters 5 and 6), while the Library Book sub-corpus is used as a diachronic corpus to observe language change in real time over a certain period of time: the 20 years from 1986 to 2005 (Chapter 8).

In these sub-corpora, different types of text, fixed-length and variable-length, are elicited. In the fixed-length data, the length of a sample is fixed at 1,000 characters, which corresponds to approximately 590 words (NINJAL 2011b: 17), starting at a set datum point. In the variable-length data, although containing a starting datum point just as a fixed-length sample does, the length of a sample varies (up to a maximum of 10,000 characters) because a sample is extracted as a complete series of sentences or paragraphs on a certain topic.

The current research uses both types of data depending on the purpose of the investigation. Since every sample is controlled for length, the fixed-length data is more suitable for a more rigorous quantitative analysis, e.g., making a frequency list to elicit basic vocabulary (NINJAL 2011b: 17, 23) (see Section 5.3). Meanwhile, the variable-length data is more suitable for a qualitative analysis of the text (for example, focusing on structure, discourse and stylistics). Since the size of variable-length data in the Publication sub-sorpus (approx. 30 million words) is four times as large as that of the fixed-length data (approx. 8 million words), the variable-length component is more useful for an in-depth study of individual lexical variables, which are relatively rare in frequency compared with phonological or syntactic variables (see Section 5.4 and Chapter 6).

3.3 CSJ: a spoken corpus

The Corpus of Spontaneous Japanese (CSJ) is a collection of spontaneous speech that was released in 2004 by NINJAL and NICT[4] (NINJAL 2006). It consists of recordings of approximately 660 hours, 7.5 million words, from 1,417 speakers under NINJAL and NICT's project conducted between 1999 and 2003.

The majority (approximately 90%) of the recorded speech belongs to the category of monologue speech, which consists of Academic Presentation Speech (APS) and Simulated Public Speech (SPS). The former is a series of recordings of academic presentations given in various fields. The latter includes recordings of public talks given by selected ordinary speakers (but not limited exclusively to non-academics). Speakers are asked to give a talk for 10–12 minutes to a small audience on everyday topics such as "the most joyful moment of my life," "the hardest moment of my life," "the town where I live," and so on.

In order to maximize a stylistic contrast between APS and SPS, the recording staff members tried to make the speech setting as relaxed as possible during the recording of SPS by having a chat with the informant before recording. They also kept trying to show a certain reaction (e.g., nodding) proactively while recoding was taking place. The two types of speech are thus often contrasted in terms of formality: SPS has more relaxed or more informal speech style than APS (NINJAL 2006: 11). Of course, a register difference may not be a direct indicator of formality. Samples in the same register may exhibit various degrees of formality in speech. On such an assumption, samples in APS and SPS are rated individually in terms of various impressionistic aspects of speech style, including Spontaneity, Speaking Rate, Clearness of Speech Articulation, Formality, and so on. Such an evaluation (what they call "impressionistic rating") of these features was done by one of the recording staff members according to a five-point scale. In addition to register distinction, the rating of Formality and Spontaneity will serve as useful factors in the study of linguistic variation (Maekawa 2003).

The use of CSJ enables us to explore spontaneous spoken language. Although it is smaller in sample size than BCCWJ, CSJ is, for the time being, largest of released spoken corpora in Japan, with rich annotation for the speaker's sociolinguitic information.

3.4 Complementary use of different sources of data

The successful account of a given variation requires a collection of data that is good for the purpose of both quantitative and qualitative analyses. In general, the fieldwork methods of observing language in the community are divided into two types: (i) face-to-face interviews and (ii) participant observations. The former technique, originally developed in Labov's study of phonological variation in New York (Labov 1966), is "means of obtaining the volume and quality of recorded speech that is needed for quantitative analysis" (Labov 1984: 29). He, however, draws our attention to the problem of the observer's paradox that sociolinguistic interviews are always faced with. The latter technique, meanwhile, attempts to minimize an observer's effect in the process of data

CHAPTER 3 DATA AND ANALYTICAL METHOD

collection. Still, Labov points out that data collected with this technique is limited in both quality and quantity, concluding that it is important to combine these complementary approaches to reduce the limitations of each (Labov 1984: 30). Consequently both methods are used complementarily throughout the book: (i) interview-based and (ii) corpus-based observations. The former concerns the volume of data required for quantitative analysis, and the latter puts emphasis on the quality of data, i.e., observations with a reduced observer's effect.

The advantage of using the interview method is, first of all, that it makes a large-scale sample immediately available for quantitative analysis. Second, a random sampling technique enables us to elicit a sample that is a good representative of the speakers of Japanese in Japan. Social attributes of speakers, e.g., age, gender, or education, can therefore expect to be well balanced. Third, questions like (ii) in Table 3.1 encourage us to investigate stylistic constraints on the use of loanwords (Chapter 7). Fourth, a real-time approach is also possible for limited items (Chapter 8). Nevertheless there are limitations in using the interview method: The major limitation is that people's self-reports do not necessarily reveal their actual behaviors, because an interview method could maximize the observer's effect on informants' responses. In an interview situation where informants are formally asked about their linguistic behavior, they are likely to become more conscious about the social value of given variants than usual. It should be kept in mind that the questions used here take the form of a direct question, where the interviewer asks informants directly about their lexical choices among prepared sets of lexical items as shown in Table 3.1. Therefore, the results of interview-based study will have to be re-examined by studying linguistic behavior with corpora.

The strength of BCCWJ is, first, that it provides a large and sufficient amount of tokens of individual lexical variables to pursue my research quantitatively. Second, a sample of each sub-corpus is a good representative of a targeted set of written text, which is why this corpus is called a "balanced" one. It is, however, noted that social attributes such as age, gender and education are not annotated for all the authors because such information may not always be traceable. Moreover, the corpus is not well-balanced in terms of social attributes of the authors. Male, well-educated or middle-/old-aged authors are predominant in this corpus. Third, it would be useful to make a contrast between different registers such as books (PB) vs. magazines (PM). It also needs to be noted, however, that although this corpus provides register distinction among books, magazines, and so on, this does not explain fully the mechanism of stylistic difference. Fourth, as BCCWJ is a collection of spontaneous writings, it is expected that the observer's effect in this corpus is reduced compared to formal face-to-face interviews, although writing convention still restricts the author's use of language in a different way. It is still important that the corpus of this scale, with information on social attributes of authors, is available for the sociolinguistic study of infrequent variables like lexical items. Lastly, the Library Book sub-corpus enables us to observe the phenomenon in real time over 20 years between 1986 and 2005.

With regard to CSJ, in contrast to the other two data sources, its sample size may not be enough for us to analyze individual lexical items quantitatively. Second, the corpus is not representative of a particular population as random sampling was not applied in the collection of the speakers. Despite these weaknesses, CSJ is more useful than the rest of the two sources in several aspects. First, the corpus is rich in annotation for social attributes of the speakers, e.g., age, gender, education, and so on. Moreover, speaker attributes are more balanced in terms of age and gender in SPS, particularly when compared with BCCWJ (although young male speakers are predominant in APS). Second, indicators of style such as formality and spontaneity in addition to the contrast between the two registers (APS vs. SPS) will contribute to elicitation of stylistic effects on the phenomenon. Third, as the corpus consists of recordings of spontaneous speech, the observer's effect is expected to be weaker than in formal interviews. It is nevertheless noted that the relatively formal nature of the two registers of public speaking would restricts the speaker's manner of speech in some way.

Taking all these advantages and limitations into account, these data sources are used complementarily in the following analyses. Each data source is worth examining to elucidate different aspects of distribution of loanwords, and it is expected that the synthetic use of these sources will lead us to gain a more comprehensive picture of the linguistic phenomenon in question.

3.5 S-curve model of language change

It is said that language change follows an s-curve pattern (Weinreich, et al. 1968: 113, Chambers & Trudgill 1980: 177–180), or a "slow-quick-quick-slow" pattern (Aitchison 2001: 91), in which a given newer linguistic variant increases slowly at the beginning, has an acceleration in the middle and then a deceleration towards the end. Previous variationist studies have described and interpreted mainly phonological and syntactic variation with an s-curve model (Labov 1972, Sankoff & Larberge 1978, Hibiya 1988b, Matsuda 1993, Nambu 2007, Sano 2008, Sano & Kawahara 2013). Studies such as Chambers (1990) and ISM[5] & NINJAL (2015) showed that lexical alternation also follows an s-shaped pattern.

The purposes of employing an s-curve model to the analysis of language

CHAPTER 3 DATA AND ANALYTICAL METHOD

change are twofold. First, in the context of variationist studies, the main purpose is to identify statistically significant variables that affect the language change in question. A logistic regression model is widely used for this. In the present research, the s-curve model is used for this purpose, i.e., to recognize significant internal and external independent variables on the occurrence of loanwords (Chapters 5 and 6).

Second, quantitative linguistics uses this mathematical model to make a prediction of change. Examples of studies for this purpose include an estimation of duration of phonological change in Yamazoe, Japan (Inoue 2000); an estimation of the period at which the rate of growth of Meiji era "scholarly *kango*" became sluggish (Sanada 2002); a prediction of diachronic process of dialect standardization in Tsuruoka, Japan (Yokoyama & Sanada 2010); a prediction of diachronic process of the use of honorifics in Okazaki, Japan (Yokoyama et al. 2008), and so on. Yokoyama & Sanada (2007) and Sanada (2008) put an emphasis on the usefulness of an s-curve model, not only for the first purpose but also for the second. In other words, they suggest that we make the best of an s-curve model in predicting language change, i.e., deductive (or hypothesis-testing) studies, in contrast to inductive (or descriptive) studies.

With regard to the diffusion of lexical items, Altman et al. (1983: 112) points out that the process of acceptance of words in real time is describable by an s-curve. Hashimoto (2010), in her study of the process of diachronic increase of the loanword stratum in newspapers in the 20th century, demonstrated that an s-curve model fits the data well. Based on these studies, the present research presupposes that loanwords, as opposed to their existing native equivalents, diffuse in an s-shaped manner in both apparent and real time. In fact, a number of previous surveys, including BBK (1999, 2000), NINJAL (2004, 2005a) and Tanaka (2007), show that there is an increase in the adoption of loanwords in apparent time. These studies, however, do not exceed a purely descriptive level. This book hence attempts to employ an s-curve model called the multiple logistic regression to the existing data, so that the resultant statistical model can be used for the prediction of the change in question (Chapters 4, 7 and 8).

The multiple logistic regression model[6] is a statistical model used to estimate the probability of a binary dependent variable based on more than one independent variable. The formula of the model is describable by [Formula 1]. [Formula 1] can be rearranged and yields [Formula 1´] to give a predicted probability p.

$$\log[p/(1-p)] = a_1 x_1 + a_2 x_2 + \ldots + a_n x_n + b \qquad \text{[Formula 1]}$$
$$p = 1/[1 + \exp(-1)(a_1 x_1 + a_2 x_2 + \ldots + a_n x_n + b)] \qquad \text{[Formula 1´]}$$

In the above formulae, p represents the probability of the occurrence of a given variant, while x_n is an independent variable, a_n is a regression coefficient of x_n and b is an intercept. a_n (a regression coefficient) represents how much effect an independent variable x_n has on the probability (See also Section 6.3.3). A positive coefficient means that an independent variable has a positive effect on p, whereas a negative coefficient refers to a negative effect of an independent variable on p. If a coefficient is 0, it refers to no significance of the effect of an independent variable on the outcome. It is important to notice that unlike ordinary linear regression, the output is between 0 and 1, following an s-shaped curve (See Figure 4.11 in Section 4.7, for an example illustration).

In this research the dependent variable is binary, i.e., the occurrence or non-occurrence of loanwords.[7] p is the probability of the occurrence of a given loanword as opposed to that of its native equivalents. Independent variables x_n include (i) Year of Birth (Age), (ii) Education, (iii) Register/Style, (iv) Gender and (v) Year of Survey.

p = Probability of the occurrence of a given loanword as opposed to its native equivalent(s)

x_1 = Year of Birth (Age)

x_2 = Education

x_3 = Register/Style

x_4 = Gender

x_5 = Year of Survey

Year of Birth (Age) is an essential factor for the study of variation and change in apparent time. The question of whether the distribution of a loanword is graded according to the age of the speakers will be examined throughout the book. The following chapter (Chapter 4) puts a primary focus on the structure of age differentiation in the adoption of loanwords. We will see that age differentiation does not show a monotonous gradient, but that it involves a delay in the acquisition process of the new variants among the youngest age group. This may sometimes complicate the description and prediction of process of change.

The effect of Education as one of indicators of social stratification has proved to play an important role in language change in Japanese. For example, more educated people show a stronger orientation toward the preservation of older forms (Tsuruoka dialect forms) than less educated people (NINJAL 2007a: 159–160). It has been shown, however, that they show a higher degree of using newer forms (standardized forms) in their attitudes when it comes to individual phonological, grammatical and lexical items (NINJAL 2007a: 117–157). An educational factor has been examined by a very limited number of researchers in the context of loanword studies. Ishiwata (1965) points out that more educated people exhibit higher levels of recognition of loanwords. The question

CHAPTER 3 DATA AND ANALYTICAL METHOD

then arises as to whether more educated people uses loanwords more frequently. This query will be examined across several chapters (Chapters 5, 6 and 7), revealing that the effect of education is modified by register/style.

Register/Style, besides age and social stratification such as education, is expected to be another important factor that determines the sociolinguistic contexts of utterances. The question of whether or not loanwords are favored in formal registers or settings will be examined in Chapters 5, 6 and 7. It will also be shown that stylistic differentiation is more prominent among more educated people (Chapter 7). These observations are useful to evaluate the sociolinguistic status of loanwords as opposed to their equivalent existing native forms.

With regard to Gender, its effect on the adoption of loan variants is not consistent across words. This is because adoption is specific to the context of the words in question. The current research will show that those that are well attested in the domain of business tend to be favored by men, whereas those that are well attested in the domain of everyday life may be favored by women (Chapter 4). On the other hand, the gender effect will not prove to be significant on the adoption of the well-attested loanwords *keesu* (< *case*) (Chapter 6) and *sapooto* (< *support*) (Chapter 7). These results seem to show that Gender is not a bona-fide variable per se.

Year of Survey is an important factor for the study of language change in real time. In particular, the combination of this factor and Age/Year of Birth allows us to examine the variability of the community as a whole over time, and, at the same time, the variability of the individual speakers under investigation over their lifespan. The examination of these variables will reveal that the process of language change cannot be described as simply as the apparent-time hypothesis presupposes (Chapter 8).

The goodness of fit of a given logistic regression model is evaluated by a value of R^2, i.e., the coefficient of determination (contribution ratio), unless otherwise noted. R^2 is the square of a coefficient of correlation between (i) observed values and (ii) predicted values under the model in question (Yokoyama & Wada 2006). It ranges from 0 to 1, and 1 represents the maximum contribution.

3.6 Issues of extending variationist methodology to lexical variation

Before looking at the distribution of any set of lexical items, we need to discuss the general problem of the study of lexical variation, i.e., the question of in what manner lexical items are treated within the framework of variationist study.

As Labov states, "the definition of a linguistic variable is the first and also the last step in the analysis of variation" (2004: 7). In its original sense, a linguistic variable is defined as "the option of saying 'the same thing' in several different ways: that is, the variants are identical in referential or truth value" (Labov 1972: 271). In other words, an alternation between competing variants should not involve a change in meaning. For instance, the presence or absence of [r] in *fourth floor* does not affect their meaning per se. In this sense, phonological variables are considered to be most useful (Lavandera 1978: 176).

Variationists are nevertheless aware that "variable elements are found at all levels of linguistic structure" (Weiner & Labov 1983: 31). The question then arises as to whether or not the original notion of *semantic equivalence* developed in the study of phonological variation could be applied in a strict sense to the analysis of non-phonological variation. This is because, although phonological alternations are meaning-preserving, alternations of different forms at non-phonological levels are not necessarily so. With regard to lexical variation, the application of the traditional notion of semantic equivalence might become even more problematic because "there are no true synonyms in an absolute sense" (Labov 1978: 8). It seems that the notion of semantic equivalence potentially poses a problem in studying variables "above and beyond phonology" (Sankoff, G. 1973).

These discussions show that the notion of semantic equivalence is not applicable to the identification of non-phonological variables (Lavandera 1978). In other words, the definition of a linguistic variable needs revising. Weiner & Labov (1983: 31), in their analysis of variation between active and passive forms, points out that, "there is no reason to confine the study of variation to alternative ways of saying the same thing, although this kind of variable has been the chief focus in the development of variable rules." Labov also admits the existence of stylistic demands that force substitution of one word for another as a stylistic variant (1978: 8). Weiner & Labov (1983: 30) states:

> But it seems to us that this concession to an idealistic semantics is needlessly unrealistic. If we isolate words from their use, we can show that there is no such thing as a precise synonym, since all words have slightly different privileges of occurrence when we consider every possible context. But in practice, the need for stylistic variation leads all speakers and writers of English to substitute one word for the other with the expectation that any differences that might arise in other contexts will not affect interpretation in that one.

Lavandera (1978: 181) and Sankoff, D. (1982: 683) suggest that, for non-phonological variables, the condition of semantic equivalence be "relaxed" and that *functional equivalence* or *discourse equivalence* be employed instead. In

CHAPTER 3 DATA AND ANALYTICAL METHOD

the study of Montreal French by Sankoff & Thibault (1980: 312), they identify environment where *avoir* ('to have') and *être* ('to be') share the same function as auxiliaries by eliminating contexts where they have other functions, e.g., the use of *être* as a copula. It would seem that the analysis of variation on a non-phonological level is not unreasonable if we accept replacing the original notion of semantic equivalence with the notion of functional or discourse equivalence. However, we should note that "we obviously have a much better chance of getting intersubjective agreement in identifying formal variants than semantic variants," or, "the possibility of accurate measurement is less immediate with semantic variation" (Weiner & Labov 1983: 31).

With the above discussion, I am attempting to apply the notion of functional equivalence to the analysis of lexical variation among the loanword *keesu* (< *case* as in *there is a case where...*) and its native equivalents *jirei*, *baai* and *rei* (Chapter 6). I will identify carefully which environments should be counted as variable contexts and which should not be, by means of having a closer look at the functions of the proposed lexical variants depending on context. It is noted that most lexical items are polysemous and have their own unique functions and any irrelevant contexts are excluded from the analysis. For example, the loanword *keesu* can refer to 'a container' as a concrete noun as opposed to its (principal) usage as a formal noun, which is shared by the four lexical variants. Furthermore, it is reported that the native form *baai* can often be used to form a hypothetical subordinate clause to mean 'if/when' whereas the loanword *keesu* and the rest of the native forms cannot be used in this function (Kim 2011). Categorical (or non-overlapped) environments like these should not fall within the scope of variationist analysis (Lavandera 1978: 178). Note that here I only focus on function, not on meaning, of a word. I disregard difference in nuance or connotation of each expression that might be recognized differently by "idiosyncratic interpretation" (Tagliamonte 2006: 74).[8]

The above procedure gives a fine-grained analysis of the diffusion of loan variants but it is also a painstaking task, since the analyst is required to identify all usages, or functions, of sets of given lexical variants by examining all tokens that occur in a corpus. The primary limitation of this approach then is that the analyst cannot observe enough loanwords at a time as to draw a general conclusion about the distribution of loanwords.

To overcome this problem, Chapters 5 and 8 will undertake a more comprehensive approach. This approach takes into account all the environments in which potential lexical variants occur. As shown later, we will find the general tendency for loan variants to replace their native equivalents in apparent time. Moreover, we will also find that loan variants are distributed differently along social dimensions such as education and style. This approach may be criticized for not excluding "noise" in the data, but it enables us to observe a larger amount of linguistic variables, with the result that the analyst can avoid the risk of drawing a general conclusion from a too small pool of data.

It is noted that the above discussion of circumscribing the variable context is regarded as a matter relevant only to the study of natural speech with a discursive context (Chapters 5 and 6). Interview-based studies (Chapters 4 and 7) primarily concern the speaker's choice between conceptually synonymous forms A and B, with no discursive context attached. In the latter cases, we are only looking at the status of a given lexical item in one's mental lexicon, and thus its distribution in natural speech is disregarded in principle.

Notes

1 Here, SUW (short unit word) is used for counting words. For more detail about morphological analyses in BCCWJ, see NINJAL (2011b: Ch4).

2 The population of each sub-corpus is calculated in terms of the number of characters (not words) contained in the publications in question.

3 Educational history of the author is not included in the official corpus DVD and therefore has to be identified by data from the questionnaire survey of authors conducted separately by NINJAL between 2006 and 2010. I obtained special permission from NINJAL to use this additional information.

4 The National Institute of Information and Communications Technology

5 The Institute of Statistical Mathematics

6 Variable rule program (Cedergren & Sankoff 1974) and SPSS are available for a multiple logistic analysis. Examples of analysis of language change in Japanese using the former include Hibiya (1988b) and Matsuda (1993), and those using the latter include Nambu (2007) and Sano (2008, 2011).

7 Although the dependent variable can have more than two values (e.g., LW, SJ, NJ), binary logistic regression is employed since the focus of the present study is on the occurrence/non-occurrence of the LW.

8 Tagliamonte (2006: 73–4) points out that there are two different levels of meaning. In regards to meaning, there is, on the one hand, "comprehensive meaning, which takes into consideration every possible inference," and which is "subject to idiosyncratic interpretation and an infinite range of potential meanings." On the other hand, there is "meaning as it is used in the speech community," which is "by definition a consensus that is shared and relatively constant." It should be noted that meaning in the latter sense should represent a narrower interpretation.

CHAPTER 4

Age as an External Factor[1]

4.1 Apparent-time approach to language change

The apparent-time approach aims to predict the existence or direction of change from age differentiation as observed in a single synchronic study. Figure 4.1 shows lexical variation in apparent time in Canadian English (Chambers 1990). The figure demonstrates that younger people tend to use the American lexical variant *couch* as opposed to the Canadian equivalent *chesterfield*.

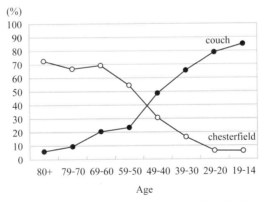

Figure 4.1: Lexical choice by the speaker's age in Canadian English
(Adapted from Chambers 1990: 162, Figure 1)

The age differentiation predicts two things here. First, the age gradient is an indication of a change in progress, so it is possible to predict that *couch* will spread further, replacing *chesterfield* according to the alternation of generations. Second, the age gradient in apparent time can be considered the rate of change in real time. These predictions are based on the well-known hypothesis that one's linguistic system, acquired during the critical period of language acquisition, is invariable throughout one's lifetime (Apparent-Time

36

Hypothesis).

The apparent-time approach is a popular way of studying language variation and change (Labov 1963, 1972; Trudgill 1974, among others) since one can predict the existence and direction of change to a certain degree even when real-time data is not immediately available. Japanese sociolinguists, such as Shibata (1978), Matsuda (1993), Hibiya (1995), Nambu (2007), Sano (2008), have also mainly used this approach in their studies of variation and change.

This chapter, using 17 loanwords as examples, examines how these loanwords spread over generations. Based on several nationwide opinion polls conducted around 2000, we will see that synchronic distributions of loanwords indicate the presence of an ongoing increase in the adoption of loanwords. I will also show that their distributions are predictable with an s-curve model.

4.2 Opinion surveys

We shall examine the diffusion of 17 loanwords based on self-reports collected from four nationwide opinion polls conducted between 1999 and 2004. Table 4.1 gives a summary of the surveys. Each survey targeted the whole Japanese-speaking population in Japan aged 15 or 16 and above. The samples are 3,000 to 4,500 people randomly selected from the population (stratified random sampling). The number of valid response ranges from 2,000 to 3,000. In a face-to-face interview, an informant was asked to choose between a loanword and its native equivalent(s), that s/he feels most familiar with (in Survey A), uses most often (in Survey B), wants to use most (in Survey C), or uses when talking to friends (in Survey D) (provided that the given variants are used in the same sense).

Survey ID	Name of survey -[Question no.]	Month/Year of survey	Targeted population	No. and % of valid response
A	Opinion Poll on the National Language: Heisei 10 (1998) (BBK 1999: 174–177) -[Q21]	Jan/1999	those aged 16 and above	2200 (73.3%)
B	Opinion Poll on the National Language: Heisei 11(1999) (BBK 2000: 18) -[Q4]	Jan/2000	those aged 16 and above	2196 (73.2%)
C	The National Survey on Attitudes to Loanwords (NINJAL 2004: 38, 43) -[Q12–13]	Oct-Nov/ 2003	those aged 15 and above	3087 (68.6%)
D	The National Survey on Attitudes to Loanwords II (NINJAL 2005a: 19) -[Q2][2]	Oct-Nov/ 2004	those aged 15 and above	3090 (68.7%)

Table 4.1: Nationwide opinion surveys on loanwords

The proportion of those who selected "loanwords" as opposed to the rest of the choices, i.e., "native equivalents," "use both," "do not use either of them" and/or "not sure," is considered to be the level of diffusion of the loanword in question. The overall level of diffusion of each loanword is provided as "LW (%)" in Table 4.2. Loanwords 1–8, 9–14, 15–16, and 17 were examined in Surveys A, B, C, and D, respectively. The distribution of each item across age and gender is provided in Appendix A.

ID	Loanwords (LW)			Native equivalents		LW (%)
	Lemma_JP	Lemma	Etymology	Lemma_JP	Lemma	
1	ニーズ	niizu	needs	必要性	hitsuyoosei	36.4
2	イベント	ibento	event	催し	moyooshi	58.2
3	メリット	meritto	merit	利点	riten	57.9
4	コンセンサス	konsensasu	consensus	合意	gooi	9.0
5	スキーム	sukiimu	scheme	計画	keikaku	3.5
6	リスク	risuku	risk	危険性	kikensei	35.5
7	ビジョン	bijon	vision	展望	tenboo	30.7
8	アカウンタビリティ	akauntabiriti	accountability	説明責任	setsumei sekinin	3.6
9	ワイン	wain	wine	ぶどう酒	budooshu	75.6
10	スーツ	suutsu	suit	背広	sebiro	52.8
11	キッチン	kitchin	kitchen	台所	daidokoro	12.1
12	オープンする	oopun-suru	(to) open	開店する	kaiten-suru	34.6
13	ゲットする	getto-suru	(to) get	獲得する	kakutoku-suru	14.0
14	トータルで	tootaru-de	(in) total	合計で	gookei-de	13.3
15	キャンセル	kyanseru	cancel	解約 取り消し	kaiyaku torikeshi	57.5
16	ハッピー	happii	happy	幸福 幸せ	koofuku shiawase	17.7
17	サポート	sapooto	support	支援 手助け	shien tedasuke	33.4

Table 4.2: The 17 selected LW variants and their native equivalents

We should pay attention to a fundamental semantic difference between a loanword and its corresponding native word(s) because such a difference may affect the distribution of paired lexical items as I discuss later in Section 4.7. I conducted keyword searches within the written corpus BCCWJ for some of the words listed in Table 4.2.[3] There appear to be two types of semantic difference.

First, there are cases in which we can find a relatively clear division of labor between a loan variant and its native variant. For example, the loanword *getto-suru* (< *get*) tends to take a concrete noun that can be obtained relatively easily in exchange for money (e.g., clothing, a car, and so on) as its object (4.1a); in contrast, the corresponding SJ word *kakutoku-suru* shows a stronger association with abstract things, that is, something that cannot be simply exchanged for money (e.g., right, status, prize, prize money, knowledge, and so on) and gives the impression that more effort is required to obtain the object (4.1b).

(4.1) a. 人気雑誌を確実にGETするには？   (PM21_00604)
      Ninki zasshi-o kakujitsuni getto-suru ni-wa?
      Popular **magazine**-ACC certainly get-do in.order.to-TOP
      'How to get a popular **magazine** certainly/successfully.'

    b. 平和と自由を獲得する   (PB34_00305)
      Heiwa to jiyuu-o *kakutoku*-suru
      Peace and freedom-ACC get-do
      'Gain **peace and freedom**'

Second, there are cases in which a loan variant covers a more general area of meaning and thus is used more widely than its native existing variant. For example, the loanword *suutsu* (< *suit*) is used to refer to clothing for both genders in the corpus (4.2a-b), while its native equivalent *sebiro* is usually used to refer to men's clothing (4.2c). Another example is the loanword *oopun-suru* (< *open*), which takes a more diverse range of things as its subject; it co-occurs not only with shops or restaurants (4.3a) but also with other locations such as galleries, institutions, facilities, and so on (4.3b). In contrast, the SJ word *kaiten-suru* ('open') is usually associated with shops as its morpheme *ten* (店 'shop') literally indicates (4.3c).

(4.2) a. 上品なスーツを着こなしたリッチそうな中年男である。   (PB13_00524)
      Joohin-na suutsu-o kikonashi-ta ritchi-souna
      chuunen otoko dearu.
      elegent-COP suits-ACC dressed.well-PAST rich-seems.to.be
      middle-aged **man** be
      'He is a middle-aged **man** dressed well in an elegant suit.'

CHAPTER 4 AGE AS AN EXTERNAL FACTOR   39

b.（母親は）子供が洋服の場合は、子供に合わせてスーツやワンピ
ースが適切である。   (PB13_00726)
(Hahaoya-wa) kodomo-ga yoofuku-no baai-wa,
kodomo-ni awasete suutsu ya wanpiisu-ga tekisetsu dearu.
(mother-TOP) child-NOM Western.clothes-GEN case-TOP,
child-to dressed.alike suit or one-piece.dress-NOM appropriate be
'(**Mother**) should wear a suit or a one-piece dress if her child is in
Western clothes.'

c. 男達の二人は背広に短靴といういでたちで、   (PB27_00160)
Otokotachi no futari-wa sebiro ni tangutsu toiu idetachi-de,
men of two.people-TOP suit with low.shoes of attire-in
'Two of those **men** were in their suits with low shoes,'

(4.3) a. 近所にアイスクリーム屋がオープンした。   (PB39_00017)
Kinjo ni aisukuriimu ya-ga oopun-shita.
neighborhood in **ice.cream shop**-NOM open-do.PAST
'A (new) **ice cream shop** has been opened in the neighborhood.'

b. 新しい保育所がオープンした。   (PN1a_00005)
Atarashii hoikusho-ga oopun-shita.
new **nurcery.school**-NOM open-do.PAST
'A new **nursery school** has been opened.'

c. シャネルブティック第1号店が開店したカンボン通り。 (PM51_00101)
Shaneru butikku daiichigoo-ten-ga kaiten-shita kanbon doori.
Chanel boutique first-shop-NOM open-do.PAST Cambon street
'Cambon Street, where **the first Chanel boutique** was opened.'

4.3 Distribution according to gender

Table 4.3 shows the average level of diffusion of each loanword by gender. The
differences between males and females are shown in bold when they are 5% or
above. Male speakers appear to have higher preference for *konsensasu* (< *con-census*), *bijon* (< *vision*) and *risuku* (< *risk*), for example (see also Figure 4.4 for
risuku). Female speakers, meanwhile, appear to have higher preference for
suutsu (< *suit*), *oopun-suru* (< *open*) and *kitchin* (< *kitchen*), and so on (see also
Figure 4.2 for *suutsu*).

ID	Loanwords	Etymology	Male	Female	Difference (M-F)
1	*niizu*	needs	37.9	35.1	2.8
2	*ibento*	event	58.3	58.1	0.2
3	*meritto*	merit	58.2	57.6	0.6
4	*konsensasu*	consensus	12.9	5.6	7.3
5	*sukiimu*	scheme	4.2	2.8	1.4
6	*risuku*	risk	38.3	33.2	5.1
7	*bijon*	vision	34.4	27.4	7.0
8	*akauntabiriti*	accountability	4.3	3.0	1.3
9	*wain*	wine	74.2	76.7	-2.5
10	*suutsu*	suit	46.3	58.1	**-11.8**
11	*kitchin*	kitchen	8.4	15.1	**-6.7**
12	*oopun-suru*	(to) open	28.7	39.3	**-10.6**
13	*getto-suru*	(to) get	11.7	15.8	-4.1
14	*tootaru-de*	(in) total	14.0	12.7	1.3
15	*kyanseru*	cancel	55.4	59.1	-3.7
16	*happii*	happy	16.8	18.4	-1.6
17	*sapooto*	support	32.5	34.2	-1.7

Table 4.3: Diffusion (%) of loanwords by gender

4.4 Distribution according to age

Self-reports show that there are two patterns of distribution by age: (i) a mono-tonically increasing s-shaped curve; (ii) an s-shaped curve that ends in a drop.

The first group shows a typical s-shaped curve, with the diffusion of loan-words monotonically increasing from older to younger generations. It includes the loanwords such as *wain* (< *wine*), *suutsu* (< *suit*), *getto-suru* (< *get*), *ibento* (< *event*) and *happii* (< *happy*). For example, the distribution of *suutsu* (< *suit*) among females shows a typical s-shaped curve, in which the diffusion is acceler-ated at the age group 50–59 and starts to decelerate at the age group 20–29 (Figure 4.2). *Wain* (< *wine*) appears to be reaching the final stage of an s-shaped growth, where the diffusion starts decelerating at the age group 40–49 and then begins to level out at almost 100% among the age groups 20–29 and below (Figure 4.3).

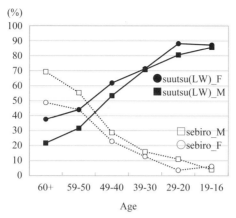

Figure 4.2: The LW *suutsu* (< *suit*) and *sebiro* by age

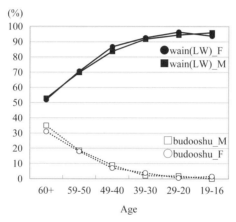

Figure 4.3: The LW *wain* (< *wine*) and *budooshu* by age

The second group, on the other hand, forms an s-shaped curve that ends in a drop in the diffusion of loanwords among those in their late teens and/or twenties. For example, Figure 4.4 shows that the diffusion of *risuku* (< *risk*) increases as the speakers become younger but there is a drop by approximately 10% between those aged 20–29 and those aged 16–19. A drop among those in their teens is also observed in loanwords such as *sapooto* (< *support*), *kyanseru* (< *cancel*), *oopun-suru* (< *open*) and *bijon* (< *vision*, male speakers only). A drop also occurs among those in their twenties. *Niizu* (< *needs*), for example, peaks at the 30–39 age group and then begin to drift downward at the age group 20–29 (Figure 4.5). A similar pattern is also observed in *meritto* (< *merit*, male speakers only).

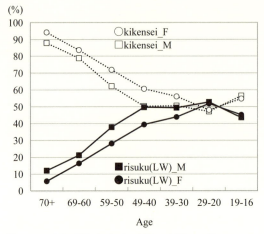

Figure 4.4: The LW *risuku* (< *risk*) and *kikensei* by age

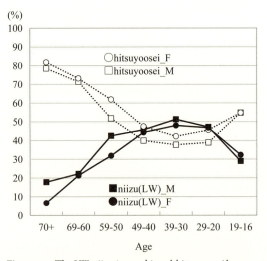

Figure 4.5: The LW *niizu* (< *needs*) and *hitsuyoosei* by age

The third group shows no pattern across age groups. This includes the loanwords such as *konsensasu* (< *concensus*), *sukiimu* (< *scheme*) and *akauntabiriti* (< *accountability*). We can see in Table 4.2 that the average level of diffusion of these loanwords is less than 10%.

4.5 Delay in loanword diffusion among the youngest age group(s)

Why does a delay in the diffusion of loanwords often occur among the youngest age group(s)? A possible reason is that they have not yet fully acquired the usage of the loanwords in question. We notice that such a delay often occurs in loanwords that are well attested in business environments, e.g., *niizu* (< *needs*) and *risuku* (< *risk*). These words appear to be less familiar to those in their late teens or early twenties, who either have not entered or are still new to the job market.[4]

In fact, a similar age distribution pattern has often been attested to in the process of dialect standardization in Japan. The studies in Shirakawa and Tsuruoka demonstrated that there is a delay in standardization of the dialects among those aged 20–24 and below (Shibata 1978: 236, see also Kunihiro, Inoue & Long (eds.) 1999: Ch11). Shibata points out that the youngest age groups tend to be delayed in acquiring standard forms because in general they have fewer social opportunities in which the use of standardized language is required than the older age groups do. He predicts from a diachronic point of view that a drop due to acquisitional delay will become gentle or disappear after a while.

Inoue (2000) shows such a process in a diagram (Figure 4.6). The figure demonstrates that the synchronic distribution in which the diffusion of an innovative variant drops at the youngest age group appears in the middle of the whole s-curve growth as shown in (b). It is then turned to a monotonically increasing s-curve at later stages of language change as shown in (c) and (d).

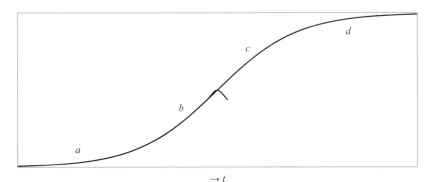

Figure 4.6: Process of language standardization over time

(Inoue 2000: 530, Figure 26-4)

Let us turn to the distribution of *niizu* (< *needs*), which shows the most striking acquisitional delay among the youngest speakers as shown in Figure 4.5.

Figure 4.7 shows diachronic shifts in the diffusion of *niizu* in terms of the level of recognition, comprehension and the actual use of the lexical item.[5] The result is based on the national survey conducted by NHK in 1995 (NHK 1995: 70) and the opinion polls conducted by BBK in 2002 and 2009 (BBK 2003: 189, 2009: 244). The upward trend over the almost 15 years from 1995 to 2009 confirms that the diffusion of the loanword is in progress in the community overall.

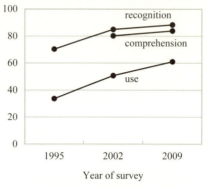

Figure 4.7: Diffusion (%) of *niizu* (< *needs*) over time
(Adapted from NHK 1995: 70; BBK 2003: 189; BBK 2009: 244)

The diffusion, however, does not progress in the same way for all age groups. Figure 4.8 compares the proportion of those who stated that they actually use *niizu* by speakers' age and year of survey.[6] The figure shows that the use of *niizu* increased in seven years from 2002 to 2009 among those aged 50–59 and above, meanwhile it remains at almost the same level for the age groups of 40–49 and below (except the age group 30–39). This implies that the change in favor of *niizu* is in progress in the former age groups. When the distribution in Figure 4.8 is sorted by speakers' year of birth as shown in Figure 4.9, we notice that the use of *niizu* between 2002 and 2009 increases among those born in the 1960s and later. This implies that the acquisitional delay in these generations in 2002 reduced in 2009.

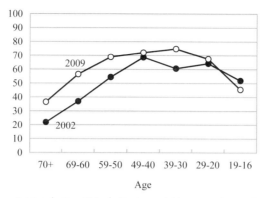

Figure 4.8: Distribution (%) of *niizu* (< *needs*) by age and year of survey
(Adapted from BBK 2003: 189; BBK 2009: 244)

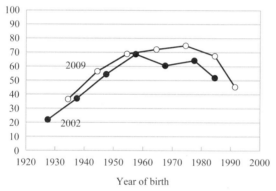

Figure 4.9: Distribution (%) of *niizu* (< *needs*) by year of birth and year of survey
(Adapted from BBK 2003: 189; BBK 2009: 244)

The above discussion leads us to conclude that this is a change in progress in the community as a whole, but, at the same time, involves *age-grading*[7] among the youngest age groups. It seems that the diffusion of the loanword *niizu* is in the middle of an s-curve growth, i.e., located in (b) in Figure 4.6. We can therefore predict that synchronic distribution of *niizu* will become a monotonically increasing s-curve pattern as shown in (c) or (d) in Figure 4.6 as the diffusion process reaches a more advanced stage.

It is then clear that the second group of loanwords, like *niizu*, should be predictable by a monotonically increasing s-curve model when viewed from a long-range perspective of language change, as is the case with the first group. This raises the question of how the influence of the acquisitional delay should be treated in an s-curve model. This point will be discussed in the following section.

4.6 Developing an s-curve model

A logistic regression analysis is employed to model the diffusion of the 17 loanwords. Before conducting analysis, we have to consider how to treat the influence of the acquisitional delay in the model. A monotonically increasing logistic curve does not fit well to the data if the loanword distribution ends in a drop among the youngest age groups, like *niizu* does. In such a case, a possible way of tackling the problem would be to exclude data from the youngest generations in which a drop occurs. Exclusion of data, however, may not be the best choice in this case as they are not completely random outliers: The observed acquisitional delay is well attested across various linguistic variables in the language (Shibata 1978). Another possibility then is the inclusion of such a disruptive effect as an independent variable. Yokoyama & Sanada (2007) suggests that a disruptive factor can be separated from independent variables of capital interest to an analyst by including it as one of the independent variables. The disruptive factor called Acquisition is therefore included in the model.

Note that Acquisition was coded as a numeral variable. The value (e.g., 0, 1, or 2) represents a distance from an age group with the highest level of loanword adoption: The higher the value is, the more striking the delay in the loanword acquisition is. For instance, if a drop in diffusion occurs between those aged 20–29 and those aged 16–19, those aged 20–29 and older are coded as "0" whereas those aged 16–19 are coded as "1." In the case of a drop occurring between the age group 30–39 and the age group of 16–19, those aged 30–39 and older are coded as "0," those aged 20–29 are coded as "1" and those aged 16–19 are coded as "2." In fact, most of those classified as "loanwords showing a monotonically increasing s-shaped curve" in Section 4.4, numerically speaking, involve a slight drop among the youngest age group. Although it seems very small, such a drop is automatically marked as "acquisitional delay" (see Appendix A for detail).

The general model of the loanword diffusion shown in Section 3.5, i.e., [Formula 1], is repeated below, with (x_1) Year of Birth, (x_2) Gender and (x_3) Acquisition included as independent variables.[8] p is the probability of the diffusion of (or preference for) a loanword as opposed to its native equivalent(s). Table 4.4 shows how samples are coded in the case of *niizu*, for example.

$$\log[p/(1-p)] = a_1 x_1 + a_2 x_2 + \dots + a_n x_n + b \qquad \text{[Formula 1]}$$

x_1 = Year of Birth (converted from age)
x_2 = Gender (M = 0, F = 1)
x_3 = Acquisition (numeral)

Gender		Age	Year of Birth (median)	Acquisition	Diffusion of LW (%)
M	o	16–19	1981.5	2	29.0
M	o	20–29	1974.5	1	47.2
M	o	30–39	1964.5	o	51.3
M	o	40–49	1954.5	o	45.7
M	o	50–59	1944.5	o	42.5
M	o	60–69	1934.5	o	22.2
M	o	70+	1924.5	o	17.8
F	I	16–19	1981.5	2	32.3
F	I	20–29	1974.5	1	46.8
F	I	30–39	1964.5	o	48.0
F	I	40–49	1954.5	o	44.3
F	I	50–59	1944.5	o	31.9
F	I	60–69	1934.5	o	21.3
F	I	70+	1924.5	o	6.6

Table 4.4: Data coding for *niizu* (< *needs*)

The logistic regression analyses (stepwise, at a significance level of 0.05) of the 17 variables were conducted with SPSS. The results are listed in Table 4.5 in order of the overall level of diffusion of the loanwords, i.e., "Diffusion of LW (%)." "Regression Coefficient (B)" and "Constant" in the table correspond respectively to a_n and b in [Formula 1] (see Section 3.5). "NA" means that the factor in question is irrelevant and thus was not incorporated into the model.

LW	Etymology	Diffusion of LW (%)	Year of Birth (a_1)	Gender (a_2)	Acquisition (a_3)	Constant (b)
wain	wine	75.6	0.0746	o	-0.9367	-144.2208
ibento	event	58.2	0.0590	o	-1.2462	-114.6673
meritto	merit	57.9	0.0497	-0.2466	-0.8044	-96.5074
kyanseru	cancel	57.5	0.0320	o	-0.8180	-62.1183
suutsu	suit	52.8	0.0632	0.4099	o	-123.4208
niizu	needs	36.4	0.0484	o	-0.8939	-94.8470
risuku	risk	35.5	0.0430	-0.2468	-0.8558	-84.4045
oopun-suru	(to) open	34.6	0.0148	0.4192	o	-29.7063
sapooto	support	33.4	0.0411	o	-0.9895	-80.9564
bijon	vision	30.7	0.0335	-0.4330	-0.7988	-66.0486
happii	happy	17.7	0.0252	o	-0.5711	-50.7461
getto-suru	(to) get	14.0	0.0786	o	NA	-155.9317
tootaru-de	(in) total	13.3	0.0193	o	o	-39.6040
kitchin	kitchen	12.1	o	0.6065	NA	-2.3075
konsensasu	consensus	9.0	o	-0.8833	NA	-2.0198
akauntabiriti	accountability	3.6	o	o	NA	-3.3621
sukiimu	scheme	3.5	o	o	NA	-3.4305

Table 4.5: Results of the regression analyses of the 17 variables: Model A

As for loanwords whose diffusion involves a delay in acquisition among the youngest generation, we contrasted the analysis that includes the variable Acquisition in the model (called "Model A," with its result shown in Table 4.5) with one that does not include it (called "Model B"). Table 4.6 compares the values of R^2 (i.e., coefficient of determination, see Section 3.5 for details) for Model A with the values of R^2 for Model B where relevant. The positive values in the difference in R^2 between Models A and B (R^2 [A–B]) show that Model A better fits to the data in most cases. The values of Regression Coefficient (B) and Constant for Model B are not shown here for this reason. Since R^2 usually increases when more independent variables are added to a model, AIC is also calculated in order to evaluate the contribution of the inclusion of the new variable. The table shows again that Model A gives better fits to the data since it almost always has the smaller AIC.

LW	Etymology	R^2			AIC		
		Model A	Model B	A–B	Model A	Model B	A–B
wain	wine	0.99	0.99	0	59.58	59.58	0
ibento	event	0.96	0.91	0.05	88.14	106.81	-18.67
meritto	merit	0.91	0.75	0.16	94.90	125.77	-30.87
kyanseru	cancel	0.90	0.64	0.26	71.13	83.81	-12.68
suutsu	suit	0.98	0.98	0	69.10	69.10	0
niizu	needs	0.89	0.39	0.50	89.86	143.61	-53.75
risuku	risk	0.89	0.76	0.13	93.99	111.84	-17.85
oopun-suru	(to) open	0.86	0.86	0	69.90	69.90	0
sapooto	support	0.93	0.72	0.21	85.28	109.62	-24.33
bijon	vision	0.93	0.83	0.10	82.89	91.58	-8.69
happii	happy	0.71	0.57	0.14	70.37	72.79	-2.41
getto-suru	(to) get	0.97	NA	NA	60.70	NA	NA
tootaru-de	(in) total	0.65	0.65	0	62.74	62.74	0
kitchin	kitchen	0.68	NA	NA	60.01	NA	NA
konsensasu	consensus	0.41	NA	NA	82.91	NA	NA
akauntabiriti	accountability	<0.01	NA	NA	64.78	NA	NA
sukiimu	scheme	0.02	NA	NA	58.88	NA	NA

Table 4.6: Comparison of Model A and Model B (*with/without* the inclusion of the variable Acquisition)

We turn to Table 4.5, where Year of Birth is shown to be significant for all but the four items at the bottom, i.e., *kitchin, konsensasu, akauntabiriti* and *sukiimu*. Note that the level of diffusion of these four loanwords remains very low (3.5–12.1%). Given that the process of linguistic change progresses in a similar manner to that of "diffusion of innovations" (Rogers 2003) as Jinnouchi (2007) points out, these four loanwords appear to have been at a very early stage of diffusion, where only a small number of people called Innovators or Early Adopters adopt an innovation as shown in Figure 4.10. According to the figure, the diffusion of a given innovation rapidly grows after being adopted by 16% of the population, where it then starts to be adopted by the Early Majority. It is thus possible that age differentiation is not significant in the case that the level of diffusion does not greatly exceed 16%.

Meanwhile, Year of Birth is shown to be a significant variable for the rest of 13 loanwords, including those of which diffusion is more or less 16% (i.e., *happii, getto-suru, tootaru-de*) as well as those of which diffusion largely exceeds 16%. A positive coefficient indicates that the younger the speakers are, the higher the probability of the diffusion of loanwords becomes. The result allows us to interpret that the diffusion of these 13 loanwords is in progress in apparent time, indicating that there is an ongoing increase in the adoption of these loanwords. Gender and Acquisition are not always significant. The effects of these factors are interpreted in the following section.

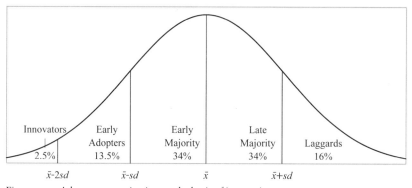

Figure 4.10: Adopter categorization on the basis of innovativeness

(Rogers 2003: 281, Figure 7-3)

4.7 Predicting change based on apparent-time distributions

This section attempts to make a prediction of loanword diffusion based on the results of the logistic regression analyses shown in Table 4.5. The probability p is calculated with [Formula 1′], which is derived from [Formula 1]. For example, the probability of the adoption of *niizu* (< *needs*) among female speakers aged 16–19 is predictable with the equation in [Formula 1″] by substituting "1981.5" for x_1 (Year of Birth), "1" for x_2 (Gender), and "2" for x_3 (Acquisition) (see Table 4.4 for data coding scheme for informants with other social attributes, and Table 4.5 for the values of a_n and b for other lexical variables). The prediction was made for 100 years of generations including the observed age groups (50 to 60 years of generations) and also the future generations following them.

$$p = 1/[1+\exp(-1)(a_1x_1 + a_2x_2 + \ldots + a_nx_n + b)] \quad \text{[Formula 1']}$$
$$p = 1/[1+\exp(-1)(0.0484(x_1) + 0(x_2) - 0.8939(x_3) - 94.8470 + b)] \quad \text{[Formula 1'']}$$

First, neither Acquisition nor Gender is shown to be significant for the loanwords *getto-suru* (< *get*) and *tootaru-de* (< *total*). In these cases, the diffusion of the loanwords is predictable from Year of Birth alone. Figure 4.11 shows the predicted probability of the preference for *getto-suru* over its native equivalent *kakutoku-suru* ('to get'). It is predicted that its diffusion will proceed without a delay among the youngest age group(s).

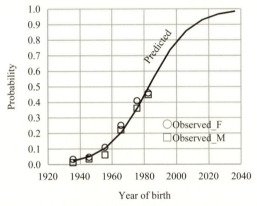

Figure 4.11: Predicted diffusion of *getto-suru* (< *get*)

Second, Acquisition is shown to be significant for all lexical items but *suutsu* (< *suit*), *oopun-suru* (< *open*) and *tootaru-de* (< *total*). In all the cases this factor has a negative effect on the loanword diffusion. The inclusion of this variable, however, does not always greatly improve the model's goodness of fit to the data. Those loanwords whose coefficient of determination (R^2) increase by 0.1 and above include *meritto* (< *merit*), *kyanseru* (< *cancel*), *niizu* (< *needs*), *risuku* (< *risk*), *sapooto* (< *support*), *bijon* (< *vision*) and *happii* (< *happy*) as shown in bold in Table 4.6.

R^2 for *niizu* (< *needs*), for example, reaches 0.89 when Acquisition is incorporated into the model (Model A), whereas it decreases to 0.39 when this variable is not included (Model B). Figure 4.12 compares the goodness of fit of the models with each other (in the case of male speakers). The figure demonstrates that Model A fits the observed values much better than the Model B (the same holds true for female speakers). This implies that the inclusion of the variable Acquisition in the model contributes to a better fit to the data.

Then we turn to Figure 4.13, where the loanword diffusion is predicted with Model A, with the effect of Acquisition disregarded (eliminated) by substituting "0" for a_3 in [Formula 1´]. By doing this we can visualize the effect of speakers' year of birth alone. Figure 4.13 clearly shows that the rate of change has a steeper rise when predicted with Model A than when predicted with Model B. In other words, Model B underestimates the rate of change.

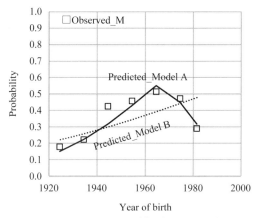

Figure 4.12: Comparing the goodness of fit of the models for *niizu* (< *needs*)

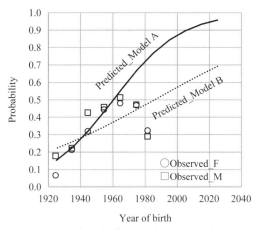

Figure 4.13: Predicted diffusion of *niizu* (< *needs*)

Finally, gender differentiation is significant for only 7 items. A negative coefficient of the variable Gender (in Table 4.5) indicates that male speakers tend to use the loanword in question more frequently than female speakers, and a positive coefficient suggests the opposite. The former group includes *meritto* (< *merit*), *risuku* (< *risk*), *bijon* (< *vison*) and *konsensasu* (< *consensus*) and the latter includes *suutsu* (< *suit*), *oopun-susu* (< *open*) and *kitchin* (< *kitchen*). We can see that male speakers are ahead of female speakers in the diffusion of *bijon* (Figure 4.14) whereas female speakers are ahead of male speakers in the adoption of *oopun-suru* (Figure 4.15).

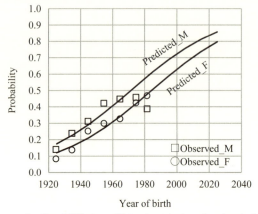

Figure 4.14: Predicted diffusion of *bijon* (< *vision*): males ahead of females

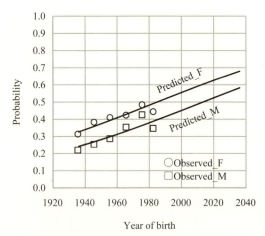

Figure 4.15: Predicted diffusion of *oopun-suru* (< *open*): females ahead of males

It is assumed that gender differentiation is caused by the context in which the loanwords in question are used: *Meritto* (< *merit*), *risuku* (< *risk*), *bijon* (< *vison*) and *konsensasu* (< *consensus*) are well attested in the domain of business and not heavily used in everyday life, whereas *suutsu* (< *suit*), *oopun-susu* (< *open*) and *kitchin* (< *kitchen*) are attested more frequently in everyday life. Since male employment rate is much higher than female employment rate[9] (men are more strongly associated with the business environment than women),

CHAPTER 4 AGE AS AN EXTERNAL FACTOR 53

they are likely to use business-related terms more often than women. It should be noted that different parameters, such as occupation, could come into play if the social advancement of women is achieved further in future.

Furthermore, it is important to pay attention to the fact that gender differentiation is induced by the semantic difference between competing variants. For example, as shown in Section 4.2, the loanword *suutsu* (< *suit*) refers to a set of clothes to be worn by both men and women, whereas its native equivalent *sebiro* often refers only to men's clothing (*Nihon Kokugo Daijiten* 2nd edition). Given that some informants assumed that the reference was to their own clothing during their interviews, women would have had only one choice, i.e., the loanword *suutsu*. This could lead to the predominance of the female speakers in selecting the loanword.

4.8 Patterns of loanword diffusion in apparent time

Self-reports in the previous nationwide surveys have shown that there are two patterns of loanword diffusion according to distribution by age. One shows a monotonically increasing s-shaped curve, and the other shows an s-shaped curve that ends in a drop among those aged 15/16–19 and/or 20–29. The delay in the acquisition of the loanwords in the latter group arguably reflects the age-specific context of use of the loanwords in question. In other words, the domain- or context-specific use of loanwords induced the acquisitional delay among the youngest age groups, who have not been in the job market for long or at all. We should note that "age is not merely the biological age, but includes concomitant social conditions" (Kunihiro et al. (eds.) 1999: 211).

We saw that those in the youngest age groups acquire the loanwords in the latter group, such as *niizu*, as they age (Figure 4.9). Consequently, I concluded that both types of loanword diffusion should be predictable with a monotonically increasing s-curve model. This raises the question as to how the influence of the acquisitional delay (or age-grading) could be separated from the speakers' birth-year effect without excluding the data of the youngest generations. The problem is shown to be solvable by incorporating an acquisition term into the model as one of the independent variables. The inclusion of this new variable, as a result, has advantages as a more accurate prediction of change: It enables us to elicit the birth-year effect alone, and in turn, corrects underestimations of the rate of change.

There are nevertheless some problems left unanswered. The previous studies suggest that we should interpret age differentiation carefully when an apparent-time distribution is the only thing we can make use of (Labov 1994: 83–84, Sankoff, G. 2006, Yokoyama & Sanada 2010, Meyerhoff 2011). In Chapter 8,

54

the limitations of an apparent-time approach and how to overcome them will be discussed.

Notes

1 This chapter is based on Kuya (2016b). Some modifications were added to the original work including tables and figures.

2 The observation is based on the raw data provided by NINJAL.

3 The searches were limited to the following context in the Publication sub-corpus.

Nouns: A word ends in *hiragana* writing + Key word + Particle/Auxiliary

Verbs: A word ends in *hiragana* writing + Key word + *suru* ('do')/*dekiru* ('be able to')

4 BBK (2014: 82–83) examined ten pairs of lexical items consisting of a loanword vs. its native equivalent in an annual opinion poll in 2014. For all the word-pairs, the proportion of those who know a native expression only, i.e., those who does not know the meaning of a loanword, gets lower as they become younger. The 16–19 age group, however, is the only exception: This age group almost always falls behind in acquisition of a loanword compared to those in their 20s (in 9 out of the 10 word-pairs under investigation). These include *niizu* (vs. *hitsuyoosei*); *kyanseru* (vs. *torikeshi*); and *risuku* (vs. *kikensei*), which are all classified in Section 4.4 as those showing a delay in acquisition among the youngest age groups. This implies that those in their teens are still in the process of acquiring these loanwords.

5 The figures in Figures 4.7–4.9 simply represent the ratio of those who *recognize, comprehend* or *use* the loanword in contrast to those who do not. Note that it is different from the proportion used throughout this chapter: the proportion of those who *prefer* the loanword over its native equivalents.

6 Age-specific proportions are not available in the report of the 1995 survey (NHK 1995), so the results of the survey for 1995 could not be included in the figure.

7 Age-grading, or age-graded variation, occurs when one changes one's linguistic behavior at different stages in one's lifetime but it does not lead to change of the community as a whole (Labov 1994: 83).

8 To avoid the problem of multicollinearity, correlations between the independent variables were evaluated for each data set. It showed that the independent variables are not highly correlated with each other (the highest correlation coefficient remains less than 0.4) and that VIF, which is one of the indicators of the risk of multicollinearity, is less than 4 in each case.

9 According to the result of the census conducted in 2000 (*Soomushoo Tookeikyoku*, Statistics Bureau, Ministry of Internal Affairs and Communications, Japan), the employment rate is 74.8% for males and 48.2% for females (for those aged 15 and above). ⟨http://www.e-stat.go.jp/SG1/estat/GL08020103.do?_toGL08020103_&tclassID=000000030587&cycleCode=0&requestSender=search⟩, retrieved on March 29, 2016.

CHAPTER 5

Other External Factors:
Gender, Education, Register, and Style

5.1 Establishing trends in loanword distribution according to social and stylistic factors

The last chapter has shown that the public attitude exhibits an upward tendency in loanword diffusion along apparent time. The purposes of this chapter are two-fold: (i) to investigates whether a similar tendency is attested to by their actual linguistic behavior using corpora; (ii) to gain a quick overview of a *general trend* in the synchronic distribution of loanwords according to a wider range of language-external contexts other than age, such as education, register and style. We will first identify loanwords that appear frequently in a corpus, and then native equivalents of the selected loan variants.

5.2 Using BCCWJ and CSJ as synchronic corpora

The Publication sub-corpus in BCCWJ and the monologue components in CSJ will be investigated as synchronic corpora. Both of the corpora were collected in the early 2000s: The former concerns written texts published between 2001 and 2005 and the latter concerns spoken data recorded between 1999 and 2003. These corpora are then considered synchronic corpora that allow us to access collections of language produced roughly in the beginning of the 21st century.

The Publication sub-corpus in BCCWJ includes information on the year of birth, gender and educational background of the authors (see Note 3 in Chapter 3 for more information on educational history of the authors). Besides, the sub-corpora consist of three types of media: books (PB), magazines (PM) and newspapers (PN), so it allows us to make a comparison of the probabilities of loanwords that appear across different registers. Among these, however, PN was excluded from the analysis since it is very small in size compared with the other two registers. (PB, PM and PN consist of approximately 28.6, 4.4 and 1.4 million words, respectively (NINJAL 2011b: 86).)

In CSJ, as already mentioned in Section 3.3, the majority of recordings are monologues uttered in two relatively formal settings: Academic Presentation Speech (APS) and Simulated Public Speech (SPS). CSJ provides the information on the speaker's year of birth, gender and educational background, and also in which register the utterance in question took place (APS or SPS). It also contains information on evaluations of stylistic aspects such as the formality, spontaneity and audience size, of each sample. Although the register difference in CSJ is considered to some extent a reflection of difference in speech style, i.e., APS has a more formal style than SPS, it will be useful for us to have a look at these factors as additional indicators of style.

Table 5.1 and Table 5.2 show the distribution of loanwords (LW[1]), Sino-Japanese words (SJ), native Japanese words (NJ) and hybrids (HB) in BCCWJ and also that in CSJ, by the author's/speaker's year of birth.[2] Figure 5.1 shows the proportion (%) of LW as opposed to the sum of all lexical strata (LW + SJ + NJ + HB) for each birth-year group based on Table 5.1. For example, by token, the proportion of LW used by those born in the 1920s is 2.3% (=4,409/189,892×100). Note that the proportion shown in the column "Sample size by age group (%)" in Table 5.1 represents the proportion of tokens collected from the authors of each age group out of the total tokens, e.g., the sample size of those born in the 1920s accounts for 8.5% of all (=189,892/2,230,782×100). The same holds true for Table 5.2 and Figure 5.2.

It should be noted that, in Table 5.1, the majority of authors are those born between the 1920s and 1960s. In contrast, the size of samples (i.e., the word counts) collected from texts written by those born in the 1910s and before, and by those born in the 1970s and after are extremely small, i.e., less than 5% of the total. Mori (2013: 279) points out that when a small-scale birth-year group shows an irregular distribution, it should be interpreted with care.[3] If we ignore such small-scale age-groups and focus on those born between the 1920s and 1960s, i.e., those marked with * in Figure 5.1, we can see a clear tendency for the proportion of LW to increase monotonically from younger generations to older ones in both token and type. The difference between those born in the 1920s and those born in the 1960s are approximately 4% by token and 7% by type.

Likewise, we find a relatively consistent trend toward an increase of LW in both token and type along apparent time in CSJ (Figure 5.2) especially when focusing on those born between 1940–44 and 1975–79, whose sample size is 5% or more of the whole sample. The difference between those born in 1940–44 and those born in 1975–79 are approximately 2% by token and 4% by type. Note that size of samples collected from those born in 1935–39 and before and those born in 1980–84 are extremely small, i.e., less than 5%, in Table 5.2 and show occasional irregularities in Figure 5.2.

These figures indicate that the vocabulary in the LW stratum as a whole is on the increase in the Japanese lexicon in both written and spoken language.

	Type					Token					Sample size
Birth year	LW	SJ	NJ	HB	Total	LW	SJ	NJ	HB	Total	by age group
1830		115	110	8	233		203	203	13	419	< 0.1%
1840		124	136	6	266		198	402	10	610	< 0.1%
1850		127	122	15	264		175	221	23	419	< 0.1%
1860	14	515	543	36	1108	27	899	1453	51	2430	0.1%
1870	24	877	1069	64	2034	45	1640	3064	103	4852	0.2%
1880	36	1120	1191	75	2422	47	2266	3499	112	5924	0.3%
1890	85	1718	1563	95	3461	147	4085	6734	185	11151	0.5%
1900	193	2652	2172	149	5166	333	6906	11942	346	19527	0.9%
1910	322	5017	3385	279	9003	648	19078	24835	815	45376	2.0%
1920	1405	11164	6929	666	20164	4409	82618	99565	3300	189892	8.5%
1930	2657	14321	8859	840	26677	12319	174353	194151	6620	387443	17.4%
1940	3623	15466	9803	976	29868	21784	251525	268852	9723	551884	24.7%
1950	3779	14451	9638	947	28815	24978	230390	266055	8994	530417	23.8%
1960	3421	11556	8310	774	24061	23154	151127	188154	6484	368919	16.5%
1970	1736	5854	4996	370	12956	6894	35296	56725	1773	100688	4.5%
1980	237	1243	1609	90	3179	470	2831	6987	212	10500	0.5%
1990	24	69	148	9	250	31	78	213	9	331	< 0.1%
Total						95286	963668	1133055	38773	2230782	100.0%

Table 5.1: Distribution of lexical strata by year of birth of the authors (BCCWJ)[4]

Figure 5.1: The LW stratum by year of birth of the authors (BCCWJ)

CHAPTER 5 OTHER EXTERNAL FACTORS 59

	Type					Token					Sample size
Birth year	LW	SJ	NJ	HB	Total	LW	SJ	NJ	HB	Total	by age group
1915–19	82	670	599	26	1377	278	2389	5265	60	7992	0.2%
1920–24	13	185	226	11	435	78	978	1259	35	2350	0.1%
1925–29	33	335	326	18	712	81	1161	1939	56	3237	0.1%
1930–34	977	5137	3731	294	10139	3815	41366	84248	2777	132206	3.9%
1935–39	1138	4993	3970	306	10407	5013	45777	101828	2204	154822	4.6%
1940–44	1431	5216	3937	312	10896	6907	56785	115222	2729	181643	5.4%
1945–49	1919	5978	4645	364	12906	10918	78546	163165	3962	256591	7.6%
1950–54	1502	5203	3756	319	10780	7684	63026	117897	2827	191434	5.7%
1955–59	2345	6596	4911	395	14247	17761	123837	221036	5716	368350	10.9%
1960–64	2423	6390	4701	453	13967	19855	135345	226960	5906	388066	11.5%
1965–69	2675	6886	5030	424	15015	26185	159319	270183	6903	462590	13.7%
1970–74	2884	7351	5607	538	16380	33636	221341	350625	9272	614874	18.2%
1975–79	2562	6637	5055	441	14695	36122	216930	320087	8194	581333	17.2%
1980–84	493	1695	1617	103	3908	1604	9980	22195	499	34278	1.0%
Total						169937	1156780	2001909	51140	3379766	100.0%

Table 5.2: Distribution of lexical strata by year of birth of the speakers (CSJ)[5]

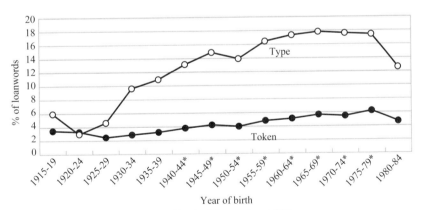

Figure 5.2: The LW stratum by year of birth of the speakers (CSJ)

5.3 Selecting potential lexical variables

Table 5.3 shows the distribution of each lexical stratum by parts of speech in the fixed-length component of PB and PM in the Publication sub-corpus, BCCWJ (particles and auxiliaries are excluded). It demonstrates that the majority of loanwords are Nouns, which are subdivided into 8 categories (i)–(viii) depending on their possible usages.

	LW	SJ	NJ	HB	Total	Example of LW	Etymology
Noun							
(i) noun	9801	21075	11479	2026	44381	*hoteru*	hotel
(ii) verbal noun	527	6393	510	64	7494	*kyanseru*	cancel
(iii) adjectival noun	209	787	115	44	1155	*orijinaru*	original
(iv) verbal/adjectival noun	9	51	7	1	68	*oopun*	open
(v) adverbial noun		236	143	18	397		
(vi) counter noun	148	124	37	11	320	*paasento*	percent
(vii) numeral noun	1	59	17	13	90	*zero*	zero
(viii) other noun			1		1		
Nominal adjective[6]	215	573	391	48	1227	*shinpuru*	simple
Pronoun		13	74	6	93		
Verb			5221	309	5530		
Adjective			549	31	580		
Adverb		105	1579	27	1711		
Adnominal			38	8	46		
Interjection	2	1	185	4	192	*bonjoruno*	Buongiorno!
Conjunction		2	29		31		
Prefix		206	25		231		
Suffix	4	491	192		687	*-chikku*	-tic
Total	10916	30116	20592	2610	64234		

Table 5.3: Lexical strata by part of speech (type, BCCWJ)

First, the most frequent category is (i) noun (9,801 types). A noun such as *hoteru* (< *hotel*) is used only as a noun followed by a postpositional particle or a copula as in Examples (5.1) and (5.2).

The second most frequent category is (ii) verbal noun (527 types). A verbal noun such as *kyanseru* (< *cancel*) is used as a noun when followed by a particle or copula as in (5.2) while it serves as a verb when compounded with a light verb such as *suru* ('do') or *dekiru* ('be able to') as in (5.1).

The third most frequent group includes (iii) adjectival noun (as a sub-category of Noun) (209 types) and Nominal adjective (215 types). A nominal adjective such as *shinpuru* (< *simple*) is used as an adjective taking an auxiliary such

CHAPTER 5 OTHER EXTERNAL FACTORS

as the copula *-na* as in (5.1). This category also serves as an adverb when followed by the copula *-ni* as *sumuuzu* (< *smooth*) shown in (5.2). An adjectival noun such as *orijinaru* (< *original*) also serves as a noun when followed by a particle as shown in (5.3).

Those in (iv) verbal/adjectival noun (9 types) are used either as a noun, verb or adjective just as (ii) verbal noun and (iii) adjectival noun.

Note that Sino-Japanese words (SJ) are integrated into Japanese in the same way as the Western loanwords as outlined above. Although LW and SJ do not have lexical items categorized as Verb nor Adjective in Table 5.3, they do serve as verbs and adjectives when relevant derivational suffixes are attached, competing with NJ verbs and adjectives that are similar in meaning.

(5.1)　最もシンプルな方法は、ホテルの予約をキャンセルすることだ。
　　　Mottomo shinpuru-na hoohoo-wa hotel-no yoyaku-o
　　　kyanseru-suru koto-da.
　　　most simple-COP way-TOP hotel-GEN reservation-ACC
　　　cancel-do thing-COP
　　　'The simplest solution is to cancel your hotel reservation.'

(5.2)　ホテルの予約のキャンセルがスムーズにできない。
　　　Hoteru-no yoyaku-no kyanseru-ga sumuuzu-ni
　　　deki-nai.
　　　hotel-GEN reservation-GEN cancellation-NOM smooth-COP
　　　be.able.to-NEG
　　　'I cannot cancel my hotel reservation smoothly (I have difficulty in canceling my hotel reservation).'

(5.3)　オリジナルの曲
　　　orijinal-no kyoku
　　　original-GEN song
　　　'The original song'

As Labov says, one of the criteria for a useful variable is being high in frequency (1966: 49). The first step is therefore to identify loanwords that are high in frequency. Three frequency lists were made by usage[7] of loanwords based on the fixed-length component of PB and PM in the Publication sub-corpus, BCCWJ. The criteria for extracting tokens of each usage are shown in Table 5.4. The most frequent loanwords in each usage are listed in Appendices B1–B3: Appendix B1 includes those in nominal usage (N) with a raw frequency of 100 and more (92 lexical items); Appendix B2 includes those in verbal usage (V) with a frequency of 30 and more (33 lexical items), and; Appendix B3 includes those in adjectival usage (A) with a frequency of 30 and more (12 lexical items). Note that verbal and adjectival usages are relatively low in frequency compared with those of nouns.

Usage	Preceding word	Key (= LW in *katakana* writing)	Following word
Nominal (N)		(i) noun (ii) verbal noun (iii) adjectival noun (iv) verbal/adjectival noun (vi) counter noun (vii) numeral noun	-Particle -Auxiliary (copula in most cases)
	A word that ends in *hiragana* writing[8]		
Verbal (V)		(ii) verbal noun (iv) verbal/adjectival noun	-*suru* ('do') -*dekiru* ('be able to')
Adjectival (A)		(iii) adjectival noun (iv) verbal/adjectival noun Nominal adjective	-Auxiliary (copula in most cases)[9]

*The numbers (i)~(vii) correspond to those in Table 5.3

Table 5.4: Criteria for making frequency lists of loanwords

In the next step, among those loanwords listed in Appendices B1–B3, those which seem to have clear, interchangeable native *single-word* equivalents have been selected by the intuition of the author, a native speaker of Japanese, as follows.[10] First, cultural borrowings are eliminated from the scope of the present study. For example, *kurikku-suru* (< *click* 'to push/press a button on a computer mouse') and *akusesu-suru* (< *access* 'to gain access to information held in a computer, to approach something or a place') are textbook examples of cultural borrowing, since they were borrowed to fill a lexical gap for computer-related terms. The definitions of these loanwords are usually given in the form of a sentence in a dictionary and so it is generally difficult to rephrase them with existing native single words. Second, abstract words are mainly selected in the case of nominal usage. Kim (2011) points out that loan nouns that are on the increase in the latter half of the 20th century belong mainly to abstract nouns. Consequently, 29 loanwords, including 16 in nominal usage (N), 10 in verbal usage (V) and 3 in adjectival usage (A), have been selected as possible loan variants that seem to be competing with their native single-word equivalents. They correspond to those marked with * / ** in the Lemma column in Appendices B1–B3.

The last step is to identify native variants of the selected 29 loanwords. Synonymy among the lexical variants is determined based on dictionaries. I consulted eight dictionaries (listed below) to find definitions of these loanwords.

CHAPTER 5 OTHER EXTERNAL FACTORS

1 *Gendai Yoogo-no Kisochishiki Katakana Gairaigo/Ruigo Jiten* (4th Edition, 1st Printing) (2011)
2 *Sanseido Kokugo Jiten* (7th Edition, 1st Printing) (2014)
3 *Shinmeikai Kokugo Jiten* (7th Edition) (2011) (web)[11]
4 *Concise Katakanago Jiten* (4th Edition) (2010) (web)
5 *Reikai Shin Kokugo Jiten* (8th Edition, 1st Printing) (2012)
6 *Kojien* (6th Edition) (2008)
7 *Nihon Kokugo Daijiten* (2nd Edition) (2000–2002)
8 *Iwanami Kokugo Jiten* (7th Edition, 1st Printing) (2009)

Only those definitions that are given in the form of single-word expressions and appear in at least four out of the eight dictionaries are considered native variants of a given loanword in this chapter. This is because it is likely that single-word expressions that consistently appear in different dictionaries could potentially serve as native variants of a given loanword. If a given loanword has even one native variant that is defined by a *phrase* or *sentence*, it is excluded from further analysis. In other words, only those of which *all* their native variants are *single-word* expressions are further investigated. As a result, 4 out of the 29 loanwords have been excluded and the 25 loanwords listed in Table 5.5 have been selected for further investigation. (The loanwords excluded at this stage are those marked with ** in the Lemma column in Appendices B1–B3.)

No.	Lemma_JP	Lemma	Etymology	Usage	Native equivalents defined by the dictionary-based approach
1	アドバイス	*adobaisu*	advice	V	*jogen, chuukoku, kankoku*
2	バランス	*baransu*	balance	N	*kinkoo, tsuriai*
3	ケース	*keesu*	case	N	*baai, jirei*
4	チャレンジ	*charenji*	challenge	V	*choosen*
5	チャンス	*chansu*	chance	N	*kikai, kooki*
6	イベント	*ibento*	event	N	*gyooji, moyooshimono, dekigoto*
7	イメージ	*imeeji*	image	V	*omoiukaberu, omoiukabu**12
8	キープ	*kiipu*	keep	V	*iji, kakuho*
9	レベル	*reberu*	level	N	*suijun, hyoojun*
10	マスター	*masutaa*	master	V	*jukutatsu*
11	メリット	*meritto*	merit	N	*riten, choosho, kooseki*
12	ニーズ	*niizu*	needs	N	*yookyuu, juyoo*
13	オープン	*oopun*	open	V	*kaiten, kaigyoo, hiraku, hirak-eru,* aku, akeru**
14	プロセス	*purosesu*	process	N	*katei, keika, tejun, hoohoo*
15	リラックス	*rirakkusu*	relax	V	*kutsurogu*
16	リスク	*risuku*	risk	N	*kiken*
17	ルール	*ruuru*	rule	N	*kisoku*
18	シフト	*shifuto*	shift	V	*ikoo*
19	シンプル	*shinpuru*	simple	A	*tanjun, kanso*
20	スムーズ	*sumuuzu*	smooth	A	*nameraka*
21	スタート	*sutaato*	start	V	*shuppatsu, kaishi, hajimeru, hajimaru*
22	サポート	*sapooto*	support	V	*shien, sasaeru, shiji*
23	テーマ	*teema*	theme	N	*shudai, daimoku*
24	タイプ	*taipu*	type	N	*ruikei, kata*
25	ユニーク	*yuniiku*	unique	A	*dokutoku, dokuji*

Alphabetically ordered by *Etymology*

Table 5.5: The 25 selected lexical variables

5.4 Analysis of the written corpus (BCCWJ)

From the variable-length component of PB and PM in the Publication sub-corpus, tokens of the 25 loanwords and their native alternatives in Table 5.5 have been elicited based on the following criteria ([Criteria 1]). Investigation is

CHAPTER 5 OTHER EXTERNAL FACTORS   65

limited to samples written by a single author. The number of tokens of each variant is shown in Table 5.6.

[Criteria 1]

    N: A word that ends with *hiragana* + Target lemma + Particle/auxiliary

    V: A word that ends with *hiragana* + Target lemma + *suru* ('do') /*dekiru* ('be able to')[13]

    A: A word that ends with *hiragana* + Target lemma + Auxiliary

Appendix C1 shows the distribution of the LW and non-LW variants by the author's year of birth. To reduce the effect of irregular distributions due to small-sized samples, especially from the youngest and oldest generations, I have chosen to focus on those born between the 1920s and 1960s, each of which, on average, contribute more than 5% of the whole sample. Note that the sample size for generations other than these groups, those born in the 1910s and before and those born in the 1970s and after, is very small (less than 5% of the whole sample, see the bottom row labeled "Sample size by age group (%)" in Appendix C1). For example, *keesu* (< *case*) shows irregular distributions among those born in the 1910s and before and also those born in the 1970s and after. By limiting the scope of investigation to these generations, a general tendency becomes more visible: The occurrence of LW increases as authors become younger.

No.	LemmaJP	Lemma	Etymology	Usage	LW	non-LW	Total	LW/Total (%)
1	アドバイス	*adobaisu*	advice	V	73	125	198	36.9
2	バランス	*baransu*	balance	N	920	186	1106	83.2
3	ケース	*keesu*	case	N	1627	21796	23423	6.9
4	チャレンジ	*charenji*	challenge	V	149	390	539	27.6
5	チャンス	*chansu*	chance	N	572	1508	2080	27.5
6	イベント	*ibento*	event	N	324	1035	1359	23.8
7	イメージ	*imeeji*	image	N	402	357	759	53.0
8	キープ	*kiipu*	keep	V	124	2274	2398	5.2
9	レベル	*reberu*	level	N	856	572	1428	59.9
10	マスター	*masutaa*	master	V	134	18	152	88.2
11	メリット	*meritto*	merit	N	450	594	1044	43.1
12	ニーズ	*niizu*	needs	N	489	1016	1505	32.5
13	オープン	*oopun*	open	V	162	7093	7255	2.2
14	プロセス	*purosesu*	process	N	523	7072	7595	6.9
15	リラックス	*rirakkusu*	relax	V	216	164	380	56.8
16	リスク	*risuku*	risk	N	606	1242	1848	32.8
17	ルール	*ruuru*	rule	N	501	230	731	68.5
18	シフト	*shifuto*	shift	V	102	432	534	19.1
19	シンプル	*shinpuru*	simple	A	450	594	1044	43.1
20	スムーズ	*sumuuzu*	smooth	A	359	190	549	65.4
21	スタート	*sutaato*	start	V	431	12706	13137	3.3
22	サポート	*sapooto*	support	V	251	2475	2726	9.2
23	テーマ	*teema*	theme	N	946	192	1138	83.1
24	タイプ	*taipu*	type	N	1260	492	1752	71.9
25	ユニーク	*yuniiku*	unique	A	187	296	483	38.7
		Total number of tokens			12114	63049	75163	

*Alphabetically ordered by *Etymology*.

Table 5.6: Distribution of LW and non-LW variants (BCCWJ)

In the following stage, we will observe the distribution of these loanwords in social and stylistic contexts. These include four language-external factors: (a) Year of Birth, (b) Gender, (c) Education, of the authors, and (d) Register, i.e., Type of Medium: books (PB) or magazines (PM). In this chapter, we shall consider "the widest possible" contexts, i.e., all the environments where the linguistic variants in question occur as outlined in Section 3.6. Although this approach is less fine-grained, it gives an analysis of a larger amount of data, which will be useful for us to gain a quick overview of a general trend in the synchronic distribution of loanwords. We will come back to the question of what the envelope of variation is considered to be in Chapter 6.

(a) Year of Birth

A regression analysis is conducted in order to verify the upward trend in the occurrence of LW in apparent time. The statistical significance of age-effect (at the 5 % level) is confirmed for 10 loanwords as shown in Figure 5.3. Each loan variant is presented by its etymology, e.g., *case*, instead of its Japanese writing *keesu*. The figure demonstrates that the occurrence of these loanwords is not independent of the author's year of birth. This means that there are changes in apparent time toward an increase in the adoption of loanwords as opposed to their native lexical variants. The rate of change, however, is different across variables. For example, *keesu* (< *case*), *oopun* (< *open*) and *purosesu* (< *process*) have relatively gentle slopes, while the rest of the loanwords show relatively steeper slopes. Figures 5.4 and 5.5 show examples of a regression model of age-distribution of LW and its goodness of fit to the data (R^2) (p refers to the p-value of an t-test). See Appendix C2 for the distribution and result of the regression analysis for each linguistic variable.

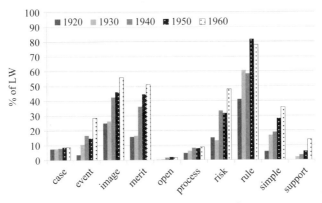

Figure 5.3: Effect of year of birth on the occurrence of LWs (BCCWJ)

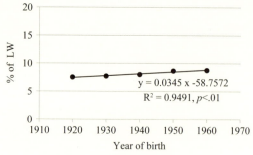

Figure 5.4: Regression analysis of *keesu* (< *case*)

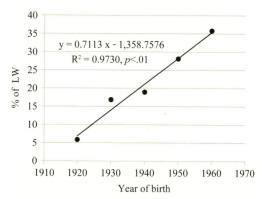

Figure 5.5: Regression analysis of *shinpuru* (< *simple*)

(b) Gender

The statistical significance of gender is evaluated by the chi-square test. The difference between men and women proved to be significant at the 5% level for 6 loanwords as shown in Figure 5.6. For a full list of the frequencies and results of the chi-square test for individual linguistic variables, see Appendix C3. Among these, 4 variables show a tendency for female authors to use a higher proportion of the loanword than male authors. The remaining two variables, marked with an asterisk (*), i.e., *rirakkusu* (< *relax*) and *risuku* (< *risk*), shows an opposite tendency. We should note that we cannot simply conclude that women are ahead of men in their use of LW as a general tendency, considering that such a tendency is observed only in 4 out of the 25 variables.

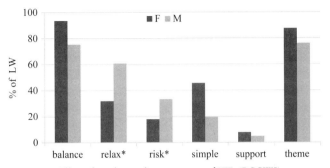

Figure 5.6: Effect of gender on the occurrence of LWs (BCCWJ)

(c) Education

Figure 5.7 shows the distribution of individual loanwords by educational background of the authors. In BCCWJ, categories of educational background of the authors consist of (1) Junior high school, (2) High school, (3) College of technology, (4) Junior college, (5) College/University, and (6) Graduate School. Here, those who graduated from (1), (2), (3), (4) or (5) are grouped together into "up to UNIV" as opposed to "GRAD," i.e., those with a graduate school education. The educational variable is binary here as the majority (more than 90%) of samples come from either university or postgraduate school educated authors.

There are 14 loanwords for which the difference between those with a postgraduate education and others proved to be significant at the 5% level by the chi-square test (for details, see Appendix C4). It should be noted that the majority of these (11 out of 14), are favored by those whose highest level of educational attainment is university or below (up to UNIV) as opposed to graduate school educated authors (GRAD). Those marked with an asterisk (*), i.e., *imeeji* (< *image*), *risuku* (< *risk*) and *shifuto* (< *shift*), however, show an opposite tendency.

The figure exhibits a general tendency for those with a university education (or below) to use loanwords more frequently than those with a postgraduate education. The reason why some loanwords are favored by those with a postgraduate education should be investigated further by consulting the use of individual words in context. For example, there may be some cases in which these loanwords are favored in academic or professional contexts.

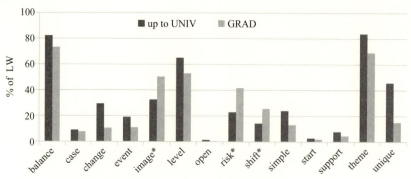

Figure 5.7: Effect of education on the occurrence of LWs (BCCWJ)

(d) Register (Type of Medium)

Figure 5.8 shows the distribution of individual loanwords by register. The difference between books (PB) and magazines (PM) proved to be significant at the 5% level by the chi-square test for 9 linguistic variables (for details, see Appendix C5). The figure shows that the occurrence of these loanwords is not independent of the effect of register, with the occurrence of LWs consistently being greater in PM than in PB.

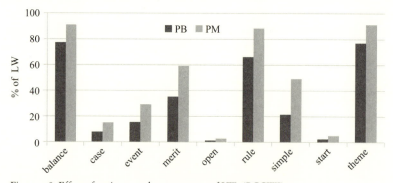

Figure 5.8: Effect of register on the occurrence of LWs (BCCWJ)

Now the question arises as to what this difference implies. One way of exploring this is to examine the correlations between register and the other factors. Table 5.7 shows (Pearson's) correlations between every pair of independent variables considered in this section. It does not reveal a very high correlation between any pairs. Provided that register is not largely dependent on the other independent variables, we should think of other possible factors that might induce the register difference.

CHAPTER 5 OTHER EXTERNAL FACTORS

	Year of Birth	Gender	Education	Register
Year of Birth	1	.149	.098	.117
Gender (M=0, F=1)	.149	1	-.059	.061
Education (up to UNIV=0, GRAD=1)	.098	-.059	1	-.119
Register (PB=0, PM=1)	.117	.061	-.119	1

Table 5.7: Correlation matrix for the independent variables (BCCWJ)

First, it is possible that the formality of a text differentiates the two registers. Tanaka (2012) points out that, among registers contained in BCCWJ, magazines and online text are characterized as having attributes such as "private," "daily," "entertaining" and "intragroup," while books and newspapers as having properties such as "public" and "social." It is then predictable that the fact of more frequent LW use in magazines than in books is an indication of greater general acceptance of the loan variants, as opposed to their native variants, with private or informal domains of writing.

It is doubtful, however, whether the difference in the type of media is directly interpretable as a difference in the degree of "formality." It may be necessary to consider empirical evidence of a stylistic difference between these media. As an example, I took a close look at the occurrence of four phonologically contracted copulas and particles across these media. Examined forms include the following: (i) *ja* (copula), (ii) *tte* (particle), (iii) *tte* (auxiliary)[14] and (iv) *n* (particle). They are contracted (therefore, colloquial) forms of (i) *de-wa* (COP-TOP 'is/are not'), (ii) the complementizer *to* ('that'), (iii) *toiu* ('what they say') and (iv) the particle *no*, respectively. Examples are presented in (5.4)–(5.7). Since contracted forms are considered to be non-standard or colloquial, a heavier use of them can be identified as a marker of a relatively lower degree of formality of text.

(5.4) *ja*_copula
    a. *Kore-wa inu ja nai.* (contracted)
    b. *Kore-wa inu de-wa nai.*
       This-TOP dog COP-TOP NEG
       'This is not a dog.'

(5.5) *tte*_particle
    a. *Inu-wa kawaii tte omoi-masu.* (contracted)
    b. *Inu-wa kawaii to omoi-masu.*
      god-TOP cute COMP think-POL
      'I think that dogs are cute.'

(5.6) *tte_* auxiliary
   a. *Inu tte no-wa hoeru kara kirai-da.* (contracted)
   b. *Inu toiu no-wa hoeru kara kirai-da.*
   dog what.they.say.about COMP-wa bark because hate-COP
   'As for dogs, I do not like them since they bark.'

(5.7) *n_*particle
   a. *Inu-wa kawaii to omou n desu.* (contracted)
   b. *Inu-wa kawaii to omou no desu.*
   dog-TOP cute COMP think COMP COP.POL
   'I do think that dogs are cute.'

The distribution of the four contracted forms (per miliom word, PMW) is shown in Figure 5.9.[15] The figure demonstrates that there is a consistent tendency for the contracted forms to occur more frequently in PM than in PB. Now it is more persuasive to say that magazines can be characterized as a medium that adopts a more colloquial or less formal style than books. So, in turn, the lower proportion of loanwords in PB than in PM implies a tendency for the loan variants to be disfavored in the more formal (or less colloquial) medium.

In summary, the difference between the two registers is interpreted, in one possibility, as the difference in the stylistic factor of formality, as represented by the presence/absence of contracted forms. In the next section, the effect of style will be further investigated with different parameters.

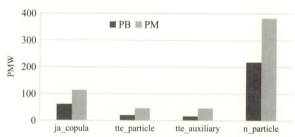

Figure 5.9: Phonologically contracted forms by register (BCCWJ)

5.5 Analysis of the spoken corpus (CSJ)

Following the discussion above, this section puts a special focus on the effect of stylistic factors on the occurrence of loanwords. CSJ provides useful information on styles based on detailed evaluation of several factors such as formality

CHAPTER 5 OTHER EXTERNAL FACTORS

and spontaneity of a talk.

Following the procedures presented in Table 5.4, frequencies of loanwords in APS and SPS were counted by their usage to make frequency lists. Appendices D1–D3 show those that occur 100 times and more in nominal usage (N) (113 words), 50 times and more in verbal usage (V) (11 words) and 50 times and more in adjectival usage (A) (4 words). Among those included in Appendices D1–D3, only those that are also listed in Table 5.5, i.e., those investigated with BCCWJ in the previous section, are left for our attention. Consequently, the 14 loanwords shown in Table 5.8, including 9 in nominal usage, 3 in verbal usage and 2 in adjectival usage, have been selected for further investigation (they correspond to those marked with * in the Lemma column in Appendices D1–D3).

No.	Lemma_JP	Lemma	Etymology	Usage	LW	non-LW	Total	LW/Total (%)
1	バランス	baransu	balance	N	110	1	111	99.1
2	ケース	keesu	case	N	185	7717	7902	2.3
3	イベント	ibento	event	N	159	290	449	35.4
4	イメージ	imeeji	image	V	68	69	137	49.6
5	レベル	reberu	level	N	446	68	514	86.8
6	メリット	meritto	merit	N	152	186	338	45.0
7	プロセス	purosesu	process	N	139	2433	2572	5.4
8	リラックス	rirakkusu	relax	V	61	5	66	92.4
9	ルール	ruuru	rule	N	458	259	717	63.9
10	シンプル	shinpru	simple	A	52	389	441	11.8
11	スムーズ	sumuuzu	smooth	A	54	40	94	57.4
12	スタート	sutaato	start	V	82	2288	2370	3.5
13	テーマ	teema	theme	N	522	145	667	78.3
14	タイプ	taipu	type	N	390	126	516	75.6
			Total number of tokens		2878	14016	16894	

*Alphabetically ordered by *Etymology*

Table 5.8: Distribution of LW and non-LW variants (CSJ)

In the following, besides the four independent variables considered in the previous section, i.e., (a) Year of Birth, (b) Gender, (c) Education, of the authors, and (d) Register, i.e., Type of Speech (APS or SPS), the following three stylistic variables are incorporated into the analysis: (e) Spontaneity, (f) Formality and (g) Audience Size of a talk. For the same reason mentioned in the previous section, age groups that do not account for more than 5% of the whole sample are not included in the analysis (see Appendix E1 for more detail). As a result, only those born between the 1940s and 1970s are included in the scope of investigation here.

(a) Year of Birth

Figure 5.10 shows the proportions of the 14 loanwords used, by the speaker's year of birth. The statistical significance of birth-year effect is evaluated by the regression analysis. The distributions of the selected loan variants in CSJ do not exhibit consistent upward tendencies in apparent time except that *ibento* (< *event*) barely shows a tendency toward significance (at the 10% level in an t-test) of birth-year effect. For the distribution and result of the regression analysis for each linguistic variable, see Appendix E2.

One of the reasons why age gradient is not visible may be attributed to the relatively small sample size of the spoken corpora. A small difference in raw frequency might have resulted in a great difference in proportion, and in turn, irregular distributions across generations. Furthermore, it is also possible that the effect of year of birth is distorted by other independent variables (this point will be discussed later in this section).

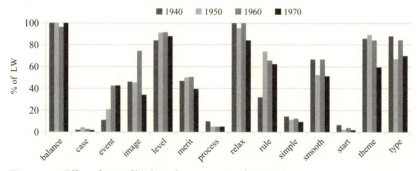

Figure 5.10: Effect of year of birth on the occurrence of LWs (CSJ)

(b) Gender

The effect of gender was evaluated by the chi-square test and proved to be significant at the 5% level for 6 out of the 14 loanwords as in Figure 5.11, with 4 of them being favored by female speakers while 2 of them (marked with an asterisk *) being favored by male speakers. (See Appendix E3 for a full list of the frequencies and results of the test for individual linguistic variables.) It seems that women tend to use loanwords more frequently than men, but we should again take care not to draw a sweeping conclusion from this small number of samples.

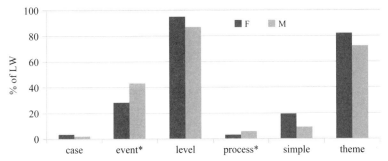

Figure 5.11: Effect of gender on the occurrence of LWs (CSJ)

(c) Education
The educational effect proved to be significant at the 5% level in the chi-square test for 5 out of the 14 variables as in Figure 5.12 (See Appendix E3 for details). In CSJ, educational categories of the speakers consist of (1) Junior high school, (2) High school, (3) College/University, and (4) Graduate School. Here, those who graduated from (1), (2) or (3) are grouped together into "up to UNIV" as opposed to "GRAD," i.e., those with a graduate school education.

There is a tendency for those in GRAD to disfavor the use of loan variants more than those in (up to) UNIV except for the use of *purosesu* (< *process*) (marked with *). Although this tendency is not very striking, it is noteworthy that this trend, i.e., the tendency for more educated people to disfavor the use of LW, is consistent with what we have seen in analysis of BCCWJ in the previous section.

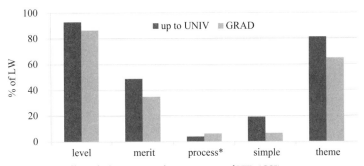

Figure 5.12: Effect of education on the occurrence of LWs (CSJ)

(d) Register (Type of Speech)
Figure 5.13 shows the distribution of loanwords by register. The effect of register was proven to be significant at the 5% level in the chi-square test for 7 out of the 14 variables, which demonstrates that the occurrence of loanwords is

generally more frequent in SPS than in APS except for *purosesu* (< *process*) (marked with *). (See Appendix E4 for details.)

Even though there is an *a priori* generalization that APS is characterized as a more formal speech setting than SPS, it would be useful to look at factors that are more closely associated with style, e.g., the degree of spontaneity or formality of the speech, in order to confirm the effect of style on the occurrence of loanwords.

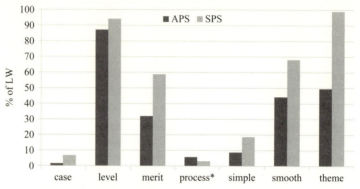

Figure 5.13: Effect of register on the occurrence of LWs (CSJ)

(e) Spontaneity

Figure 5.14 shows the occurrence of LWs by the degree of spontaneity of the talk. Spontaneity was originally evaluated on a five-point scale: (1) Not spontaneous—(2) Not really spontaneous—(3) Neither—(4) Somewhat spontaneous—(5) Highly spontaneous. Here (4) and (5) are grouped together into "Spontaneous" as opposed to "Others" including (1), (2) and (3).

The effect of spontaneity proved to be significant at the 5% level in the chi-square test for 7 out of the 14 variables (see Appendix E4 for details). The figure shows that the use of LWs is more frequent in spontaneous speech except for *keesu* (< *case*) (marked with *). It implies that the loan variants are more strongly associated with spontaneous speech.

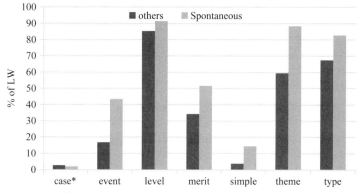

Figure 5.14: Effect of spontaneity on the occurrence of LWs (CSJ)

(f) Formality

Figure 5.15 shows the distribution of LWs by the degree of formality of the speech. Formality in CSJ was originally evaluated on a five-point scale: (1) Casual—(2) Somewhat casual—(3) Neither—(4) Somewhat formal—(5) Formal. Here (4) and (5) are grouped together into "Formal" as opposed to "Others" including (1), (2) and (3).

The effect of formality on the occurrence of a loan variant proved to be significant at the 5% level in the chi-square test for 7 out of the 14 variables (see Appendix E5 for details). It demonstrates that loanwords are disfavored in formal speech except for *purosesu* (< *process*) (marked with *). This implies that LW use is more strongly associated with informal speech.

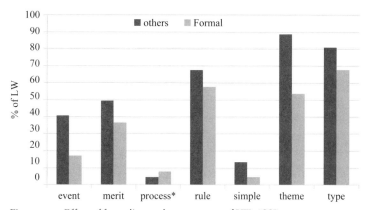

Figure 5.15: Effect of formality on the occurrence of LWs (CSJ)

(g) Audience Size

Figure 5.16 shows the distribution of LWs by audience size (Small: less than 10, Medium: 10–30, and Large: 50 and more). The effect of audience size proved to be significant at the 5% level in the chi-square test for 8 out of the 14 variables (see Appendix E5 for details). Although the distribution is not always hierarchically ordered from small audience to large audience, it is often the case that the loan variants are least frequent in front of the largest audience, except for *puro-sesu* (< *process*) (marked with *). It implies that LWs are less frequently used in front of a larger audience.

It is not difficult to imagine that audience size tends to affect the speaker's attention to the formality level of the setting, or in other words, the speaker's attention to speech. A larger audience would mean that the speaker is required to show more consideration to the various linguistic backgrounds of the addressees, such as age, for instance. For a similar discussion on the relationship between audience size and the occurrence of loanwords, see Chapter 7.

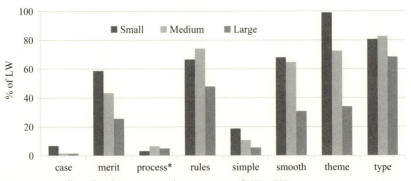

Figure 5.16: Effect of audience size on the occurrence of LWs (CSJ)

Although data from CSJ has showcased the roles of different stylistic variables, it should be noted that they are likely to be correlated with each other. Table 5.9 shows a correlation matrix of the seven independent variables considered in this section. It is notable that many pairs of independent variables are moderately/strongly correlated.

Most noticeably, Register or Audience Size is moderately/strongly correlated with many factors. First, Register has a very strong correlation with Audience Size ($r = 0.862$), where the academic presentation speech (APS) predicts a larger audience size. Second, both Register and Audience Size show moderate/strong correlations with Education, where more educated speakers are associated with APS ($r = 0.612$) and speech with a larger audience ($r = 0.519$). Third, these two factors, Register or Audience Size, also show weak/moderate correlations with Gender, where female speakers are associated with SPS ($r = -0.355$) and speech

CHAPTER 5 OTHER EXTERNAL FACTORS

with a smaller audience (r = –0.306). Lastly, Register and Audience Size have weak/moderate correlations with Formality and Spontaneity, where APS is associated with more formal speech (r = 0.221) and with less spontaneous speech (r = –0.180), and speech with a larger audience is associated with more formal speech (r = 0.264) and with less spontaneous speech (r = –0.161). It can also be noted that Formality and Spontaneity are weakly correlated with each other (r = –0.261).

These observations imply that factors such as Audience Size, Education, Gender, Formality and Spontaneity affect the phenomenon as subcategories of Register (for similar dicussions on correlations among external factors in CSJ, see Sano 2009: 136). In other words, register differentiation is attributed to these factors. The fact that SPS shows higher proportions of LWs than APS is attributed to the predominance of a smaller audience, less educated speakers, female speakers, and less formal or more spontaneous speech in SPS.

	Register	Year of Birth	Gender	Education	Spontaneity	Formality	Audience Size
Register (SPS=0, APS=1)	1	.135	-.355	.612	-.180	.221	.862
Year of Birth	.135	1	-.033	-.028	-.174	.040	.154
Gender (M=0, F=1)	-.355	-.033	1	-.210	-.079	.019	-.306
Education (up to UNIV=0, GRAD=1)	.612	-.028	-.210	1	-.039	.143	.519
Spontaneity (Others=0, Spontaneous=1)	-.180	-.174	-.079	-.039	1	-.261	-.161
Formality (Others=0, Formal=1)	.221	.040	.019	.143	-.261	1	.264
Audience Size (Small=1, Medium =2, Large=3)	.862	.154	-.306	.519	-.161	.264	1

Table 5.9: Correlation matrix for the independent variables (CSJ)

As for Year of Birth, it only shows a very weak correlation with Register (r = 0.135), Spontaneity (r = –0.174) and Audience Size (r = 0.154), where younger speakers are weakly associated with APS, less spontaneous speech and a larger audience, all of which generally disfavor the use of LWs. This explains to some degree why age gradient is not observed in CSJ.

5.6 Summary of the factor-by-factor analyses

In this chapter, individual linguistic variables have been examined with regard to synchronic distribution by gender, education, register, and several stylistic parameters as well as generation. Table 5.10 shows the summary of the factor-by-factor analyses, where the effect of an external factor proven to be significant is marked either with ** ($p < 0.01$), * ($p < 0.05$), + ($p < 0.1$), or "ns" if not significant. A result is bracketed if it shows a pattern that is different from the general tendency.

In BCCWJ, many linguistic variables showed a tendency for younger generations to use loanwords more often than older generations (Younger > Older). This means that the claim that there is an ongoing change toward heavier use of loanwords, which had previously only been attested to by questionnaire-based studies of language attitudes, has been further supported by empirical evidence from people's actual linguistic behavior. In CSJ, however, this generational tendency was not visible, partly because the correlations between Year of Birth and other factors. We have seen that age distribution might be distorted because younger speakers are associated with factors that prevent the use of LW, such as APS, low spontaneity and larger audience. Another possibility is that the diffusion of loanwords is not in progress in the spoken mode, or, that it is in progress but too slow to be captured by observing just a 40-year period.

With regard to other language-external factors, it has been shown that loanwords are disfavored by more educated people and in more formal settings. First, the effect of Education proved to be significant for many lexical variables under consideration. In both BCCWJ and CSJ, those from GRAD use loanwords less frequently than those from (up to) UNIV (UNIV > GRAD).

Second, the effect of Register was attested in both corpora. In the written corpus, the occurrence of LWs is greater in magazines (PM) than in books (PB) (PB < PM). I pointed out that the difference between PB and PM may possibly be due to stylistic difference; for example, the formality of a text, evaluated by the frequency of non-standard contracted forms. To examine the effect of stylistic factors by means of other parameters, CSJ has also been investigated. The spoken corpus also exhibited the significance of the effect of Register (APS < SPS), Spontaneity (Others < Spontaneous), Formality (Others > Formal) and Audience Size (Small > Large) on the occurrence of loan variants. However, these results should be interpreted with care because various external factors are moderately/strongly correlated with each other. In particular, the correlations between Register and (i) Audience Size, (ii) Education, (iii) Spontaneity and (iv) Formality could imply that the register difference is attributable to these factors.

Lastly, the effect of Gender was not as consistent as that of the above external

Table 5.10: Summary of the factor-by-factor analyses

Factor	BCCWJ				CSJ						
General tendency	Year of Birth Younger > Older	Gender M<F	Education UNIV > GRAD	Register PB < PM	Year of Birth Younger > Older	Gender M<F	Education UNIV > GRAD	Register APS < SPS	Spontaneity Others < Spontaneous	Formality Others > Formal	Audience Size Small > Large
advice	+	ns	ns	-	ns	-	-	-	-	-	-
balance	**	**	ns	**	ns	**	+	**	(*)	ns	**
case	**	+	*	**	ns	**	+	**	(*)	ns	**
challenge	ns	ns	+	ns							
chance	ns	ns	**	ns							
event	*	ns	**	**	+	(**)	ns	ns	**	**	+
image	**	ns	(**)	ns	ns	ns	ns	ns	ns	ns	ns
keep	ns	-	-	-							
level	ns	ns	**	ns	ns	*	*	*	*	+	ns
master	+	-	-	-							
merit	**	ns	ns	**	ns	ns	*	**	**	*	**
needs	+	ns	ns	ns							
open	*	ns	*	*							
process	*	ns	ns	+	ns	(*)	(*)	(*)	ns	(**)	(*)
relax	ns	(**)	(**)	ns	ns	-	-	-	-	-	-
risk	*	(**)	ns	*							
rule	ns	ns	(*)	ns	ns	ns	ns	ns	+	**	**
shift	ns	-	**	**							
simple	**	**	**	**	ns	**	**	**	**	*	**
smooth	ns	ns	ns	ns	ns	ns	+	*	ns	ns	**
start	ns	ns	*	**	ns	+	+	ns	ns	ns	ns
support	*	*	ns	ns							
theme	ns	**	**	**	ns	**	**	**	**	**	**
type	+	+	ns	ns	ns	ns	+	+	**	**	**
unique	+	ns	**	+	ns						

( ) indicates that it shows tendency different from a general one.

variables. It seems that the gender differentiation is specific to the context of the words in question rather than a universal tendency.

It is noteworthy that, despite the limitation of the method (i.e., the inclusion in the analysis of "the widest possible" contexts where the selected variants occur) as discussed in Section 3.6, the results succeeded to some extent in eliciting general sociolinguistic patterns in the distribution of the selected loan variants not only by age but also by other social and stylistic factors. This approach, however, still has room for improvement. While the dictionary-based approach that I used to identify lexical variants (near-synonyms) is objective, we should note that dictionaries put an emphasis on "the denotational meaning of these synonymous words, not their usage" (Xiao & McEnery 2006: 111) within various linguistic contexts. To tackle this problem, we go a step further in Chapter 6, in which the envelope of variation is identified in a more careful manner.

Notes

1 Note that the majority of words dubbed "LW" in BCCWJ and CSJ are taken from Western languages, but this also includes a minority from non-Western languages such as Sanskrit, Korean, and so on.

2 In addition to (i) particles and (ii) auxiliaries, (iii) fillers, which are particularly frequent in spoken language, are excluded in both cases (BCCWJ, CSJ). In BCCWJ, the investigation is limited to the fixed-length samples written by a single author whose year of birth is available. In CSJ, the investigation is limited to the samples uttered by a speaker whose year of birth is available.

3 According to Mori (2013), the social distributions of authors in BCCWJ are imbalanced. He shows that birth year of the author is available only in 71.4% of the whole sample in the Library Book sub-corpus (LB). Among those, the majority of authors were those born between the 1920s and 1960s and the proportion of those born before or after that period account for only a small portion. Some attention is thus required when treating data related to these birth-year groups. He also points out that samples collected from those born in the 1910s and before are likely to be of reprinted books, since those born in the 1910s should be in their 90s in 2001–2005. It appears that the same holds true for the Publication sub-corpus, which is examined here.

4 The BCCWJ data is analyzed with UniDic, an electronic dictionary that annotates Japanese texts with morphological information. Here, SUW (short unit word) is used for counting words. See NINJAL (2011b: Ch4) for more detail.

5 I examined the UniDic version of CSJ (not the original DVD version) in order to use SUW (short unit word) that is also used in BCCWJ for counting words. It is noted that, since I used the available in-progress data as of November 2014 (with permission from NINJAL), the results shown here will be slightly different from what will be the finalized UniDic version.

CHAPTER 5 OTHER EXTERNAL FACTORS   83

The finalized UniDic version was made available to corpus DVD holders from 1st September 2016. For more detail about the UniDic version of CSJ, see Watanabe, Tanaka & Koiso (2015).

6 This category corresponds to *keiyoodooshi* in Japanese linguistics and is called *keijooshi* in BCCWJ.

7 Note that some loanwords have different native alternatives depending on its usage. For example, *imeeji* (< *image*) is a near-synonym of the NJ/SJ nouns *inshoo, kanji* and *gazoo* ('impression, feeling, image') in its nominal usage while its verbal usage *imeeji-suru* is synonymous with the NJ verb *omoiukaberu* ('to imagine'). That is why it is important to make frequency lists by usage.

8 The scope of investigation is limited to the case where a preceding word ends with *hiragana*. This is to effectively identify the cases where the loanwords in question are used independently and eliminate the cases where they are used as part of compounds or nonce words (*rinji ichigo*), e.g., 脳死ケース (*nooshi-keesu*, brain.death-case, 'the case of a brain death'). Note that words ending with *kanji* or *katakana* in writing are in most cases nouns and thus tend to form compounds or nonce words with the loanwords following them.

9 Samples extracted with these criteria are not completely exclusive to each other. For example, a context like "[adjectival noun] + [auxiliary]" does not distinguish adjectival usages (e.g., *orijinaru-na/da* 'original-COP') from nominal usages (e.g., *orijinaru-no* 'original-COP').

10 Although using one's intuition is subjective, this procedure is essential to effectively reduce linguistic variables to a reasonable number for further investigations. The final decision on native alternatives of the selected loanwords will be made by a more objective and rigorous method in the following stage.

11 Web dictionaries (3 and 4) are available at: ⟨http://www.sanseido.net/⟩ (accessed on May 4–16, 2015, and June 7–17, 2016).

12 Note that a LW/SJ verbal noun like *imeeji* ('(to) image') serves as both a *transitive* verb taking *suru* ('do') and an *intransitive* one taking *dekiru* ('be able to') or *sa-reru* ('do-PASS'), whereas the NJ verbs have different inventories for each usage: *omoiukaberu* (tr.)/*omoiukabu* (intr.). Therefore, in some cases, when a dictionary shows only an NJ transitive verb, e.g., *omoiukaberu*, as a definition of a given loanword, the intransitive NJ counterpart, e.g., *omoiukabu* is automatically added to the list of native equivalents and are marked with an asterisk (*) in the table.

13 If "Target lemma" is a NJ verb, e.g., *sasaeru* ('to support'), the following word, i.e., + *suru* ('do')/*dekiru* ('be able to'), is disregarded.

14 UniDic distinguishes the two *tte* forms: (i) the one called "particle" as in Example (5.5), which is the colloquial form of the complementizer *to* followed by a verb, such as *iu* ('say'), *omou* ('think'), and so on, and (ii) the one called "auxiliary" as in Example (5.6), which is the merger of *toiu* ('what they say') followed by a noun or the particle *no*.

15 I used the variable-length component of the Publication sub-corpus. The criteria for eliciting these forms are as follows:
> (i) *ja_copula*: *ja* + *nai* (NEG)
> (ii) *tte_particle*: *tte* + {*iu* ('say') / *omou* ('think') / *kiku* ('hear') / *kangaeru* ('think')}
> (iii) *tte_auxiliary*: *tte* + {*koto* ('thing') / *no* (particle) / *kanji* ('feeling') / *wake* ('reason') / *yatsu* ('thing, fellow') / *mono* ('thing') / *tokoro* ('place')}
> (iv) *n_particle*: *n* + {*da* (COP) / *desu* (COP.POL)}

As quotations tend to promote the occurrence of these colloquial forms, tokens occurring in quotations are excluded by using the two tags: "Quotation" and "Quotes" (see Note 7 in Chapter 6 for more detail about these tags). This allows us to eliminate the effect of direct and indirect speech by people other than the author.

CHAPTER 6

Incorporating Internal and External Factors into Analysis: A Case Study of *Keesu* (< *Case*)[1]

6.1 Towards a more fine-grained analysis of lexical variation

This chapter attempts to make a more fine-grained analysis of lexical variation, by investigating the question of the extent to which one should limit the envelope of variation based on usage. I will conduct a case study of *keesu* (< *case*) and its native alternatives in BCCWJ and CSJ. Based on the previous in-depth study of this loanword (Kim 2011), I will first provide a more detailed description of the selected linguistic variable, including the shared function of the variants, by observing all the contexts where the variants that I identified appear. I will then identify internal and external factors that affect the occurrence of the loan variant and introduce a multivariate model to incorporate both types of factors into analysis.

The reason for choosing *keesu* as a linguistic variable is four-fold. First, previous studies such as Kim (2011) and Hashimoto (2010: 52) confirm an upward tendency in the occurrence of *keesu* in real time. This means that the diffusion of this loanword is a bona-fide example of an ongoing change. Second, the loanword in question is high in frequency, guaranteeing the necessary volume for a quantitative analysis. Note that *keesu* is the most frequently occurring loanword among those examined in Chapter 5 (see Table 5.6). Third, the distribution pattern of this loanword is not inconsistent with the overall tendencies of the distributions of the 25 variables considered in Chapter 5. Last but most importantly, the loanword and its native equivalents have been fully investigated in terms of their usages and functions based on a corpus (Kim 2011). The last point is particularly crucial in identifying the envelope of variation. Consequently, *keesu* is a good example of lexical variable to be studied within the framework of variationist approach.

6.2 Identifying envelope of variation

Kim (2011) suggests that some loan nouns, including *keesu* (< *case*), have become "basic words"[2] in spite of the existence of native equivalents in competition with them. Figure 6.1 shows that *keesu* first appears in newspapers in the 1960s[3] and shows a consistent increase over the latter half of the 20th century as opposed to its native equivalents: *baai*, *rei*[4] and *jirei*.

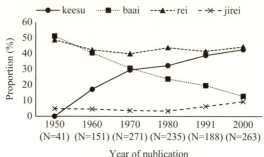

Figure 6.1: Diachronic distribution of *keesu*, *baai*, *rei*, and *jirei* (newspapers)
(Adapted from Kim 2011: 107, Table 1a, modified by the author[5])

According to Kim (2011: 93), *keesu*, *jirei*, *rei*, and *baai* are synonymous in that they all serve as a formal noun, in particular as a head of a gap-less relative clause (see Section 6.3.1 for more detail) as in Examples (6.1a–d). In the examples below, each variant forms a nominal phrase (NP), modified by the preceding square-bracketed gap-less relative clause.

(6.1) (Kim 2011: 93, Examples (1)–(4))
 a. [_{NP} [_{RC} 債務超過状態でも認められた] _N ケース] がある。
 [_{NP} [_{RC} *saimuchookajootai-de-mo mitome-rare-ta*] _N *keesu*]-*ga aru*.
 [[in.the.state.of.insolvency-COP-too admit-PASS-PAST] case]-NOM exist
 'There is [a case [in which one obtained a permission even in the state of insolvency]].'

b. [$_{NP}$ [$_{RC}$「情報教育」を掲げながら、実際はパソコンの利用法の習得
どまりとなる] $_N$事例] もある。

[$_{NP}$ [$_{RC}$ *"Joohoo-kyooiku"-o kakage-nagara jissai-wa*
pasokon-no riyoo-hoo-no shuutoku-domari tonaru]
$_N$ *jirei*]-*mo aru.*

[[information-education-ACC emphasize-although actual-TOP
computer-GEN use-method-GEN acquisition-mere remain]
case]-too exist

'There are [cases [in which students learn merely how to use a computer in spite of the emphasis in education being on promoting their
comprehensive skills of making the best use of information]].'

c. 植物状態のような慢性の意識障害では、[$_{NP}$ [$_{RC}$ 目は開いているが
話せないなど、JCSが適合しない] $_N$例] がある。

Shokubutsu-jootai-no yoona mansei-no
ishiki-shoogai-de-wa, [$_{NP}$ [$_{RC}$ *me-wa ai-teiru ga*
hanase-nai nado, JCS-*ga*
tekigoo-shi-nai] $_N$ *rei*]-*ga aru.*

vegetative-state-GEN such.as chronic-GEN
consciousness-disturbance-in-TOP [[eyes-TOP open-PROG but
can.speak-NEG such.as JCS(Japan Coma Scale)-NOM
be.applicable.to-do-NEG] case]-NOM exist

'JCS is sometimes not applicable to chronic disturbance of consciousness such as post-coma unresponsiveness (vegetative state); for example, there are [cases [in which the patient cannot speak a word despite
the fact that his/her eyes are open]].'

d. 水汲みは子供たちの仕事。[$_{NP}$ [$_{RC}$ 数キロ離れた所からやってくる]
$_N$場合] もある。

Mizukumi-wa kodomotachi-no shigoto.
[$_{NP}$ [$_{RC}$ *Suu-kiro hanareta tokoro kara yattekuru*] $_N$ *baai*]-*mo aru.*
Fetching.water-TOP children-GEN routine.

[[Several-kilometers distant place from come] case]-too exist.

'Fetching water is a daily routine for children. There are [cases [in
which they come from several kilometers away to do this]].'

Based on Kim's observation, we will regard this function (as the formal noun
'case') as one that the four variants typically share. In contrast, the context in
which these variants are used in other functions does not fall within the scope
of further investigation. For example, as Kim (2011: 94–95) points out, environments where the variants have idiomatic or word-specific meanings are to

be excluded from the analysis. First, unlike the other three variants, *baai*, if not followed by a particle, can be used to refer to (i) 'as for,' simply raising the topic of the sentence as in (6.2a), or (ii) 'if/when,' adding a hypothetical subordinate clause to the sentence as in (6.2b). Second, the four variants occur in their own idiomatic usages. These include the cases in which (i) *baai* refers to 'time' as in (6.2c), (ii) *rei* refers to 'in question' or 'that' as a demonstrative determiner as in (6.3a) and 'as usual' as in (6.3b), and (iii) *keesu* refers to 'container' as a concrete noun as in (6.4). These usages are distinguished from the usage as the general formal noun 'case.' In addition, cases where (iv) these words serve as a component of a compound or a nonce word (*rinji ichigo*) as in (6.5) are also excluded from the analysis. Examples (6.2)–(6.3) were taken from BCCWJ.

(6.2) *baai*

    a. Topicalizing ('as for')

      船橋警察署の場合、   (PB13_00095)

      Funabashi keisatsu-sho-no baai,

      Funabashi police-office-GEN case

      'As for Funabashi police office,'

    b. Hypothetical subordinate clause ('if/when')

      対馬でタクシーを利用する場合は、島が大きくそのまま利用する

      と非常に交通費が高くなってしまうため、   (PM51_00890)

      Tsushima-de takushii-o riyoo-suru baai-wa,

      shima-ga ookiku sonomama riyoo-suru-to

      hijoo-ni kootsuuhi-ga takaku-natteshimau tame,

      Tsushima-in taxi-ACC use-do case-TOP,

      island-NOM big without.consideration use-do-if

      very-COP travel.expenses-NOM expensive-result.in because,

      'If/when you use a taxi on Tsushima Island, traveling expenses can get very high if you keep riding without thinking since the island is so big,'

    c. 'time'

      だが、今はそんなことを言っている場合ではない。 (PB43_00366)

      Daga, ima-wa sonna koto-o it-teiru baai-de-wa-nai.

      but, now-TOP such thing-ACC say-PROG case-COP-TOP-NEG

      'It is not the time to be talking about a thing like that.'

CHAPTER 6 INCORPORATING INTERNAL AND EXTERNAL FACTORS INTO ANALYSIS 89

(6.3) *rei*
a. Demonstrative determiner ('in question/that')
そして、例の十字路に着いた。 (PB22_00242)
Soshite, rei-no juujiro-ni tsui-ta.
then in.question-GEN crossroad-at arrive-PAST
'Then I got to that crossroads (the crossroads in question).'

b. 'as usual'
ところが、例によってエレベーター前のドアには鍵がかかってい
る。 (PB52_00020)
Tokoroga, rei-niyotte erebeetaa mae-no doa-ni-wa
kagi-ga kakat-teiru.
however, as.ussal lift front-GEN door-on-TOP
key-NOM locked-PROG
'However, as usual, the door in front of the lift is locked.'

(6.4) *keesu*
Concrete noun ('container')
革製のケース
kawa-sei-no keesu
lether-made.of-GEN container
'A container made of leather'

(6.5) Part of a compound
モデルケース、具体的事例、典型例
moderu keesu, gutaiteki jirei, tenkei rei
model case, specific case, typical case
'model case,' 'specific example,' 'typical example'

Kim (2011: 115) points out that *keesu* co-occurs with the predicates listed in Table 6.1, particularly with *ooi* ('many') and *aru* ('present'). Noticing that these predicates assign the nominative particle *ga* to the noun *keesu*, I will focus on the contexts where *keesu* and the other variants are used in a subject position followed by these predicates. Examples (6.6a–f) from BCCWJ provide sentences with each predicate.

Type of predicate	Examples[6]
Present/Absent	*aru* ('present'), *mi-rareru/miuke-rareru* ('can be observed'), *nai* ('absent'), *mitome-rare-nai* ('cannot be observed'), etc.
Many/Few	*ooi/medatsu/hotondo-da/attooteki-da/ooku mirareru* ('many'), *ippanteki-da* ('(the most) common'), *sukunai* ('few'), *mezurashii/hotondo nai* ('rare'), etc.
Increase/Decrease	*fueru/zooka-suru* ('increase'), *heru* ('decrease'), etc.
Occur	*okiru/shoojiru/hassei-suru* ('occur'), etc.
Assume	*sootei-sareru* ('be assumed'), *kangae-rareru* ('be predicted'), *yosoo-sareru* ('be expected'), etc.
Report	*age-rareru* ('be given as an example'), *hooji-rareru* ('be reported'), etc.

Table 6.1: Type of predicate that co-occurs with *keesu*

(Summarized from Kim 2011: 115)

(6.6)   a. Present/Absent

手順7の写真の方が自然なケースもありますので、 (PB10_00109)

Tejun 7-no shashin-no hoo-ga shizen-na
*keesu- mo **ari-masu** node,*

procedure 7-GEN photo-GEN this.way-NOM natural-COP
case-too **exist-POL** so

'There **is** a <u>case</u> in which the photo taken in the procedure 7 looks natural, so...'

   b. Many/Few

また回線料も現状の専用線やVANと比べると安くできるケースが
多い.   (PB10_00063)

Mata kaisen-ryoo-mo genjoo-no sen'yoo-sen ya VAN
*to kuraberu to yasuku dekiru <u>keesu</u>-ga **ooi**.*

also connection-fee-too present.state-GEN special-line or VAN
with compare if cheap can.do <u>case</u>-NOM **many**

'There are **many** <u>cases</u> in which the connection fee is cheaper than that of an existing line or VAN.'

CHAPTER 6 INCORPORATING INTERNAL AND EXTERNAL FACTORS INTO ANALYSIS 91

c. Increase/Decrease

最近は地方銀行が「株主優遇定期作成優待券」を贈呈したり、地元の名産品を贈る<u>ケース</u>も**増えています**。　　(PB23_00254)

*Saikin-wa chihoo-ginkoo-ga "kabunushi yuuguu
teiki sakusei yuutaiken"-o zootei-shi tari,
jimoto-no meisanhin-o okuru <u>keesu</u>- mo* **fue-tei-masu**.

nowadays local-bank-NOM stockholder preferential.treatment
periodical preparation discount.coupons-ACC give-do or
local-GEN specialty-ACC give <u>case</u>-too **increase-PROG-POL**

'Nowadays the <u>cases</u> in which local banks give "stockholder discount coupons" or specialties of the district (to stockholders) are **increasing**.'

d. Occur

最近では、こうした危機管理以前の「安全管理」に問題ある<u>ケース</u>が**続発**している。　　(PB13_00434)

*Saikin-de-wa, kooshita kiki-kanri izen-no
"anzen-kanri"-ni mondai aru <u>keesu</u>-ga*
zokuhatsu-shi -teiru.

nowadays-in-TOP this risk-management rather.than-GEN
safety-manegement-in problem exist <u>case</u>-NOM
occur.in.succession-do-PROG

'Nowadays <u>cases</u> **occur in succession** in which there is a problem of "safety management" rather than risk management.'

e. Assume

銀行で借り直すことになる<u>ケース</u>も**考えられる**　　(PB13_00381)

Ginkoo-de kari-naosu koto ninaru <u>keesu</u>-mo **kangae-rareru**

bank-in ask.for.loan-again thing result.in <u>case</u>-too **expect-PASS**

'It is **expected** that they have to ask a bank for a loan again'

f. Report

ネグレクトが疑われるという<u>ケース</u>も**報告**されている。(PB13_00249)

Negurekuto-ga utagaw-areru toiu <u>keesu</u>-mo **hookokus-are-teiru**.

neglect-NOM suspect-PASS COMP <u>case</u>-too **report-PASS-PROG**

'The <u>cases</u> in which there is some suspicion of neglect (of children) are also **reported**.'

Based on the above discussions, the envelope of variation is limited to the contexts below in [Criteria 2], in which the four variants serve as formal nouns in subject positions, followed by either the nominative case marker *ga* (NOM), its topicalized variation *wa* (TOP) or its emphasized version *mo* ('too'), and then followed by the predicates that have the semantic features of [Present/Absent, Many/Few, Increase/Decrease, Occur, Assume, Report].

[Criteria 2]

Subject (as a formal noun) {*keesu, jirei, baai, rei*}

+ Particle {*ga, wa, mo*}

+ Predicacte { Present/Absent, Many/Few, Increase/Decrease, Occur, Assume, Report}

6.3 *Keesu* in BCCWJ

The language-internal criteria for eliciting data have now been identified. Now, tokens that satisfy the above criteria will be extracted from the variable-length component of PB and PM in the Publication sub-corpus in BCCWJ.[7] Articles written by a single author for whom birth year, gender and educational history are all identified are counted. The resultant number of tokens is shown in Table 6.2. There are 1,405 in total, including 312 of *keesu* (22.2%), 76 of *jirei* (5.4%), 776 of *baai* (55.2%) and 241 of *rei* (17.2%). We first notice that *keesu* accounts for approximately 20% of the total tokens; in contrast, it accounts for only 8% in the approach taken in the previous chapter. This is mainly due to the exclusion of a great number of examples of *baai* when it is used in the topicalizing or hypothetical usages shown in Examples (6.2a) and (6.2b).

Lemma	N	%
keesu	312	22.2%
jirei	76	5.4%
baai	776	55.2%
rei	241	17.2%
Total	1405	100.0%

Table 6.2: Tokens of *keesu* and its native variants (BCCWJ)

6.3.1 Internal factors:
syntactic structure and co-occurring predicate

Kim (2011: 101) demonstrated that *keesu* is often modified by a gap-less relative clause as shown earlier in Example (6.1a). She adds that *keesu*, however, is also used independently (without a modifier) as in (6.7). It can otherwise be preceded by a non-clause modifying component, such as a nominal phrase

CHAPTER 6 INCORPORATING INTERNAL AND EXTERNAL FACTORS INTO ANALYSIS 93

marked by the genitive case *no* (6.8a), an adjectival phrase (6.8b), and an adnominal (6.8c). In Table 6.3, one would notice that the occurrence of *keesu* in the usage with a clause modifier exhibits a clearer and sharper upward tendency in real time, compared with that in the remaining two usages.

(6.7) 男女の賠償額にケースによっては1000万円近い差が生じている。

(Kim 2011: 99, Example (15))

danjo-no baishoo-gaku-ni
keesu-niyotte-wa 1000-man-yen chikai
sa-ga shooji-teiru.
men.and.women-GEN compensation-amount.of-in
case-depending.on-TOP 1000-ten.thousand-JPY nearly
difference-NOM occur-PROG
'As the average wage for women is lower than that for men, the difference in the amount of compensation could be as much as 10 million yen in some cases.'

(6.8) (Kim 2011: 99)
  a. 京都市のケース
   Kyooto-shi-no keesu
   Kyoto-city-GEN keesu
   'the case of Kyoto'

  b. 悪質なケース
   akushitsu-na keesu
   vicious-COP case
   'a vicious case'

  c. そんなケース
   sonna keesu
   that case
   'such a case'

Year of publication	1950	1960	1970	1980	1991	2000
Without a modifier						
keesu	0.0	11.8	33.3	42.9	25.0	16.7
baai	25.0	35.3	9.5	14.3	0.0	5.6
rei	75.0	52.9	57.1	42.9	75.0	77.8
Total	100.0	100.0	100.0	100.0	100.0	100.0
With a non-clause modifier						
keesu	0.0	13.5	30.3	29.5	35.8	38.3
baai	50.0	44.6	23.2	14.1	35.8	15.0
rei	50.0	41.9	46.5	56.4	28.3	46.7
Total	100.0	100.0	100.0	100.0	100.0	100.0
With a clause modifier						
keesu	0.0	16.9	25.4	33.1	60.2	63.2
baai	52.6	35.4	39.2	33.1	22.7	17.4
rei	47.4	47.7	35.4	33.8	17.0	19.4
Total	100.0	100.0	100.0	100.0	100.0	100.0

Table 6.3: Diachronic distribution of *keesu* by usage (%)
(Adapted from Kim 2011: 112, Tables 5, 7 and 8, modified by the author[8])

Furthermore, Kim (2011: 101) emphasizes that the majority, i.e., 225 out of 233, of *keesu* used with a clause modifier serve as a head of a gap-less relative clause. This is clearly distinguished from an ordinary relative clause construction in that the noun *keesu* does not fill the grammatical gap in the preceding relative clause. In (6.9a), *keesu* fills the object position of the preceding bracketed relative clause. While in (6.1a), repeated here as (6.9b), there is no syntactic gap for *keesu* to fill in the preceding bracketed relative clause. We call the latter case the "Gap-less Relative Clause Head" (henceforth, Gap-less RCH) construction and distinguish it from the rest of the cases called "Others." Since such a distinction results from syntactic (grammatical) structure in which the variants occur, we name this independent variable "Structure."

(6.9) a. 参照すべきケース

$[_{NP} [_{RC}$ *sanshoo-su beki*$]_N$ *keesu*$]$
[[refer.to-do should] case]
'[A case$_i$ [$_{RC}$ that we should refer to <gap$_i$>]]'

b. 債務超過状態でも認められたケースがある。   (Kim 2011: 93)

$[_{NP} [_{RC}$ *saimuchookajootai-de-mo mitome-rare-ta*$]_N$ *keesu*$]$-*ga aru.*
[[in.the.state.of.insolvency-COP-too admit-PASS-PAST] case]-NOM exist
'There is [a case [$_{RC}$ in which one obtained permission even in the state of insolvency]].'

Based on Kim's observation, the present data shown in Table 6.2 will be distinguished by structure: Gap-less RCH or Others. Figure 6.2 shows the proportion of *keesu* and its native equivalents by structure. It is most noticeable that *keesu* is more frequently used as a Gap-less RCH (23.1%) than Others (15.5%). *Baai* also show a similar distribution whereas *jirei* and *rei* shows the opposite tendency. Table 6.4 confirms the statistical significance of the effect of syntactic structure on the occurrence of the LW.

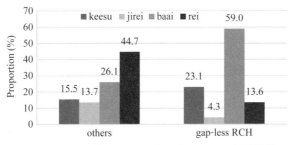

Figure 6.2: *Keesu* and its native variants by structure (BCCWJ)

		Others	Gap-less RCH	Total
LW	N	25	287	312
	%	15.5%	23.1%	22.2%
non-LW	N	136	957	1093
	%	84.5%	76.9%	77.8%
Total	N	161	1244	1405
	%	100.0%	100.0%	100.0%

$X^2 = 4.695$, d.f. = 1, $p < 0.05$

Table 6.4: Effect of structure on the occurrence of *keesu* (BCCWJ)

Figure 6.3 demonstrates that *keesu* shows a relatively high proportion of use with the predicates [Increase/Decrease] (54.1%) and [Occur] (60.5%). *Baai* shows a relatively high proportion of use with [Present/Absent] (63.1%), [Many/Few] (50.5%) and [Assume] (56.0%), whereas *jirei* and *rei* often co-occur with [Report] (45.8% and 37.5%, respectively). Table 6.5 indicates that the occurrence of the LW is not independent of the type of co-occurring predicate.

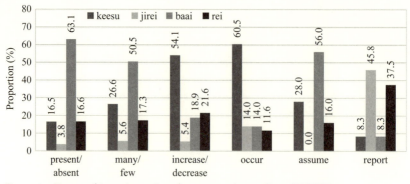

Figure 6.3: *Keesu* and its native variants by co-occurring predicate (BCCWJ)

		Present/ Absent	Many/ Few	Increase/ Decrease	Occur	Assume	Report	Total
LW	N	134	123	20	26	7	2	312
	%	16.5%	26.6%	54.1%	60.5%	28.0%	8.3%	22.2%
non-LW	N	679	340	17	17	18	22	1093
	%	83.5%	73.4%	45.9%	39.5%	72.0%	91.7%	77.8%
Total	N	813	463	37	43	25	24	1405
	%	100.0%	100.0%	100.0%	100.0%	100.0%	100.0%	100.0%

$X^2 = 81.832$, d.f. $= 5$, $p < 0.001$

Table 6.5: Effect of co-occurring predicate on the occurrence of *keesu* (BCCWJ)

6.3.2 External factors: year of birth, gender, education, register, and genre

In light of the existence of an ongoing change in favor of the newer lexical variant *keesu* in the latter half of the 20th century as reported by Kim (2011), it is expected that the proportion of the loan variant systematically increases as the authors' generation becomes younger. The hypothesis proved to be true as shown in Figure 6.4. The proportion of *keesu* increases from the oldest birth-year group (–1930, 19.7%) to the youngest birth-year group (1960–70, 29.2%). We notice, in contrast, that *rei* shows a systematic decrease, being surpassed largely by *keesu* among the youngest authors. *Baai* retains the highest proportion, while *jirei* shows the lowest proportion throughout generations without striking tendencies. Table 6.6 confirms the statistical significance of the effect of year of birth on the preference for the LW.

CHAPTER 6 INCORPORATING INTERNAL AND EXTERNAL FACTORS INTO ANALYSIS   97

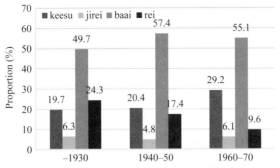

Figure 6.4: *Keesu* and its native variants by year of birth (BCCWJ)

		–1930	1940–50	1960–70	Total
LW	N	59	162	91	312
	%	19.7%	20.4%	29.2%	22.2%
non-LW	N	241	631	221	1093
	%	80.3%	79.6%	70.8%	77.8%
Total	N	300	793	312	1405
	%	100.0%	100.0%	100.0%	100.0%

$X^2 = 11.320, \text{d.f.} = 2, p < 0.01$

Table 6.6: Effect of year of birth on the occurrence of *keesu* (BCCWJ)

Figure 6.5 shows that women (22.9%) are ahead of men (22.1%) in the use of *keesu*, but it does not seem to be a striking difference. Table 6.7 shows, as expected, the difference is not statistically significant.

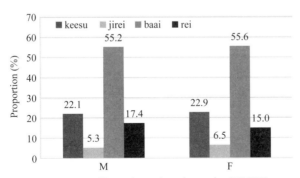

Figure 6.5: *Keesu* and its native variants by gender (BCCWJ)

		M	F	Total
LW	N	277	35	312
	%	22.1%	22.9%	22.2%
non-LW	N	975	118	1093
	%	77.9%	77.1%	77.8%
Total	N	1252	153	1405
	%	100.0%	100.0%	100.0%

$X^2 = 0.045$, d.f. = 1, $p = 0.833$

Table 6.7: Effect of gender on the occurrence of *keesu* (BCCWJ)

Figure 6.6 shows that the proportion of *keesu* systematically decreases from left to right: from those whose highest obtained education is high school or below (HS, 33.8%),[9] then university educated authors (UNIV, 25.2%) to postgraduate school educated authors (GRAD, 18.1%). *Baai*, in contrast, decreases leftwards consistently. It implies that there is a tendency for the more educated people to refrain from using the LW. Table 6.8 confirms the significance of the effect of education on the use of the loanword.

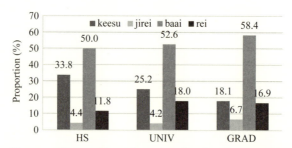

Figure 6.6: *Keesu* and its native variants by education (BCCWJ)

		HS	UNIV	GRAD	Total
LW	N	23	168	121	312
	%	33.8%	25.2%	18.1%	22.2%
non-LW	N	45	499	549	1093
	%	66.2%	74.8%	81.9%	77.8%
Total	N	68	667	670	1405
	%	100.0%	100.0%	100.0%	100.0%

$X^2 = 15.412$, d.f. = 2, $p < 0.001$

Table 6.8: Effect of education on the occurrence of *keesu* (BCCWJ)

Figure 6.7 shows that the proportion of *keesu* is rather higher in magazines (PM) (35.6%) than in books (PB) (21.5%). Table 6.9 shows that the effect of register (type of medium) on the occurrence of the loanword is significant.

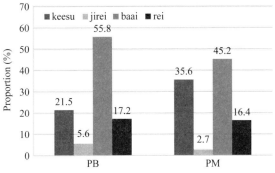

Figure 6.7: *Keesu* and its native variants by register (type of medium) (BCCWJ)

		PB	PM	Total
LW	N	286	26	312
	%	21.5%	35.6%	22.2%
non-LW	N	1046	47	1093
	%	78.5%	64.4%	77.8%
Total	N	1332	73	1405
	%	100.0%	100.0%	100.0%

$X^2 = 8.016$, d.f. = 1, $p < 0.01$

Table 6.9: Effect of register (type of medium) on the occurrence of *keesu* (BCCWJ)

Table 6.10 shows the proportion of the LW and the non-LWs by genre (PB only). The effect of genre proved to be significant on the occurrence of the LW ($X^2 = 27.711$, d.f. = 1, $p < 0.01$). The residual analysis shows that Social Science ($r = 2.3$, $p < 0.05$) has a positive effect on the occurrence of the LW whereas Technology & Engineering ($r = -2.6$, $p < 0.01$) and Language ($r = -3.0$, $p < 0.01$) have a negative effect on it. The positive effect of Social Science on the occurrence of the LW is apparently because *keesu* is associated more closely with the contexts in which social or legal problems are described as in (6.10a–b).[10]

		General	Philos-ophy	History	Social Sciences	Natural Sciences	Tech.& Engineer-ing	Industry	Arts	Lan-guage	Litera-ture	Total
LW	N	10	20	14	131	39	13	30	13	8	7	285
	%	19.2%	26.7%	15.7%	24.7%	18.8%	11.8%	28.6%	31.0%	9.0%	29.2%	21.5%
	r	-0.4	1.1	-1.4	*2.3	-1.0	**-2.6	1.8	1.5	**-3.0	0.9	
non-LW	N	42	55	75	399	168	97	75	29	81	17	1038
	%	80.8%	73.3%	84.3%	75.3%	81.2%	88.2%	71.4%	69.0%	91.0%	70.8%	78.5%
	r	0.4	-1.1	1.4	-2.3	1.0	2.6	-1.8	-1.5	3.0	-0.9	
Total	N	52	75	89	530	207	110	105	42	89	24	1323
	%	100.0%	100.0%	100.0%	100.0%	100.0%	100.0%	100.0%	100.0%	100.0%	100.0%	100.0%

$X^2 = 27.711$, d.f. = 1, $p < 0.01$

r refers to adjusted residual. p ** < 0.01, * < 0.05 in the residual analysis.

Table 6.10: Effect of genre on the occurrence of *keesu* (BCCWJ, PB only)

(6.10) a. このごろは家事事件に弁護士が関わる<u>ケース</u>が増えてきたが、

(PB43_00044)

Konogor-wa kaji-jiken-ni bengoshi-ga kakawaru
<u>keesu</u>-ga fue-tekita ga,
recently-TOP family-affairs-DAT lawyer-NOM be.involved
<u>case</u>-NOM increase-has.been but
'Recently, <u>cases</u> in which a lawyer gets involved in family affairs have increased,'

b. また、日本と外国との商慣習のズレにより国際問題になる<u>ケース</u>もあり、

(PB43_00557)

Mata, nihon to gaikoku to-no shoo-shuukan-no
zure-niyori kokusai-mondai ninaru <u>keesu</u>-mo ari,
Also, Japan and foreign.country and-GEN business-practice-GEN
difference-due.to international-problems result.in <u>case</u>-too exist
'There also are <u>cases</u> in which differences in business practices can develop into international problems,'

6.3.3 Multivariate analysis

A multiple logistic regression analysis was conducted to evaluate the statistical significance of the independent variables examined above. A multivariate analysis examines the effect of an independent variable on a dependent variable while the other independent variables are controlled; this is not immediately observable in a univariate cross-tabulation analysis. We can also include an interaction term in a model to see whether the given independent variables interact with each other. The model takes the form of [Formula 1] (as shown in

CHAPTER 6 INCORPORATING INTERNAL AND EXTERNAL FACTORS INTO ANALYSIS   101

Section 3.5 and repeated below), where p corresponds to the probability of the occurrence of the LW *keesu* (< *case*) as opposed to that of the non-LWs: *jirei*, *baai* and *rei*.

$$\log[p/(1-p)] = a_1 x_1 + a_2 x_2 + \dots + a_n x_n + b \qquad \text{[Formula 1]}$$

The dependent variable is binary: the occurrence (=1) or non-occurrence (=0) of the loanword *keesu*. There are six independent variables, including two language-internal ones: (x_1) Structure and (x_2) Predicate, as well as four language-external ones: (x_3) Year of Birth, (x_4) Gender, (x_5) Education and (x_6) Register (Type of Medium). All independent variables are categorical and the reference categories are those coded with the smallest numbers. Table 6.11 demonstrates that each independent variable is not highly correlated with any of the others.

x_1 = Structure (Others = 0, Gap-less RCH = 1)
x_2 = Predicate (Present/Absent = 1, Many/Few = 2,
         Increase/Decrease = 3, Occur = 4, Assume = 5, Report = 6)
x_3 = Year of Birth (−1930 = 1, 1940–50 = 2, 1960–70 = 3)
x_4 = Gender (M = 0, F = 1)
x_5 = Education (HS = 1, UNIV = 2, GRAD = 3)
x_6 = Register (Type of Medium) (PB = 0, PM = 1)

	Structure	Predicate	Year of Birth	Gender	Education	Register
Structure	1.000	-.187	.076	-.003	-.034	-.006
Predicate	-.187	1.000	.004	.012	.022	-.044
Year of Birth	.076	.004	1.000	.151	.068	.099
Gender	-.003	.012	.151	1.000	.088	.103
Education	-.034	.022	.068	.088	1.000	-.018
Register	-.006	-.044	.099	.103	-.018	1.000

Table 6.11: Correlation matrix for the independent variables: *keesu* in BCCWJ

Table 6.12 shows the result of the logistic regression analysis (stepwise, at a significance level of 0.05) using SPSS. It demonstrates that the all independent variables except for Gender: Structure, Predicate, Year of Birth, Education and Register, proved to be significant.[11]

First, we notice that, taking Others as a reference, the Gap-less RCH structure promotes the occurrence of the LW. Second, the occurrence of the LW is higher with predicates referring to [Many/Few], [Increase/Decrease] and [Occur], compared with the reference category [Present/Absent]. Third, taking the oldest birth-year group as a reference, the LW occurs more frequently in those born in the 1960–70s but the difference between the reference category and those born in the 1940–50s does not prove to be significant. Fourth, it is shown that GRAD disfavors the use of the LW in comparison with the reference category HS but the difference between HS and UNIV are not significant. Lastly, the LW occurs more frequently in PM than in PB. The coefficient of determination (R^2) is 0.33.

		B	S.E.	Wald	df	Sig.	Exp(B)
Structure	Others						
	Gap-less RCH	.595	.249	5.703	1	*	1.814
Predicate				76.784	5	**	
	Present/Absent						
	Many/Few	.609	.144	17.867	1	**	1.839
	Increase/Decrease	2.224	.338	43.408	1	**	9.246
	Occur	2.078	.362	32.925	1	**	7.991
	Assume	.815	.477	2.916	1	+	2.259
	Report	-.421	.755	.310	1		.656
Year of Birth				9.988	2	**	
	−1930						
	1940–50	.095	.179	.285	1		1.100
	1960–70	.552	.203	7.404	1	**	1.737
Gender		0					
Education				17.284	2	**	
	HS						
	UNIV	-.267	.286	.875	1		.765
	GRAD	-.802	.290	7.629	1	**	.448
Register	PB						
	PM	.727	.267	7.401	1	**	2.070
Constant		-1.928	.376	26.343	1	**	.145

p ** < 0.01, * < 0.05, + < 0.10

R^2 = 0.33 (Nigelkerke R^2 = 0.120)

Table 6.12: Result of the logistic regression analysis: *keesu* in BCCWJ

6.4 Additional analysis: *keesu* in CSJ

In order to examine further the effect of stylistic factors, the spoken corpus, CSJ, is also investigated. Following the criteria shown at the end of Section 6.2 (i.e., [Criteria 2]), tokens of the four variants are collected (Table 6.13). The table shows that after eliminating irrelevant contexts, the loanword *keesu* accounts for 12.0% of the all tokens, which is less frequent than that in the written corpus (BCCWJ), i.e., 22.2%.

Lemma	N	%
keesu	87	12.0
jirei	24	3.3
baai	431	59.4
rei	183	25.2
Total	725	100.0

Table 6.13: Tokens of *keesu* and its native variants (CSJ)

Table 6.14 shows that the LW occurs as a Gap-less RCH (13.2%) more frequently than as Others (8.1%) but this does not prove to be significant at the 5% level despite a tendency toward significance. Table 6.15 shows that the LW occurs more often with the predicate [Many/Few] (23.1%) than with the predicate [Present/Absent] (9.4%). There was no occurrence of the LW with the predicate [Increase/Decrease].

		Others	Gap-less RCH	Total
LW	N	14	73	87
	%	8.1%	13.2%	12.0%
non-LW	N	158	480	638
	%	91.9%	86.8%	88.0%
Total	N	172	553	725
	%	100.0%	100.0%	100.0%

$X^2 = 3.182$, d.f. $= 1, p = 0.074$

Table 6.14: Effect of structure on the occurrence of *keesu* (CSJ)

		Present/ Absent	Many/ Few	Increase/ Decrease	Occur	Assume	Report	Total
LW	N	52	28	0	4	2	1	87
	%	9.4%	23.1%	0.0%	20.0%	20.0%	5.9%	12.0%
non-LW	N	503	93	2	16	8	16	638
	%	90.6%	76.9%	100.0%	80.0%	80.0%	94.1%	88.0%
Total	N	555	121	2	20	10	17	725
	%	100.0%	100.0%	100.0%	100.0%	100.0%	100.0%	100.0%

Chi-square test is not conducted as there are several cells with expect count less than 5.

Table 6.15: Effect of co-occurring predicate on the occurrence of *keesu* (CSJ)

Table 6.16 shows that the occurrence of the LW is not independent from the speaker's year of birth. The use of the LW decreases from older generations to younger ones, indicating a decrease of the use of the LW, opposite to what we saw in Section 6.3.2.

Table 6.17 shows that the difference between genders proved to be significant, with the LW favored more by female speakers (17.4%) than male speakers (10.2%). Table 6.18 shows that the educational effect proved to be significant, with the LW occurring less frequently among GRAD (9.1%) in particular. This is consistent with the result in Section 6.3.2

		−1940	1950–60	1970–80	Total
LW	N	20	46	21	87
	%	17.2%	14.2%	7.5%	12.1%
non-LW	N	96	277	258	631
	%	82.8%	85.8%	92.5%	87.9%
Total	N	116	323	279	718
	%	100.0%	100.0%	100.0%	100.0%

$X^2 = 9.750$, d.f. = 2, $p < 0.01$

Table 6.16: Effect of year of birth on the occurrence of *keesu* (CSJ)

		M	F	Total
LW	N	56	31	87
	%	10.2%	17.4%	12.0%
non-LW	N	491	147	638
	%	89.8%	82.6%	88.0%
Total	N	547	178	725
	%	100.0%	100.0%	100.0%

$X^2 = 6.553$, d.f. = 1, $p < 0.05$

Table 6.17: Effect of gender on the occurrence of *keesu* (CSJ)

		HS[12]	UNIV	GRAD	Total
LW	N	9	42	36	87
	%	16.7%	15.8%	9.1%	12.2%
non-LW	N	45	223	361	629
	%	83.3%	84.2%	90.9%	87.8%
Total	N	54	265	397	716
	%	100.0%	100.0%	100.0%	100.0%

$X^2 = 7.962$, d.f. = 2, $p < 0.05$

Table 6.18: Effect of education on the occurrence of *keesu* (CSJ)

Tables 6.19–6.22 show the effect of register, spontaneity, formality and audience size on the occurrence of the LW. The effect of these variables proved to be significant except for formality (Table 6.21). First, the LW is more frequent in SPS (25.3%) than in APS (7.0%). Second, the LW is disfavored more in less spontaneous speech (5.9% in Low Spontaneity) than in more spontaneous speech (14.0% in Neither and 14.2% in High Spontaneity).[13] Third, the LW is used more frequently in front of small audience (24.3% in Small) than in front of larger audiences (5.6% in Medium and 8.9% in Large).

CHAPTER 6 INCORPORATING INTERNAL AND EXTERNAL FACTORS INTO ANALYSIS 105

		SPS	APS	Total
LW	N	50	37	87
	%	25.3%	7.0%	12.0%
non-LW	N	148	490	638
	%	74.7%	93.0%	88.0%
Total	N	198	527	725
	%	100.0%	100.0%	100.0%

$X^2 = 45.303$, d.f. = 1, $p < 0.001$

Table 6.19: Effect of register (type of speech) on the occurrence of *keesu* (CSJ)

		Low Spontaneity	Neither	High Spontaneity	Total
LW	N	10	25	52	87
	%	5.9%	14.0%	14.2%	12.2%
non-LW	N	159	154	313	626
	%	94.1%	86.0%	85.8%	87.8%
Total	N	169	179	365	713
	%	100.0%	100.0%	100.0%	100.0%

$X^2 = 8.175$, d.f. = 2, $p < 0.05$

Table 6.20: Effect of spontaneity on the occurrence of *keesu* (CSJ)

		Casual	Neither	Formal	Total
LW	N	12	44	28	84
	%	13.5%	13.9%	10.6%	12.6%
non-LW	N	77	272	236	585
	%	86.5%	86.1%	89.4%	87.4%
Total	N	89	316	264	669
	%	100.0%	100.0%	100.0%	100.0%

$X^2 = 1.523$, d.f. = 2, $p = 0.467$

Table 6.21: Effect of formality[14] on the occurrence of *keesu* (CSJ)

		Small (1–10)	Medium (20–50)	Large (100–300)	Total
LW	N	53	18	14	85
	%	24.3%	5.6%	8.9%	12.2%
non-LW	N	165	301	144	610
	%	75.7%	94.4%	91.1%	87.8%
Total	N	218	319	158	695
	%	100.0%	100.0%	100.0%	100.0%

$X^2 = 44.211$, d.f. = 2, $p < 0.001$

Table 6.22: Effect of audience size on the occurrence of *keesu* (CSJ)

Table 6.23 shows correlations between the above-mentioned independent variables. Register, Audience Size and Education have relatively strong correlation with each other ($r > 0.5$). Spontaneity and Formality are moderately correlated ($r = -0.483$). To avoid the multicollinearity problem, Audience size and Education are excluded from the analysis, considering that Register serves as a good indicator of these two variables. By the same token, Formality is excluded from the analysis, considering that Spontaneity serves as a good indicator of this variable.[15]

	Structure	Predicate	Year of Birth	Gender	Education	Register	Spontaneity	Formality	Audience
Structure	1.000	-.151	.101	-.006	-.141	-.073	.099	-.118	-.088
Predicate	-.151	1.000	.015	.015	.105	.102	-.006	.017	.132
Year of Birth	.101	.015	1.000	.012	.054	.224	-.077	.039	.188
Gender	-.006	.015	.012	1.000	-.163	-.172	-.067	.044	-.151
Education	-.141	.105	.054	-.163	1.000	.648	-.169	.258	.556
Register	-.073	.102	.224	-.172	.648	1.000	-.289	.365	.804
Spontaneity	.099	-.006	-.077	-.067	-.169	-.289	1.000	-.483	-.288
Formality	-.118	.017	.039	.044	.258	.365	-.483	1.000	.399
Audience	-.088	.132	.188	-.151	.556	.804	-.288	.399	1.000

Table 6.23: Correlation matrix for the independent variables: *keesu* in CSJ

Consequently, the following internal and external factors are incorporated into a multivariate analysis (the reference categories are those coded with the smallest numbers). An interaction term (Register×Spontaneity) is added in order to examine the existence of an interaction effect between the two variables. It is noted that the tokens with the value [Increase/Decrease] for the variable Predicate are excluded from the analysis, since the occurrence of the LW was categorical with this predicate (Table 6.15).

x_1 = Structure (Others = 0, Gap-less RCH = 1)
x_2 = Predicate (Present/Absent = 1, Many/Few = 2, Occur = 4,
    Assume = 5, Report = 6)
x_3 = Year of Birth (−1940 = 1, 1950–60 = 2, 1970–80 = 3)
x_4 = Gender (M = 0, F = 1)
x_5 = Register (SPS = 0, APS = 1)
x_6 = Spontaneity (Low Spontaneity = 1, Neither = 2,
    High Spontaneity = 3)
$x_5 x_6$ = Register×Spontaneity (interaction term)

CHAPTER 6 INCORPORATING INTERNAL AND EXTERNAL FACTORS INTO ANALYSIS   107

Table 6.24 shows the result of the logistic regression analysis (stepwise, at a significance level of 0.05) by SPSS. It demonstrates that the effect of Predicate, Register and the interaction term Register×Spontaneity proved to be significant. Structure, Year of Birth, Gender and Spontaneity have been shown not to be significant. The coefficient of determination (R^2) is 0.24.

		B	S.E.	Wald	df	Sig.	Exp(B)
Structure		o					
Predicate				21.873	4	**	
	Present/Absent						
	Many/Few	1.082	.277	15.288	1	**	2.951
	Occur	1.645	.627	6.875	1	**	5.179
	Assume	1.632	.838	3.791	1	+	5.116
	Report	-.047	1.065	.002	1		.954
Year of Birth		o					
Gender		o					
Register	SPS						
	APS	-2.692	.543	24.611	1	**	.068
Spontaneity		o					
Register×Spontaneity				8.788	2	*	
	SPS×Low Spontaneity						
	SPS×Neither						
	SPS×High Spontaneity						
	APS×Low Spontaneity						
	APS×Neither	1.690	.579	8.512	1	**	5.419
	APS×High Spontaneity	1.122	.572	3.847	1	*	3.071
Constant		-1.339	.185	52.204	1	**	.262

p ** < 0.01, * < 0.05, + < 0.10
R^2 = 0.24 (Nigelkerke R^2 = 0.179)

Table 6.24: Result of the logistic regression analysis: *keesu* in CSJ

First, the LW occurs more frequently with the predicates [Many/Few] and [Occur], compared with [Present/Absence] as a reference category. The result is consistent with what we have seen in the analysis of BCCWJ (Table 6.12).

Second, there is an interaction between Register and Spontaneity. Figure 6.8 illustrates the relation between Register and Spontaneity by showing the predicted probabilities of the occurrence of *keesu* followed by the predicate [Many/Few] as an example. The predicted values were calculated with the regression equation shown in [Formula 1′] in Section 3.5 (see Section 4.7 for the detailed explanation of how predictions are made with the formula). We can see that Spontaneity comes into play in APS, with [APS×Neither] and [APS×High Spontaneity], as compared with [APS×Low Spontaneity], showing higher probabilities of the occurrence of the LW. In contrast, Spontaneity does not play a role in SPS. This indicates that a higher degree of spontaneity promotes the use of the LW only in APS. SPS, however, shows higher probabilities of the occurrence of the LW than APS does, regardless of the degree of spontaneity.

Last but not least, it is noted that the variable Year of Birth, which showed a slightly odd distribution in the univariate analysis (Table 6.16), did not prove to be significant in the multivariate one.

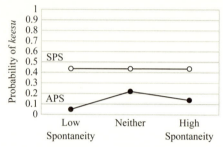

Figure 6.8: Interaction between Register and Spontaneity (Those co-occurring with Predicate [Many/Few])

6.5 Sociolinguistically asymmetric distributions of *keesu*

This chapter attempted to incorporate both language-internal and external factors into analysis of lexical variation. We have witnessed that the loan variant *keesu* and its native variants *jirei*, *baai* and *rei* overlap in function as a formal noun (in particular as a Gap-less RCH). The four variants also have their own unique functions (or show division of labor) but such environments were excluded from the analysis.

As a result of the multivariate analyses, two internal variables: (i) Structure and (ii) Predicate, proved to have an influence on the occurrence of the loan variant. First of all, the loanword proved to be more strongly associated with the Gap-less RCH structure (BCCWJ). This provided statistical evidence in favor of Kim's (2011) observation. Second, compared wih the predicate [Present/Absent], predicates referring to (a) [Many/Few], (b) [Increase/Decrease] and (c) [Occur] co-occur more often with the loan variant (BCCWJ, CSJ). It may be worth mentioning that, as opposed to the predicate [Present/Absent], (a) [Many/Few] and (b) [Increase/Decrease] are characterized having the semantic feature of *quantitative evaluation* (+), while (b) [Increase/Decrease] and (c) [Occur] having the feature of *change of state* (+) as shown in Table 6.25. This may imply that *keesu* tends to be used in the context in which the occurrence or a quantitative aspect of a certain event is emphasized, co-occurring with the predicates (a) [Many/Few], (b) [Increase/Decrease] and (c) [Occur]. In contrast, *baai* occurs most frequently with the predicate [Present/Absent], indicating that it is used more often in the context in which only the existence/non-existence of a certain fact matters.

	Change of state (−)	Change of state (+)
Quantitative evaluation (−)	Present/Absent	(c) Occur
Quantitative evaluation (+)	(a) Many/Few	(b) Increase/Decrease

Table 6.25: Semantic features of co-occurring predicates

With regard to external factors, (i) Year of Birth, (ii) Education (of the author/speaker), (iii) Register and (iv) Spontaneity (of the talk) proved to have impacts on the use of the loan variant. First, there is a tendency for the youngest generation to use the loanword more often (BCCWJ). This can be considered an indication of a generational change in favor of *keesu* as opposed to its Japanese counterparts. Second, the effect of the level of education also proved to be significant, with the loanword *keesu* being disfavored by the most educated authors (BCCWJ). Third, register is another significant factor, with the proportion of *keesu* being higher in magazines than in books (BCCWJ). In other words, the loanword is disfavored in more formal text like books, compared with magazines (as I also pointed out in Chapter 5).

Additional analysis with the spoken corpus (CSJ) provided a more comprehensive understanding of the relationship between register and stylistic parameters such as Spontaneity. In the present data, the use of the LW is inhibited in APS, which is characterized having a more formal speech style than SPS. Recall that APS is associated with larger audiences and speakers with higher educational backgrounds, implying that the loan variant is disfavored in such environments. Furthermore, Spontaneity is in interaction with Register, with more spontaneous speech promoting the use of the LW in APS. The results imply that, roughly speaking, the occurrence of the LW is more closely associated with more informal and more spontaneous speech, and, additionally, smaller audiences and those with lower educational backgrounds.

To conclude, a more detailed anlaysis of lexical variation has revealed that the occurrence of the LW *keesu* is dependent on both *language-internal* and *external* factors. In addition to distribution based on internal factors, sociolinguistically asymmetric distributions of *keesu* as a loan variant give an interesting insight into its status as opposed to its native counterparts in contemporary written and spoken Japanese. The tendency for more educated people and more formal (or less spontaneous) settings to disfavor the loan variant implies that the loanword is not fully established in certain social categories or settings. This asymmetry implies, although *keesu* may have become an integral part of basic Japanese vocabulary in some respect (Kim 2011), it still remains non-standard and subject to various sociolinguistic restrictions to a certain degree. Among these restrictions, stylistic constraints on loanword use will be discussed further in Chapter 7.

Notes

1 This chapter is based on Kuya (2013b) and has been further developed, with Section 6.3.3 and Section 6.4 newly added.

2 According to her explanation, "basic words" are defined as those being frequently and broadly used in certain registers by shifting from the periphery to the core of the lexicon of a language. She showed in her case studies that (i) *toraburu* (< *trouble*) and (ii) *keesu* (< *case*) have established their status as "basic words" in newspapers by expanding their meaning and usage.

3 According to Irwin (2011: 60), the first written attestation of *keesu* is in 1872.

4 *Rei* is not included in the dictionary-based approach in the previous chapter.

5 The figures are given in per million word (PMW) in Kim but I modified them by converting PMW into proportions to show the probabilities of the occurrence of a given variant as opposed to the other variants.

6 Note that mainly those examples that assign the nominative particle to the subject are shown in the table. See Kim (2011) for the complete list of examples.

7 I would like to draw attemtion to the following two issues in using BCCWJ as a source of synchronic data, in order to make our anlysis more fine-grained.

First, there is sometimes a discrepancy between the publication date of a book and its first printed date. Generally, unlike magazines or newspapers, books published at a certain point include those reprinted from their previous, original publications. That is, there is a risk that language originally written and published, say, in the 1980s, is treated as language written in the 2000s. Moreover, it is not necessarily the case that a given book was firstly and exclusively written for publication as a book. In other words, it is possible that it was formerly written and first made public elsewhere, e.g., in magazines, newspapers, and so on, but later published as a book. In other words, in the Publication sub-corpus there is always a certain proportion of text from reprinted books or from articles that were originally written for other types of media. NINJAL made the maximum effort to trace and provide the first publication date of texts and to mark samples when they know that the text in question was originally made public before or originally written for other types of media (Maruyama 2012). To reduce the effect of these types of text, I will consider only those that were first published during the period 2001–2005. If clearly indicated, those that were originally written for other sources of

CHAPTER 6 INCORPORATING INTERNAL AND EXTERNAL FACTORS INTO ANALYSIS   111

media are also excluded. Note that the total number of tokens shown in Table 6.2 is smaller than that shown in Kuya (2013b) mainly because of this additional procedure.

Second, quotations should be excluded from the analysis because language that appears in such environments cannot be treated as the language of the author. BCCWJ marks such components by the tags "Quotation" and "Quote" (Yamaguchi et al. 2011: 117–124). These tags allow us to exclude the direct and indirect speech of people other than the author. By the same token, translated articles are also excluded.

8 The figures are given in per million word (PMW) in Kim but I modified them by converting PMW into proportions to show the probabilities of the occurrence of a given variant as opposed to the other variants.

9 Recall that educational categories of the authors in BCCWJ consist of (1) Junior high school, (2) High school, (3) College of technology, (4) Junior college, (5) University, and (6) Graduate School. Here, the category "HS" includes those who graduated from (1), (2), (3), or (4).

10 This does not necessarily mean that *keesu* has been developed particularly as a technical term used by professionals in legal or other related fields.

11 "B" (Regression coefficient) corresponds to a_n in [Formula 1]. "Wald" is a test statistic that is used for testing the significance of B. The significance of a Wald statistic is evaluated based on a degree of freedom "df" and its p-value shown in the column "Sig." A positive coefficient indicates that a given category has a higher probability of the occurrence of the LW than its reference category whereas a negative coefficient indicates that it has a lower probability than its reference category. "0" indicates that the effect of the independent variable in question on the output is not significant (at the 5% level).

"Exp(B)" represents the odds ratio, which is the value converted from B. The interpretation of Exp(B) is easier than that of B; for example, Exp(B)=2.070 in the independent variable Register means that the probability of occurrence of LW is 2.070 times stronger in PM than that in its reference category PB. The effect size is smallest (i.e., none) when Exp(B)=1 and grows as Exp(B) becomes distant from 1 (Exp(B)=10 would mean that the effect size is 10 times more, and, Exp(B)=0.1 would mean that it is 10 times less, in contrast to a reference category). In the logistic regression model, unlike the linear regression model, the effect size of an independent variable on a dependent variable is not understood from the value of B by intuition, since B represents the amount of change in the left-hand side of [Formula 1], i.e., log[p/$(1-p)$], not the probability p itself, when x_n is in an increment of 1.

"Constant" corresponds to b (an intercept) in [Formula 1].

12 Recall that educational categories of the speakers in CSJ consist of (1) Junior high school, (2) High school, (3) College/University, and (4) Graduate School. Here, the category "HS" includes (1) and (2).

13 Recall that spontaneity was originally evaluated on a five-point scale: (1) Not spontaneous—(2) Not really spontaneous—(3) Neither—(4) Somewhat spontaneous—(5) Highly spontaneous. Here, (1) and (2) are grouped together into "Low Spontaneity" as opposed to "High Spontaneity" including (4) and (5). Those choosing (3) "Neither" are in between Low Spontaneity and High Spontaneity.

14 Recall that formality was originally evaluated on a five-point scale: (1) Casual—(2) Somewhat casual—(3) Neither—(4) Somewhat formal—(5) Formal. Here, (1) and (2) are grouped together into "Casual" as opposed to "Formal" including (4) and (5). Those choosing (3) "Neither" are in between Casual and Formal.

15 The value of VIF is 3.553 for Register, 2.990 for Audience size, 1.793 for Education, 1.346 for Spontaneity, 1.468 for Formality, and less than 1.1 for the rest if all the variables in Table 6.23 are included. After eliminating the variables in the shaded cells in Table 6.23, however, the values for the remaining variables become lower (1.181 at the highest).

CHAPTER 7

Stylistic Constraints on Lexical Choice: A Case Study of *Sapooto* (< *Support*)[1]

7.1 Elucidating the impact of style on lexical choice

The influence of age on the adoption of loanwords has been repeatedly reported in previous surveys (BBK 1999, 2000, 2003, 2008, 2013; NINJAL 2004, 2005a; Tanaka 2007; Jinnouchi 2007). However, stylistic effect on the phenomenon has not yet been investigated sufficiently in spite of its importance to an extensive elucidation of the theory of language change. Inoue (2000: 557) points out that linguistic change progresses in different manners across different speech styles. In order to express this, he proposed a three-dimensional model: the Water Tank Model,[2] in which the diffusion of a given variant is captured by two independent variables: time and speech style (Inoue 2000: 556, Figure 27-7).

According to NINJAL (2004: 32), 36.5% of people turned out to decide the use or non-use of loanwords depending on where the utterance takes place and to whom the utterance is directed. This implies that the diffusion of a given loanword progresses over a speech community at different speeds across different speech styles. This chapter, therefore, will take into consideration a stylistic effect on the use of loanwords, in order to elucidate a more elaborate process of loanword diffusion.

The first part of the chapter provides a quantitative analysis of the phenomenon with a statistical model that predicts the use/non-use of the loanword *sapooto* (< *support*) according to speech style (Sections 7.4 and 7.5). This model will help give a multidimensional view of how the loanword spreads into a community across different styles. The latter part of the chapter describes a qualitative aspect of stylistic variation (Section 7.6). It concerns the question of how and why individual speakers switch from one lexical item to another. An in-depth analysis of individual speakers will let us discuss the nature of the observed style-shifting and also speakers' evaluation of the loanword in question.

7.2 Previous studies on style

The study of style, i.e., *intra-speaker* variation, as opposed to *inter-speaker* variation, is an attempt to understand variation that occurs within one speaker's language depending on various contexts. In spite of a number of studies on the relation between language and style, a unified theory of stylistic variation has not been reached (Takano 2012). The earliest approaches, such as Labov (1972) and Trudgill (1974), claim that one's linguistic behavior is determined by the level of formality of speech style or, in other words, the amount of attention paid to speech (Attention to Speech Model). This model predicts that a prestigious variant is favored in a formal setting as a result of an increased amount of attention paid to speech (careful speech).

In contrast, the Audience Design Model (Bell 1984) points out that stylistic variation occurs in response to audience. For example, Rickford & McNair-Knox (1994) reported that the probability of the occurrence of vernacular speech varies depending on to whom the utterance is addressed.

The Speaker Design Model (Schilling-Estes 2002) puts more emphasis on the speaker's intention. A speaker uses language selectively in order to prove his/her social identity. Ekert (1988: 206) points out that the high school student group called "Burnouts" in Detroit tends to adopt ongoing urban sound changes proactively as a result of their motivation to orient themselves to the urban community that they are associated with.

The previous studies have shown that stylistic variation is interpretable from various perspectives. Analysts have to consider which model is most convincing to explain the process in which certain stylistic variation occurs. However, it should also be noted that the mechanism of a given style-shifting is sometimes not fully explainable by a single model (Section 7.6).

Furthermore, we should aware that stylistic factors often interact with other external factors. Figure 7.1 shows the distribution of the variable /ng/ in Norwich by socioeconomic class and style (Trudgill 1974: 92). Index score /ng/ represents the proportion of [n] to the standard [ŋ] (Trudgill 1974: 84). Different speech styles are arranged along a scale of formality: the most formal Word List Style (WLS), Reading Passage Style (RPS), Formal Speech (FS) to the least formal Casual Speech (CS). The consistent tendency for the index to decrease from CS to WLS indicates that the occurrence of the variable /ng/ is not independent from the social context in which a speech is delivered, i.e., speech style. It should also be noted that the gradient of the data is different across social classes. For example, the two middle-class (MC) groups show the greatest amount of stylistic differentiation between CS and FS, whereas the three working-class (WC) groups do not make a clear stylistic difference between these two speech styles; they instead show the sharpest stylistic differentiation between FS and RPS. Trudgill (1974: 93) points out that this appears to show the ability of the MC groups to control the (ng) forms in FS to a level nearer to that of the more formal styles, i.e., RPS and WLS.

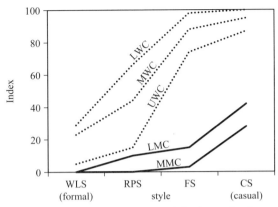

Figure 7.1: Variable /ng/ in Norwich by class and style
(Adapted from Trudgill 1974: 92, Figure 14)

Here there is an interaction between social class and style, with the stylistic effect on the variable /ng/ modified by social class. In other words, the manner in which the stylistic factor affects this variation is different across social classes. An interaction effect can sometimes demonstrate the *crossover* pattern. We can see the most famous example of this in a study of New York English (Labov 1972: 114, see also Labov 1994: 87), wherein people from the second highest socioeconomic class use the prestigious variant of the variable /r/ more frequently than those from the highest socioeconomic class in formal settings, although the use of this /r/ by these two groups in more informal settings is the other way around (hypercorrection). Since previous studies on variation in Japanese (e.g., Sano 2008, 2011) have also reported the presence of an interaction between style and other social factors, this chapter will also take this point into consideration (Section 7.5).

7.3 *The National Survey on Attitudes to Loanwords II*
(NINJAL 2005a)

NINJAL (2005a) conducted *The National Survey on Attitudes to Loanwords II* in 2004.[3] The targeted population is the entire Japanese-speaking population in Japan who are aged 15 and above. The statistical sample is 4,500 people selected randomly with a stratified sampling method (stratified by administrative divisions and area). There were valid responses from 3,090 people (68.7%),

1,421 males and 1,669 females. The survey was conducted in the form of a face-to-face interview in which an informant was interviewed individually based on the prepared questionnaire.

This survey was the second attempt by NINJAL to investigate the public attitudes to loanwords, following their first survey conducted in 2003: *The National Survey on Attitudes to Loanwords* (NINJAL 2004). The first survey concerns people's overall attitudes to loanwords in general. For example, it includes questions on whether or not they usually use loanwords, and whether they have a positive attitude towards a further influx of loanwords in the future. The second survey, by contrast, puts more focus on the question of how speech style or social setting affects the use of loanwords. Lexical choice between (i) the LW サポート (*sapooto < support*), (ii) its SJ equivalent 支援 (*shien*), and (iii) its NJ counterpart 手助け (*tedasuke*), all referring to 'support/help,' was used by NINJAL as a case study. As shown below in Example (7.1), the example sentence with a blank was presented to the informants to help them make choices more easily. They were then asked to select one lexical item among the above three in the following distinct speech settings: (i) when talking to friends (Friends), (ii) when talking in public (Public) and (iii) when talking to elderly people (Elders).

(7.1) Example context (NINJAL: 2005a: 125)
       新しく農業を始めるには、地域の（　　　）が必要です。
       Atarashiku noogyoo-o hajimeru ni-wa,
       chiiki-no [　]-ga hitsuyoo-desu.
       newly farming.business-ACC to.start in.order.to-TOP
       community-GEN [　]-NOM necessary-COP.POL
       '[　] should be given at the community level when one starts a new farming business.'

The informants were subsequently asked the reason why they chose that word in each setting from two different perspectives A and B (they were asked to select one each from A and B). Those categorized as "A" are concerned purely with the linguistic meanings that a word delivers, including "it is (i) Concise, (ii) Easy to understand, (iii) Precise in meaning, or (iv) Familiar to me." Those categorized as "B" are concerned with things outside of a purely linguistic meaning, i.e., the nuances socially embedded in each word, including "it sounds (i) Novel, (ii) Intelligent, (iii) Stylish, (iv) Colloquial, or (v) Dignified." (NINJAL 2005a: 125)

Table 7.1 shows that the distribution of each word varies across settings. The LW *sapooto* occurs most frequently in Friends (33.4%). In contrast, the use of the LW is least frequent in Elders (3.3%). The LW is selected in Public (27.3%) at a level little lower than that for Friends.

	LW サポート sapooto	SJ 支援 shien	NJ 手助け tedasuke	Not sure	Total
Friends	1033 33.4%	790 25.6%	1204 39.0%	63 2.0%	3090 100%
Public	843 27.3%	1455 47.1%	708 22.9%	84 2.7%	3090 100%
Elders	102 3.3%	402 13.0%	2520 81.6%	66 2.1%	3090 100%

Table 7.1: Lexical choice across different settings: Friends, Public, and Elders (Adapted from NINJAL 2005a: 18)

Henceforth, the focus is put on two of the three settings originally studied by NINJAL: Friends and Public. The reason for focusing only on these two settings is that it is difficult to align the three settings, i.e., Friends, Public and Elders, on the same continuum of style. Based on the traditional definition of style, in which various speech settings are aligned along the continuum of formality (Casual vs. Careful, Labov 2001b), we are likely to place a setting like Friends close to the Casual pole (Labov 1972: 85). Speech addressed to a general audience, what Labov (2001b: 91) calls "Soapbox," is in contrast placed closer to the Careful pole.

However, a setting like Elders, which is defined as a situation where one talks to elderly people one is unfamiliar with, cannot be placed on the continuum of informal-formal. In addition, we see that the occurrence of the loanword in Elders is too rare across all generations to be applicable to the research being undertaken (Figure 7.2).

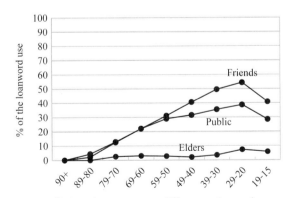

Figure 7.2: Diffusion of *sapooto* across different settings and age groups

One of the advantages of using the present data is that the sample is a good representative of the population: We are reasonably able to extend the result obtained here to the whole population, i.e., the entire Japanese-speaking population in Japan.

In addition, the loanword *sapooto* is regarded as a typical example of a well-attested loanword in Japanese. First, according to NINJAL (2007b: 275), people understand the meaning of this word 81.8% of the time on average and even the oldest age group (aged 60 and above) shows a relatively high level of comprehension (61.8%). Moreover, the loanword has been shown to be well attested in written and spoken language (Chapter 5).[4] Second, the distribution pattern of *sapooto* is not inconsistent with the general trend that the loanwords under investigation in Chapter 5 have exhibited. These studies provide evidence in support of the assumption that it is not unreasonable to generalize a conclusion from an analysis of *sapooto*, within the bounds of these well-adopted kinds of loanwords.

7.4 Effect of age, education, gender, and style

This section examines the effect of individual social factors on the choice to use the loanword using cross tabulation.

(a) Age
Figure 7.3 shows the distribution of the LW, SJ and NJ across age groups and styles. In Friends, the proportion of the LW increases from older to younger age groups, with those in their 40s or younger selecting the LW as their first choice. Likewise, there is a similar age gradient in Public, but the LW is no longer the first choice for any age group as a result of the jump in the relative frequency of the SJ in all the age groups.

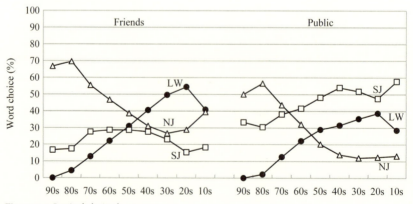

Figure 7.3: Lexical choice by age

CHAPTER 7 STYLISTIC CONSTRAINTS ON LEXICAL CHOICE   119

It is notable that, in both Friends and Public, those in their teens use the LW less frequently than those in their twenties in spite of the general tendency for younger people to favor loanwords. This phenomenon is, as discussed in Chapter 4, explainable in terms of a delay in lexical acquisition among teens: They have not acquired the loanword *sapooto* to the same extent as older generations have. The example sentence presented to the informants in the interview (see Example 7.1 in the privious section) describes a rather social or political issue, which is unlikely to be a common topic of conversations for teens. Hence, it is possible that they are not familiar enough with the loanword in question to judge whether it can be used in this specific context.

Henceforth, those in their teens (N=137) are excluded from the analysis as they are shown to behave differently from those in other age groups. Moreover, those in their 80s (N=46) and 90s (N=6) are also excluded from further analysis because of their very small sample size. The number of the remaining informants (those aged 20s–70s) is 2,901. Table 7.2 shows the use and non-use of the LW across age groups (the occurrence of the SJ and NJ are grouped together as "Non-LW"). The chi-square test shows that age is not independent from the occurrence of the LW in both Friends and Public.

		20s	30s	40s	50s	60s	70s	Total	
Friends	LW	149	252	193	192	138	51	975	$X^2(5) = 238.163$
	Non-LW	125	256	283	427	487	348	1926	$p < 0.001$
	Total	274	508	476	619	625	399	2901	
Public	LW	106	180	150	179	138	50	803	$X^2(5) = 91.332$
	Non-LW	168	328	326	440	487	349	2098	$p < 0.001$
	Total	274	508	476	619	625	399	2901	

Table 7.2: Effect of age on the use/non-use of *sapooto*

(b) Education

Figure 7.4 shows the distribution of lexical items by speakers' educational background with JHS, HS and UNIV referring to elementary/junior high school graduates, high school graduates and university graduates, respectively. It demonstrates the tendency for those with higher educational backgrounds to use the LW more frequently. It is remarkable that those in UNIV select the LW as their first choice in Friends, but its proportion in Public drops largely to a level close to that of HS. Instead, their first choice switches to the SJ. Statistical testing shows that, as shown in Table 7.3, the effect of one's educational background on the occurrence of the LW is significant in both Friends and Public.

We should, however, pay attention to the possibility that the educational factor is interrelated with the age factor. Table 7.4 shows that the order of the educational categories in LW use, i.e., JHS < HS < UNIV in Friends and JHS < HS ≤

UNIV in Public, holds true for most of the age groups, even when each educational category is stratified by age. It is then not unreasonable to claim that the educational factor is independent of the age factor to a certain degree (see also Section 7.5).

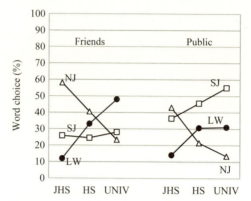

Figure 7.4: Lexical choice by education

		JHS	HS	UNIV	Total	
Friends	LW	62	482	425	969	$X^2(2) = 190.499$
	Non-LW	456	976	460	1892	$p < 0.001$
	Total	518	1458	885	*2861	
Public	LW	73	446	274	793	$X^2(2) = 58.646$
	Non-LW	445	1012	611	2068	$p < 0.001$
	Total	518	1458	885	*2861	

*Samples whose educational background is unknown (N=40) are excluded.

Table 7.3: Effect of education on the use/non-use of *sapooto*

		20s	30s	40s	50s	60s	70s	All age groups
Friends	JHS	38.9	16.7	30.8	9.0	11.9	9.5	12.0
	HS	49.3	49.0	33.6	29.7	25.2	14.8	33.1
	UNIV	63.5	52.4	49.8	44.9	30.2	26.3	48.0
Public	JHS	16.7	25.0	30.8	21.8	13.0	10.5	14.1
	HS	40.7	37.9	33.2	29.7	27.3	12.6	30.6
	UNIV	39.1	34.0	29.2	30.5	21.7	23.7	31.0

Table 7.4: Proportion (%) of LW to non-LW by education and age

(c) Gender

Gender differentiation does not appear to be very striking for the LW, compared with that for the SJ or NJ (Figure 7.5). The chi-square test (Table 7.5) indicates that gender is independent of the occurrence of the LW.

CHAPTER 7 STYLISTIC CONSTRAINTS ON LEXICAL CHOICE 121

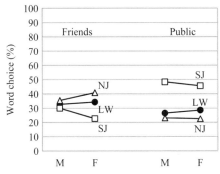

Figure 7.5: Lexical choice by gender

		Male	Female	Total	
Friends	LW	434	541	975	$X^2(1) = 0.798$
	Non-LW	891	1035	1926	$p = 0.372$
	Total	1325	1576	2901	
Public	LW	352	451	803	$X^2(1) = 1.512$
	Non-LW	973	1125	2098	$p = 0.219$
	Total	1325	1576	2901	

Table 7.5: Effect of gender on the use/non-use of *sapooto*

(d) Style

As we saw earlier in Table 7.1, the occurrence of the LW varies across the two speech styles. Table 7.6 confirms that the difference reaches statistical significance.

Figures 7.6 and 7.7 are provided to examine the interaction between style and other social factors: (i) age and (ii) education. In Figure 7.6, style-shifting occurs only among those aged 40s and below. Likewise, Figure 7.7 shows that style-shifting occurs only among those from UNIV. These figures imply the possibility that the effect of style on the use of the LW comes into play in interaction with the effect of age and/or education.

	Friends	Public	Total	
LW	975	803	1778	$X^2(1) = 23.991$
Non-LW	1926	2098	4024	$p < 0.001$
Total	2901	2901	5802	

Table 7.6: Effect of style on the use/non-use of *sapooto*

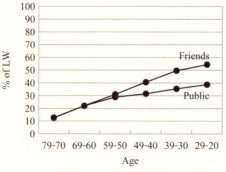

Figure 7.6: Distribution of *sapooto* by age and style

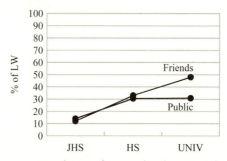

Figure 7.7: Distribution of *sapooto* by education and style

7.5 Predicting the diffusion of *sapooto* in a multi-dimensional space

A multiple logistic regression model is employed to evaluate the effect of each independent variable on the phenomenon. In the general formula of the model, i.e., [Formula 1], *p* represents the probability of the occurrence of the LW *sapooto* as opposed to its native equivalents *shien* and *tedasuke*.

$$\log[p/(1-p)] = a_1 x_1 + a_2 x_2 + \ldots + a_n x_n + b \qquad \text{[Formula 1]}$$

The dependent variable is considered to be binary, i.e., the occurrence (= 1) or non-occurrence (= 0) of the LW. There are six independent variables[5] including two interaction terms as follows:

CHAPTER 7 STYLISTIC CONSTRAINTS ON LEXICAL CHOICE

x_1 = Year of Birth (converted from age)
x_2 = Education (1 = JHS, 2 = HS, 3 = UNIV)
x_3 = Style (1 = Friends, 2 = Public)
x_4 = Gender (1 = Male, 2 = Female)
x_1x_3 = Year of Birth×Style (interaction term)
x_2x_3 = Education×Style (interaction term)

The year of birth of the speakers (converted from their age) is inputted as a numeral variable. In practice, a median value is adopted to represent each age range: 1929.5 (70–79), 1939.5 (60–69), 1949.5 (50–59), 1959.5 (40–49), 1969.5 (30–39), 1979.5 (20–29). The other variables: Education, Style and Gender, are all categorical ones, and reference categories are those having the lowest value (=1). As discussed in Section 7.4, two interaction terms, i.e., Year of Birth×Style and Education×Style, are added into the model. Table 7.7 is provided to show how samples are coded, with those in their 20s as an example.

Age Range	Year of Birth (median)	Gender	Education	Style	Occurrence of LW	No. of Samples
20–29	1979.5	1	1	1	1	4
20–29	1979.5	1	2	1	1	31
20–29	1979.5	1	3	1	1	28
20–29	1979.5	2	1	1	1	3
20–29	1979.5	2	2	1	1	38
20–29	1979.5	2	3	1	1	45
20–29	1979.5	1	1	1	0	3
20–29	1979.5	1	2	1	0	40
20–29	1979.5	1	3	1	0	22
20–29	1979.5	2	1	1	0	8
20–29	1979.5	2	2	1	0	31
20–29	1979.5	2	3	1	0	20
20–29	1979.5	1	1	2	1	1
20–29	1979.5	1	2	2	1	26
20–29	1979.5	1	3	2	1	18
20–29	1979.5	2	1	2	1	2
20–29	1979.5	2	2	2	1	31
20–29	1979.5	2	3	2	1	27
20–29	1979.5	1	1	2	0	6
20–29	1979.5	1	2	2	0	45
20–29	1979.5	1	3	2	0	32
20–29	1979.5	2	1	2	0	9
20–29	1979.5	2	2	2	0	38
20–29	1979.5	2	3	2	0	38

Table 7.7: Example of data coding (Samples of those in their 20s)

Table 7.8 shows the result of the logistic regression analysis (stepwise, at a significance level of 0.05) using SPSS. "B" (Regression coefficient) and

"Constant" in the table correspond to an and b (an intercept) in [Formula 1]. (For the interpretaion of "B," "Wald," "Exp(B)," and so on, see Note 11 in Chapter 6.) The analysis shows that the three variables: (i) Year of Birth, (ii) Education and (iii) Education×Style, are significant. The coefficient of determination (R^2) is 0.67.[6]

First, the interaction between Year of Birth and Style is not statistically significant. We can see then, that Year of Birth alone has a positive effect on the occurrence of the LW, which indicates that the use of the LW increases as speakers' year of birth does.

Second, there is an interaction between Education and Style. This means that the effect of Education, in spite of its statistical significance, should not be discussed alone, because it is modified by the stylistic factor. The interpretation of the effect of this interaction term on the occurrence of the LW is illustrated in the following section.

		B	S.E.	Wald	df	Sig.	Exp(B)
Year of Birth		.0258	.002	147.806	1	**	1.026
Education					2	**	
	JHS			121.865			
	HS	.8462	.112	56.873	1	**	2.331
	UNIV	1.3366	.121	121.690	1	**	3.806
Style		0					
Gender		0					
Year of Birth×Style		0					
Education×Style				56.819	2	**	
	JHS×Friends						
	HS×Friends						
	UNIV×Friends						
	JHS×Public						
	HS×Public	-.1174	.081	2.112	1		.889
	UNIV×Public	-.7431	.100	54.712	1	**	.476
Constant		-51.9468	4.121	158.910	1	**	<.001

$**p < 0.01$
($R^2 = 0.67$)

Table 7.8: Result of the logistic regression analysis: *sapooto*

Figure 7.8 shows the predicted probabilities of the occurrence of the LW by Education, Style and Year of Birth. This prediction is not only for those aged 20s to 70s, but also for those excluded from the analysis in Section 7.4, i.e., those in the age groups 15–19, 80–89 and 90–94. In addition to that, future generations, i.e., those born in 1997 and 2007, 10 and 20 years after the youngest surveyed group are also taken into consideration. This enables us to predict the diffusion of *sapooto* across 100 years of age. The predicted values were calculated with the regression equation shown above in [Formula 1] (see Section 4.7 for the explanation of how predictions are made with the formula).

The lines with filled marks (●/■) represent the predicted probabilities of the occurrence of the LW, and the empty marks (○/□) represent the observed values. The round marks (○/●) represent the occurrence of the LW in Friends and the square marks (□/■) represent the same in Public. It should be noted that there are two observed values for each birth-year group as samples are divided by gender. The predicted values are the same for both genders as the effect of the variable Gender has been shown not to be significant.

Note that JHS shows more discrepancy between the predicted and observed values than HS or UNIV, apparently because JHS is more sensitive to the effect of outliers due to the relatively smaller sample size among the three (the sample sizes of JHS, HS and UNIV are N = 518, N = 1,458 and N = 885, respectively. See Table 7.3). Especially for those in their 20s, 30s and 40s, i.e., those born in the 1960s–1980s, it is rare that their highest obtained education is JHS. We observe, accordingly, the largest discrepancy in these age groups in JHS.

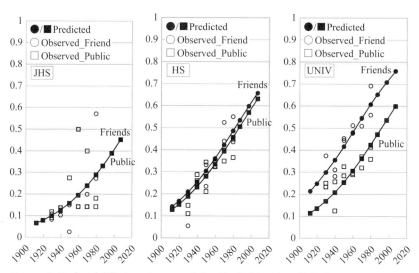

Figure 7.8: Predicted diffusion of *sapooto* defined by (i) Education, (ii) Style, and (iii) Year of Birth

The figure shows that the probability of the occurrence of the LW increases from older generations to younger ones in every educational and stylistic category, forming part of an s-curve. However, such linguistic change progresses at different rates depending on the combination of [Education×Style], as a result of the interaction between these variables.

JHS exhibits no stylistic difference in the use of the LW: The two curves completely overlap each other. In HS, there is a very small difference in the use of the LW between Friends and Public, though the difference is shown not to be significant. Notice that [HS×Public] in Table 7.8 does not show significance at the 5% level. On the other hand, the stylistic effect comes into play in UNIV, where the probability is approximately 0.1–0.2 lower in Public than in Friends. Figure 7.8 shows that loanword adoption is greatest in the category [UNIV×Friends]. It appears that this group is reaching the advanced stage of the s-curve, where the rate of change starts to slow down at the youngest generations, such as those born in 1997 and 2007. In [UNIV×Public], in contrast, the spread of the LW is delayed for 20–30 years: The diffusion reaches 0.6 among those born in 1979 in [UNIV×Friends] whereas it reaches the same level among those born in 2007 in [UNIV×Public].

Figure 7.9 illustrates the relation between Education and Style in the case of those in the 30s age group by showing predicted values. As seen above, those in [UNIV×Friends] shows the greatest adoption of the LW, though it drops largely in [UNIV×Public] to a level slightly lower than that of [HS×Public] (*crossover* pattern). Consequently, the ranking of the educational categories seen in Friends, i.e., JHS < HS < UNIV, is no longer maintained in Public. This implies that the effect of Education varies as a function of Style.

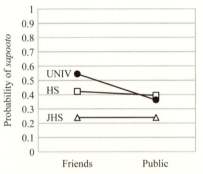

Figure 7.9: Interaction between Education and Style
(Those in their 30s)

The multivariate analysis has confirmed that the use of the LW is context-bound: People use the LW quite selectively depending on where the utterance is taking place or to whom it is directed. Following Inoue's model (2000: 556, Figure 27-2), Figure 7.10 is provided to illustrate a three-dimensional model of the loanword diffusion (in the case of those born in 1987). It succeeds in capturing the spread of the loanword *sapooto* in a three-dimensional space by Style and Education in interaction. It shows that the change spreads at different rates across different speech style; people's readiness to use the LW becomes weaker when talking in public (Public) than when chatting with friends (Friends). The stylistic variable, however, is shown to work in interaction with the educational one and that such a tendency is prominent only among the most educated group (UNIV).

As a result, the present study has succeeded in providing another piece of evidence in support of the claim made in the previous variationist studies that it is often the case that style interacts with other social variables (e.g., class, education, gender) (Labov 1972, Trudgill 1974, Sano 2008, Sano 2011, among others).

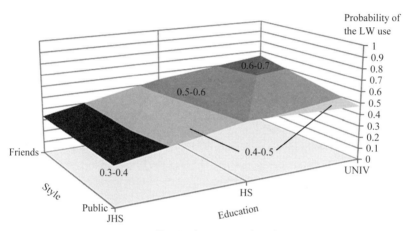

Figure 7.10: Diffusion of *sapooto* in three dimensions
(Those born in 1987)

7.6 Motivations for switching *from* or *to* the loanword

This section aims to describe the mechanism of style-shifting, i.e., the reason why such shifting occurs, by contrasting those who alternate between LW and non-LW across different styles with those who do not.

We first observe what types of word-switching occur when speech style shifts, say, from Friends to Public.[7] Table 7.9 shows that there are 9 (3×3) types of switching/non-switching (excluding the cells "Not sure"). The shaded cells, i.e., those numbered as [2], [3], [4], [6], [7], [8], represent the groups that had shifting in lexical choice. In total, half of the informants (48.9%) made some sort of switch across different styles. The major patterns are the switches from non-SJ to SJ, including the switch from NJ to SJ ([6]: 15.6%) and the switch from LW to SJ ([4]: 13.8%). The switch from LW to non-LW is 17.5% in total ([4]: 13.8% + [7]: 3.7%) whereas the switch from non-LW to LW is 11.7% in total ([2]: 4.6% + [3]: 7.1%). Because of the overall decrease in the proportion of LW use from 33.6% in Friends to 27.7% in Public, we tend to assume that the switch from LW to non-LW occurred. However, the proportion of switching in the opposite direction, i.e., from non-LW to LW, is not negligible.

| | | Public | | | | |
		LW	SJ	NJ	Not sure	Total
	LW	[1]	[4]	[7]		
		461	401	107	6	975
		15.9%	13.8%	3.7%	0.2%	33.6%
	SJ	[2]	[5]	[8]		
		132	500	121	3	756
		4.6%	17.2%	4.2%	0.1%	26.1%
Friends	NJ	[3]	[6]	[9]		
		206	453	429	26	1114
		7.1%	15.6%	14.8%	0.9%	38.4%
	Not sure	4	6	4	42	56
		0.1%	0.2%	0.1%	1.4%	1.9%
	Total	803	1360	661	77	2901
		27.7%	46.9%	22.8%	2.7%	100.0%

Table 7.9: Patterns of word-switching

Table 7.10 shows the proportion (%) of types of word-switching (switching/ non-switching) by education. It shows that the total proportion of switching from LW to non-LW, of which the majority comes from the switching to SJ (LW→SJ), increasing from JHS (5.6%) to UNIV (28.0%). On the other hand, the occurrence of switching from non-LW to LW remains more or less at 10% for all educational categories. Focusing on the difference between switching to non-LW (LW→non-LW) and switching to LW (non-LW→LW), it is less than 3% in JHS (5.6 – 7.9 = –2.3%) and HS (15.7 – 13.2 = 2.5%), whereas the difference is outstanding (28.0 – 11.0 = 17%) in UNIV. A clear stylistic difference in LW use among UNIV is then attributed to the predominance of switching to non-LW over switching to LW. This is visualized in Figure 7.11 with a little simplification, where SJ and NJ are grouped together as non-LW. The solid lines represent the proportions of switching across styles whereas the dotted lines represent the proportions of non-switching. It shows that the smaller amount of word-switching across styles in HS and JHS does not mean that no style-shifting occurred in these groups. Both types of switching (LW→non-LW and non-LW→LW) in fact occurred, but canceled each other out.

	Friends → Public	JHS	HS	UNIV	Others	All educational categories
[1]	LW → LW	6.2	17.1	19.9	7.5	15.9
	LW → non-LW	5.6	15.7	28.0	5.0	17.5
[4]	LW → SJ	3.5	12.1	23.1	5.0	13.8
[7]	LW → NJ	2.1	3.6	5.0	0.0	3.7
	non-LW → LW	7.9	13.2	11.0	17.5	11.7
[2]	SJ → LW	1.5	4.9	5.4	10.0	4.6
[3]	NJ → LW	6.4	8.3	5.5	7.5	7.1
	non-LW → non-LW	73.4	50.9	40.3	60.0	51.8
[5]	SJ → SJ	18.0	15.5	19.1	30.0	17.2
[8]	SJ → NJ	6.2	3.9	3.5	2.5	4.2
[6]	NJ → SJ	14.5	17.8	12.8	15.0	15.6
[9]	NJ → NJ	34.7	13.7	5.0	12.5	14.8
	Others	6.9	3.0	0.8	10.0	3.1
	Total (%)	100.0	100.0	100.0	100.0	100.0
	(N)	(518)	(1458)	(885)	(40)	(2901)

Table 7.10: Patterns of word-switching by education (%)

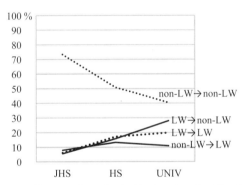

Figure 7.11: Patterns of word-switching by education (Simplified)

(a) Switching from LW to non-LW
It is assumed that, among those who choose LW in Friends, those who do not show word-switching in Public and those who do show switching in Public, each have different reasons for their word choice in Public.

First, let us focus on those who choose LW in Friends ([1][4][7] in Table 7.9). Table 7.11 demonstrates that the reasons for word choice in Public are different for those who show switching to SJ ([4]: from LW to SJ) and those who do not ([1]: from LW to LW), with the difference significant at the 0.1% level in the chi-square test.[8] The residual analysis shows that the former puts more emphasis on "Easy to understand" and "Precise in meaning" in Reason A and

"Intelligent" and "Dignified" in Reason B than the latter. "Easy to understand" and "Precise in meaning" seem to represent the speakers' consideration for the addressees. The other two, "Intelligent" and "Dignified," in contrast, seem to reflect the speakers' attention to the formality of the setting, in which they are required to sound proper for the occasion. In summary, those who switch from LW to SJ seem to consider SJ more suitable to use in Public than LW in terms of addressees' ease of understanding and the formality of the setting.

Table 7.12 demonstrates that the reasons for word choice in Public among those who show switching to NJ ([7]: from LW to NJ) are different from the reasons given by those who do not ([1]: from LW to LW), with the difference significant at the 0.1% level in the chi-square test. The data shows that the former group consider "Easy to understand" in Reason A and "Colloquial" in Reason B more important than the latter.[9] Both "Easy to understand" and "Colloquial" seem to reflect the speakers' consideration for the addressees. Therefore, those who switch from LW to NJ seem to consider NJ more suitable to use in Public than LW in terms of addressees' ease of understanding.

Patterns of switching		Reason A					Reason B					
		Concise	Easy	Precise	Familiar	Total	Novel	Intelligent	Stylish	Colloquial	Dignified	Total
[1] from LW to LW	N	122	147	18	170	457	121	52	33	152	9	367
	%	26.7	32.2	3.9	37.2	100.0	33.0	14.2	9.0	41.4	2.5	100.0
	Residual	5.5	-5.8	-10.9	11.6		9.7	-6.0	4.2	-.4	-6.9	
[4] from LW to SJ	N	47	206	128	17	398	11	106	5	135	57	314
	%	11.8	51.8	32.2	4.3	100.0	3.5	33.8	1.6	43.0	18.2	100.0
	Residual	-5.5	**5.8	**10.9	-11.6		-9.7	**6.0	-4.2	.4	**6.9	
Total	N	169	353	146	187	855	132	158	38	287	66	681
	%	19.8	41.3	17.1	21.9	100.0	19.4	23.2	5.6	42.1	9.7	100.0
		$X^2(3) = 248.315, p < 0.001$					$X^2(4) = 163.536, p < 0.001$					

** $p < 0.01$ in residual analysis

Table 7.11: Reasons for word choice in Public: those choosing LW in Friends (1)

CHAPTER 7 STYLISTIC CONSTRAINTS ON LEXICAL CHOICE

Patterns of switching		Reason A				Reason B				
		Concise	Easy	Familiar	Total	Novel	Intelligent	Stylish	Colloquial	Total
[1] from LW to LW	N	122	147	170	439	121	52	33	152	358
	%	27.8	33.5	38.7	100.0	33.8	14.5	9.2	42.5	100.0
	Residual	4.4	-9.1	5.7		5.5	2.2	3.0	-8.0	
[7] from LW to NJ	N	7	83	9	99	4	5	0	79	88
	%	7.1	83.8	9.1	100.0	4.5	5.7	0.0	89.8	100.0
	Residual	-4.4	**9.1	-5.7		-5.5	-2.2	-3.0	**8.0	
Total	N	129	230	179	538	125	57	33	231	446
	%	24.0	42.8	33.3	100.0	28.0	12.8	7.4	51.8	100.0
		$X^2(2) = 83.695$, $p < 0.001$				$X^2(3) = 64.533$, $p < 0.001$				

** $p < 0.01$ in residual analysis

Table 7.12: Reasons for word choice in Public: those choosing LW in Friends (2)

(b) Switching from non-LW to LW

Now let us turn to those who choose non-LW in Friends but switch to LW in Public ([2] and [3] in Table 7.9). Table 7.13 looks at those who choose SJ in Friends. It demonstrates that reasons for word choice in Public are different for those who show switching ([2]: from SJ to LW) and those who do not ([5]: from SJ to SJ), with the difference significant at the 0.1% level in the chi-square test. The residual analysis shows that the former group places more stress upon "Concise" in Reason A and "Novel" and "Stylish" in Reason B than the latter. Evaluations like "Concise" seem to indicate consideration of the speakers' ease of use and also their consideration for the addressees. "Novel" and "Stylish" seem to be associated with the question of how the speakers want to express themselves in front of unspecified general audience. In summary, those who switch from SJ to LW seem to consider LW more suitable to use in Public than SJ in terms of the ease of use for the speakers themselves, the ease of understanding of the addressees, and the speakers' identity construction.

Table 7.14 looks at those who choose NJ in Friends. It demonstrates that the reasons for word choice in Public are different for those who make switching ([3]: from NJ to LW) and those who do not ([9]: from NJ to NJ), with the difference significant at the 0.1 % level in the chi-square test. The residual analysis shows that the former group considers "Concise" and "Precise in meaning" in Reason A and "Novel," "Intelligent" and "Stylish" in Reason B more important than the latter group. In summary, those who switch from NJ to LW seem to consider LW more suitable to use in Public than NJ in terms of the ease of use for the speakers themselves or the addressees ("Concise" and "Precise in meaning"), the speakers' identity construction ("Novel" and "Stylish"), and the formality of the setting ("Intelligent").

Patterns of switching		Reason A					Reason B					
		Concise	Easy	Precise	Familiar	Total	Novel	Intelligent	Stylish	Colloquial	Dignified	Total
[5] from SJ to SJ	N	47	281	70	98	496	13	77	11	184	32	317
	%	9.5	56.7	14.1	19.8	100.0	4.1	24.3	3.5	58.0	10.1	100.0
	Residual	-8.1	4.0	1.7	0.9		-8.9	-1.0	-3.5	7.5	1.5	
[2] from SJ to LW	N	50	48	11	21	130	41	33	14	19	6	113
	%	38.5	36.9	8.5	16.2	100.0	36.3	29.2	12.4	16.8	5.3	100.0
	Residual	**8.1	-4.0	-1.7	-0.9		**8.9	1.0	**3.5	-7.5	-1.5	
Total	N	97	329	81	119	626	54	110	25	203	38	430
	%	15.5	52.6	12.9	19.0	100.0	12.6	25.6	5.8	47.2	8.8	100.0

$X^2(3) = 66.726, p < 0.001$ $\qquad$ $X^2(4) = 113.043, p < 0.001$

** $p < 0.01$ in residual analysis

Table 7.13: Reasons for word choice in Public: those choosing SJ in Friends

Patterns of switching		Reason A					Reason B				
		Concise	Easy	Precise	Familiar	Total	Novel	Intelligent	Stylish	Colloquial	Total
[9] from NJ to NJ	N	18	292	21	96	427	3	8	5	293	309
	%	4.2	68.4	4.9	22.5	100.0	1.0	2.6	1.6	94.8	100.0
	Residual	-10.9	8.8	-4.9	2.3		-10.7	-9.5	-5.4	17.5	
[3] from NJ to LW	N	76	63	34	30	203	65	61	25	32	183
	%	37.4	31.0	16.7	14.8	100.0	35.5	33.3	13.7	17.5	100.0
	Residual	**10.9	-8.8	**4.9	-2.3		**10.7	**9.5	**5.4	-17.5	
Total	N	94	355	55	126	630	68	69	30	325	492
	%	14.9	56.3	8.7	20.0	100.0	13.8	14.0	6.1	66.1	100.0

$X^2(2) = 161.986, p < 0.001$ $\qquad$ $X^2(3) = 308.116, p < 0.001$

** $p < 0.01$ in residual analysis

Table 7.14: Reasons for word choice in Public: those choosing NJ in Friends

Based on the discussion above, we should revisit the question of what actually induces style-shifting in the present data. First, there is evidence that style-shifting occurs as a response to the speakers' attention to their speech (Attention to Speech Model). This includes the cases where a speaker chooses LW in Friends but switches to SJ in Public in order to sound intelligent or dignified in response to the formality of the setting. Based on the fact that SJ is in general associated with social prestige (Ishiwata 2001: 9), we can conclude that an increase in the level of formality of the setting leads to switching to the more prestigious form, SJ. Evaluations like "Intelligent" or "Dignified," however, are also interpretable as speakers' spontaneous acts of developing their identity in public speaking (Speaker Design Model). This means that it is possible that style-shifting occurs when a speaker wants to show him-/herself to be intelligent or dignified in front of an anonymous general audience.

Second, some data show that style-shifting occurs as a response to addressees (Audience Design Model). For example, there are cases where a speaker chooses LW in Friends but switches to non-LW in Public in order to help their addressees understand the speaker more easily. In general, speakers feel a need to consider their addressees more strongly when talking to an anonymous general audience in public than when chatting with well-acquainted friends, as they cannot expect as much linguistic homogeneity when talking to the former group as when talking to the latter group. It appears that speakers tend to become more careful about the use of loanwords when talking to a variety of people in a setting like "Public," considering, for example, that not all generations are equally familiar with loanwords.

The above descriptions point out that the stylistic difference between the two settings, which is often intuitively contrasted in terms of formality (Section 7.2), must in fact be interpreted from multiple perspectives. It is therefore important to apply several models complimentarily or simultaneously to the data in order to gain an integrated understanding of the nature of style and style-shifting.

7.7 Elaborate process of loanword diffusion across different styles

This chapter has examined how a stylistic variable influences the diffusion of the LW *sapooto* as opposed to its native equivalents. The data showed that the diffusion of the loanword is interpreted as an ongoing change with stylistic variation. It also revealed that a stylistic variable comes into play in interaction with the educational variable: Stylistic difference in word choice is significant only for the most educated group. The multivariate analysis enables us to provide a Water Tank Model (Inoue 2000), in which the diffusion of the loanword is captured multi-dimensionally by stylistic and other veriables (Figure 7.10). The model is shown to be useful in predicting probabilities of the phenomenon for future generations as well as those excluded from analysis due to lack or insufficiency of data, verifying its practical utility as a "tool for predicting probability" (Yokoyama & Sanada 2007: 82).

In-depth observation of individual speakers revealed that when speech style shifts from Friends to Public, switching from LW to non-LW occurs as the most prominent pattern, but at the same time, a significant minority of people switch from non-LW to LW. Switching from LW to non-LW tends to occur when speakers want to add *intelligence* and *dignity* to their speech by using SJ in def-erence to the formality of the setting. It also occurs when speakers want to make understanding *easier* for the addressees by using non-LW variants, which are characterized by the evaluations like "Easy to understand" and "Colloquial." On the other hand, switching from non-LW to LW tends to occur when speakers want to place emphasis on the *novelty* and *stylishness* of their speech by selecting LW. In addition, speakers' intention of adding *intelligence* to their speech in deference to the formality of the setting sometimes induces a switch from NJ to LW. Their motives for intra-speaker variation tell us that both types of style-shifting are not fully explainable by a single traditional model and need to be interpreted from various perspectives.

To conclude, examining stylistic variation both quantitatively and qualita-tively serves as a clue to elucidate the elaborate process of loanword diffusion according to speech style.

CHAPTER 7 STYLISTIC CONSTRAINTS ON LEXICAL CHOICE   135

Notes

1 This chapter is based on Kuya (2016a). Some modifications were added to the original work including tables and figures.

2 It shows that the higher the level of formality of a setting is, the faster an innovative form spreads. Note that his model is based on dialect standardization, i.e., change from *above*. In the case of change from *below*, it is expected that the lower the level of formality of a setting is, the faster an innovation spreads.

3 I owe this chapter to the generosity of NINJAL, who allowed me to access the raw data of this survey.

4 Kim (2011: 26) also points out that the loanword in question has become a basic word in written Japanese.

5 It seems that these independent variables do not have high multicollinearity. Correlation matrix for the given independent variables showed that the highest correlation exists between Year of Birth and Education: $r = -0.421$ (a low-moderate correlation). However, the highest VIF remains below 2. Hence, both Year of Birth and Education are treated as distinct variables here.

6 The goodness of fit for *sapooto* in Table 7.8 ($R^2 = 0.67$) is higher than that for *keesu* in Table 6.12 ($R^2 = 0.33$) and in Table 6.24 ($R^2 = 0.24$). It seems that this results from the difference in the nature of the data used here. The data examined for *sapooto* is relatively large in size (N = 2,901) and well controlled for linguistic context and balanced in terms of the social factors that we examine. In contrast, the data examined for *keesu*, collected from the two corpora, is relatively small in size (N = 1,405 from BCCWJ and N = 725 from CSJ) and not well-controlled for linguistic context nor well-balanced in terms of the social factors we examine. Thus, the samples from the corpora show more discrepancy between the observed and predicted values than the samples from the interviews.

7 Shifting does occur in the opposite direction too. Here, the more informal setting Friends is interpreted as the reference (default) category since an interpretation of the results seems to become more straightforward when we look at the shift from the less formal setting (Friends) to the more formal setting (Public) than the other way around.

8 Those who chose "No applicable choice" and "Not sure" are excluded from the analysis. Consequently, the total number of each switching group is not equal to that in Table 7.9.

9 "Precise in meaning" in Reason A and "Dignified" in Reason B are excluded from the analyses in Table 7.12, because these categories include cells in which the expected number of occurrence is less than 5. By the same token, "Dignified" in Reason B is excluded from the analysis in Table 7.14.

CHAPTER 8

Loanword Diffusion in Real Time

8.1 The apparent-time hypothesis revisited

The previous chapters have provided statistical evidence of a change in apparent time toward an increase in the adoption of the loan variants. In spite of the fact that apparent time is "a truly powerful concept in locating the presence of change" (Sankoff, G. 2006: 113, see also Bailey et al. 1991), a number of studies reveal that the apparent-time approach has its limitations.

First, age gradient is only an indication, but not evidence, of change in progress: It could be the reflection of *age-grading*.[1] In order to interpret a given age differentiation as an ongoing change, the evidence from real-time observation is essential. In the study of language change in Japanese, there are two famous series of real-time studies: the study of dialect standardization in Tsuruoka (ISM & NINJAL 2014, 2015) and the study of the use of honorifics in Okazaki (NINJAL 2010a–d). The survey of language standardization in Tsuruoka, for example, has been conducted every two decades since 1950 (followed by 1971, 1991 and 2011).[2]

Figure 8.1 illustrates the diachronic process of phonological standardization in the community, in which the non-standard (centralized) form of the variable /u/ (as in *karasu* 'a crow') is being replaced by its standard form over the 60 years between 1950 and 2011. The degree of standardization of the variable ranges 40–65% across generations in 1950 but it seems to have nearly completely standardized by 2011 with most age groups selecting the standard form 100% of the time. We see that the four s-shaped curves form a larger s-curve as a whole, demonstrating that the change in question is in progress in the community overall.

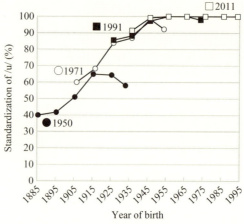

Figure 8.1: Standardization of the variable /u/ in Tsuruoka, Japan
(Adapted from ISM & NINJAL 2014: 51, modified by the author[3])

Second, although Figure 8.1 illustrates the case in which a distribution in apparent time is "a faithful reproduction of changes in real time," the apparent-time approach often fails to capture transition across speakers' lifetimes (Labov 1982: 67). The apparent-time hypothesis, i.e., the assumption that one's linguistic system is invariable throughout one's lifetime, might lead to an underestimation of the rate of change (Sankoff, G. 2006: 115). For example, Pope, Meyerhoff & Ladd (2007: 622–623) points out, in their follow-up study of Labov (1963, revised as 1972: Ch1), that phonological change in Martha's Vineyard is progressing at a higher rate than the apparent-time distribution indicates. Such acceleration occurs when individuals change their language over their lifetimes in the direction of a change in progress in the community as a whole (Sankoff, G. 2005: 1011). This type of change is called "lifespan change" and it is said to be well-attested for vocabulary too (Meyerhoff 2011: 152) because, in general, "people can easily add to their vocabulary throughout their lives" (Meyerhoff 2011: 160). In Table 8.1 "Lifespan change" is added as a new category of change to refine the classification of language change originated in Labov (1994: 83).

Meanwhile, Yokoyama & Sanada (2010: 40) demonstrates that the rate of change is "decelerated" when individual speakers change in the direction *opposite* to a change in progress in the community as a whole (e.g., towards *dialectalization* as opposed to *standardization* in the case of Tsuruoka). Decelerated change is also attested to by the example of verbal conjugation in Japanese (Matsuda 2013: 87). This type of change, by definition shown in Table 8.1, should also fall into a category of lifespan change. Yokoyama et al. (2008: 65) highlights the concept of "life-long memory," i.e., memory accumulated after one's critical period, which induces acceleration/deceleration of change. This sort of memory is considered to be dependent on, as they call, "aging" and a "trend of the times." They suggest that we pay more attention to the effect of these factors in predicting change in order to avoid miscalculations of the rate of change.

	Age differentiation	Variability of the individuals	Variability of the community
1 Stability	–	–	–
2 Age-grading	+	+	–
3 Lifespan change	+	+	+
4 Generational change	+	–	+
5 Communal change	–	+	+

Table 8.1: Types of language change defined by (i) Age differentiation, (ii) Variability of the individuals, and (iii) Variability of the community (Adapted from Meyerhoff 2011: 153, Table 7.2, modified by the author)

In summary, as Table 8.1 shows, there are three possibilities when we observe age differentiation (+) in apparent time. First, it can be interpreted as *age-grading* if the community overall is invariable (–). Second, it is interpreted as *generational change* if the community as a whole changes (+) but individual speakers remain invariable (–). The phonological change in Tsuruoka in Figure 8.1 is an example of this type of change. The Third possibility is *lifespan change*, in which both the whole community and individuals are variable (+). This highlights the importance of investigation into variability of the community and that of individuals over time. This chapter thus attempts a real-time approach to the diffusion of loanwords. We will examine two questions: (i) whether the attested age gradient in the previous chapters is indeed interpretable as change in progress; (ii) whether individual speakers are stable over their lifetimes in their receptiveness to loanwords, provided that the change is indeed in progress.

Here, the important independent variables to be examined are (i) Age, (ii) Year of Birth, and (iii) Year of Survey. The variable Gender is not investigated in this chapter since proportions by gender are not always provided in the reports of the surveys that we examine here.

8.2 Using interview- and corpus-based data in diachronic analyses

With regard to the studies of loanword diffusion, several institutes and organizations have conducted one-off surveys since the 1970s. However, there has never been a sufficient systematic attempt to integrate the results of these surveys into a comprehensive whole within a framework of the real-time approach. I will therefore pick up mutually related items from these surveys and analyze them as real-time data.

First, Table 8.2 shows three nationwide sampling surveys that were conducted in 1979, 1996 and 2000 on the use of two loanwords: *wain* (< *wine*) and *oopun-suru* (< *open*). Between a loanword and its native equivalent: *wain* vs. *budoshu* ('wine'); *oopun-suru* vs. *kaiten-suru* ('to open'), informants were asked to choose one that they use more frequently. The level of diffusion of these loanwords is defined by the proportion of those who chose the loanwords as opposed to those who chose their native equivalents and, if applicable, other choices including "Use both," "Do not use either of them," or "Not sure" (See Appendix F1). The surveys employed a face-to-face interview technique and the results can reasonably be contrasted with each other to observe change in the community over 20 years.

Name of survey -[Question No.]	Month/Year of survey	Targeted population	No. and (%) of valid response
A survey on public attitudes to language (NHK 1980: 5, 15)	Sept/1979	those aged 16 and above	2639 (73.3%)
The 10th survey on the linguistic awareness: The Japanese people and spoken language (NHK 1996: 55, 66, 69) -[Q1]	Mar/1996	those aged 20 and above	1251 (69.5%)
Opinion Poll on the National Language in Heisei 11 (1999) (BBK 2000: 18) -[Q4]	Jan/2000	those aged 16 and above	2196 (73.2%)

Table 8.2: Surveys on individual lexical items: *wain* and *oopun-suru*

Second, Table 8.3 provides information on surveys concerning the question of how people feel about their present use of loanwords in general in their everyday lives. This question has been repeatedly asked in annual opinion polls by BBK between the 2000s and 2010s. The same question was also asked in the opinion poll conducted back in 1977 by NSDKK.

People were asked to evaluate their feelings about the recent use of loanwords in written and spoken Japanese according to a three-point scale: "(1) Like—(2)Neither like nor dislike—(3)Dislike," and (4)"Not sure" (Appendix F2). Those who chose (1) and (2) are grouped into one that shows a *positive* attitude as opposed to the "Dislike" group, that can be grouped into one that shows a *negative* attitude, as the former two groups always show similar age distribution patterns (see also Ishiwata 2001: 122).

The whole data set enables us to examine change in the proportion of those who display a positive attitude toward the present loanword use in the com-

CHAPTER 8 LOANWORD DIFFUSION IN REAL TIME 141

munity over 35 years.

Name of survey -[Question No.]	Month/Year of survey	Targeted population	No. and (%) of valid response
Opinion Poll on the National Language (NSDKK 1977:140) -[Q22]	Aug/1977	those aged 20 and above	8170 (81.7%)
Opinion Poll on the National Language in Heisei 11 (1999)　(BBK 2000:23) -[Q6]	Jan/2000	those aged 16 and above	2196 (73.2%)
Opinion Poll on the National Language in Heisei 14 (2002)　(BBK 2003:140) -[Q17]	Nov/2002	those aged 16 and above	2200 (73.3%)
Opinion Poll on the National Language in Heisei 19 (2007)　(BBK 2008:144) -[Q16]	Mar/2008	those aged 16 and above	1975 (57.3%)
Opinion Poll on the National Language in Heisei 24 (2012)　(BBK 2013:92) -[Q8]	Mar/2013	those aged 16 and above	2153 (61.1%)

Table 8.3: Surveys on preference *for* or *against* the present loanword use

Third, Table 8.4 provides information on surveys concerning the question of how people feel about a further expansion of the use of loanwords in future. This question was asked in an opinion poll conducted in 1995 by BBK and another conducted in 2003 by NINJAL.

People were asked to evaluate their feelings about a further expansion of loanwords in the Japanese language in the future according to a four-point scale. Note that each survey uses slightly different wordings for its rating. The survey conducted in 1995 provided the choices: "(1)Further expansion is acceptable—(2)Only moderate expansion is acceptable—(3)No more expansion is acceptable—(4)They should be decreased," and (5)"Not sure," whereas the one conducted in 2003 introduced the options: "(1)Like—(2)Somewhat Like—(3)Somewhat Dislike—(4)Dislike," and (5)"Not sure." In each case, the first two choices, i.e., (1) and (2), are grouped into one that shows a *positive* attitude to the phenomenon in contrast to the last two choices, i.e., (3) and (4), that can be grouped into one that shows a *negative* attitude.

We can observe change in the proportion of those who display a positive attitude toward a further expansion of loanwords in the community roughly over a decade (Appendix F3).

Name of survey -[Question No.]	Month/Year of survey	Targeted population	No. and (%) of valid response
Opinion Poll on the National Language in Heisei 7 (1995)　(BBK 1995:48) -[Q16]	Apr/1995	those aged 16 and above	2212 (73.7%)
The National Survey on Attitudes to Loanwords　(NINJAL 2004:16) -[Q2]	Oct–Nov/2003	those aged 15 and above	3087 (68.6%)

Table 8.4: Surveys on preference *for* or *against* a further expansion of loanwords

In addition to the above interview-based data, data collected from the variable-length components of the Library Book sub-corpus (LB) in BCCWJ is used to see the diachronic process of loanword diffusion. This sub-corpus contains books published between 1986 and 2005, so it is possible to observe language produced over the two decades.

We will have a look at the distribution of both individual loanwords and the loanword stratum as a whole. Three lexical variables are selected for real-time investigations: (i) *keesu* (< *case*), (ii) *sapooto-suru* (< *support*) and (iii) *shinpuru* (< *simple*) and their native equivalents (I have chosen one variable from nominal, verbal and adjective usage each). These loan variants have shown a relatively consistent age gradient in their distributions in Chapter 5 and are thus considered to be good candidates for those in the process of change in progress.

Native equivalents of these loanwords and criteria of data elicitation are consistent with those shown in Table 5.5 in Section 5.3 and [Criteria 1] in Section 5.4, respectively. The scope of investigation is limited to a sample written by a single author whose year of birth is available. In order to reduce irregularity of small-sized samples, birth-year groups that contribute less than 5% of the whole samples within each publication year range (i.e., 1986–1990, 1991–1995, 1996–2000, and 2001–2005) are excluded, following the discussions in Section 5.2. The majority of samples are from those born between the 1920s and 1960s.

Table 8.5 shows the summary of the number of tokens for each linguistic variable by publication year. The table demonstrates a general tendency for the proportion of the loan variants (LW/Total (%)) to increase consistently over the two decades (except for *keesu* in 1996–2000). (See Appendix F4 for LW use sorted according to age group in each publication year.)

LW (as opposed to non-LW)	Year of Publication	LW (N)	non-LW (N)	Total (N)	LW/Total (%)
keesu (< *case*)	1986–2005	979	8328	9307	11.8
	1986–1990	105	1301	1406	8.1
as opposed to	1991–1995	222	1851	2073	12.0
baai and *jirei*	1996–2000	301	2560	2861	11.8
	2001–2005	351	2616	2967	13.4
sapooto-suru (< *support*)	1986–2005	60	1600	1660	3.8
	1986–1990	1	270	271	0.4
as opposed to *shien*,	1991–1995	6	382	388	1.6
sasaeru and *shiji*	1996–2000	23	516	539	4.5
	2001–2005	30	432	462	6.9
shinpuru (< *simple*)	1986–2005	89	450	539	19.8
	1986–1990	6	70	76	8.6
as opposed to	1991–1995	19	106	125	17.9
tanjun and *kanso*	1996–2000	30	150	180	20.0
	2001–2005	34	124	158	27.4
The LW stratum (token)	1986–2005	81547	2183863	2265410	3.7
	1986–1990	11825	348792	360617	3.4
as opposed to SJ,	1991–1995	19332	548541	567873	3.5
NJ[4] and HB	1996–2000	24781	661547	686328	3.7
	2001–2005	25609	624983	650592	4.1

Table 8.5: Distribution of *keesu*, *sapooto*, *shinpuru*, and the LW stratum in LB, BCCWJ (1986–2005)

8.3 Examining the variability of the community overall

The variability of the community as a whole can be observed by examining the effect of year of survey when the speaker's age at the time of survey is controlled. See Appendices F1–F4 for the full data sets examined in this chapter.

Figure 8.2 shows that there is a jump in the level of diffusion of *wain* (< *wine*) between 1979 and 1996, but a further rise does not occur between 1996 and 2000—perhaps due to a too small interval between the two surveys. We can see that the replacement of *budooshu* by *wain* is near completion among those aged 20s and below: The age gradients in 1996 and 2000 start to level off at 90–100% among these age groups.

Figure 8.3 also shows that there is a big jump in the level of diffusion of the loanword *oopun-suru* (< *open*) between 1979 and 1996. There is a rise between 1979 and 2000, though a clear rise occurs only among those aged 40s or below. The problem is that the curve in 1996 is at a level notably higher than that in 2000. This leads to a conclusion that, oddly enough, the adoption of the loanword sharply rose between 1979 and 1996 but suddenly fell over the only 4-year period after that. This fall is actually explainable by the fact that the informants were provided with the example sentence shown in Example 8.1 in making their word choice in the 1996 survey. It is possible that this particular context contributed to the enhanced preference for the loanword in 1996. We will soon return to this point to discuss how to deal with the effect of this in statistical analysis (Table 8.6).

(8.1) 新しいスーパーが{オープン／開店}する。
Atarashii suupaa-ga {oopun / kaiten}-suru.
New supermarket-NOM open-do
'A new supermarket will be opened.'

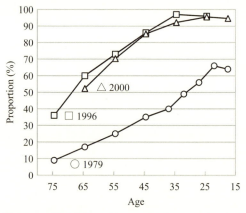

Figure 8.2: Variability of the community: *wain* (< *wine*)

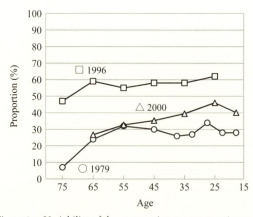

Figure 8.3: Variability of the community: *oopun-suru* (< *open*)

Figure 8.4 demonstrates an overall tendency for those who have a positive attitude toward the current use of loanwords to increase in 35 years from 1977 to 2013, although shifts between any other two years are not immediately clear.

Figure 8.5, in contrast, shows a clear drop (more or less 20%) between 1995 and 2003 in the proportion of those who have a positive attitude toward a further expansion of loanwords. This is the case where, despite the fact that each age gradient indicates generational change toward an increase in the adoption of loanwords in future, the community as a whole is moving in the opposite direction in real time. We call this "reversed" change (reversed generational change) henceforth.

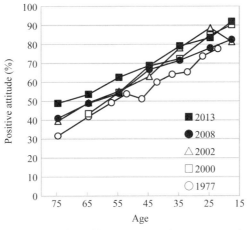

Figure 8.4: Variability of the community: the present use of LWs

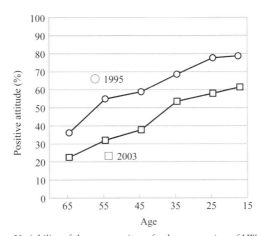

Figure 8.5: Variability of the community: a further expansion of LWs in future

Due to relatively small-sized samples, the lines for the individual loanwords *keesu* (< *case*), *sapooto-suru* (< *support*), *shinpuru* (< *simple*) are not as smooth as those based on the interview data above. Diffusions of these loan variants however generally show rises along publication year (the distribution of *keesu* is shown in Figure 8.6 as an example). The loanword stratum as a whole in BCCWJ also exhibits a jump between 1986 and 2001 (Figure 8.7).

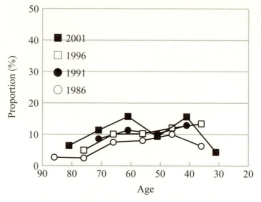

Figure 8.6: Variability of the community: *keesu* (< *case*)

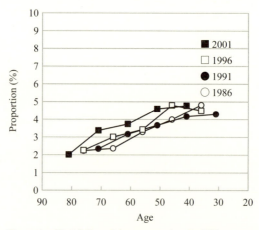

Figure 8.7: Variability of the community: the LW stratum

In order to verify the statistical significance of the variability of the community we have observed above, a logistic regression analysis was conducted. The model takes the form of [Formula 1] in Section 3.5. The dependent variable is in all the cases binary: the preference for, or use of, loanwords (=1) or not (=0). Independent variables are (i) Year of Survey (Year of Publication) and (ii) Age

CHAPTER 8 LOANWORD DIFFUSION IN REAL TIME   147

of the speakers (at the time of survey). The disruptive factor (iii) Context is added to the analysis of *oopun-susu*, since, as discussed above, the presence or absence of the particular context seems to have an influence on the word choice to a certain degree.[5] The inclusion of a disruptive factor into a model helps us to elicit the effect of factors in interest (Yokoyama & Sanada 2007). (See also the discussion in Section 4.6 for the application of a disruptive factor.) Table 8.6 shows the results of the logistic regression analysis with SPSS (stepwise, at a significance level of 0.05). It is shown that Year of Survey and Age are both significant. The coefficient of determination (R^2) is generally high except that for *keesu*.

First, the negative coefficients for Age indicate that the age effect inhibits the adoption of loanwords; in other words, preference for loanwords over native variants increases as one becomes younger. Second, Context appears to have a positive effect on the choice of the loanword *oopun-suru*, which means that the presence of the specific context enhanced the preference for the loanword. Third, Year of Survey is shown to have a positive influence on the preference for loanwords in most cases. This means that the receptiveness to loanwords in the community overall has been grown over time. This confirms that the diffusion of the loanwords examined in the earlier chapters, i.e., *wain* and *oopun-suru* (Chapter 4), *keesu* (Chapter 6), and *sapooto* (Chapter 7), is indeed an example of change in progress. However, this factor comes into play in the opposite direction when it comes to people's attitude toward a further expansion of loanwords. It indicates that the community as a whole has become less receptive to further adoption of loanwords over time. This example tells that it is possible that a change progresses in the direction opposite to what the distribution in apparent time suggests (reversed change).

	Year of Survey	Age	Context	Constant	R^2
Interview-based					
wain	0.119189	-0.058587	NA	-233.957192	0.96
oopun-suru	0.022899	-0.012489	1.022264	-45.846686	0.90
Present use	0.014477	-0.038376	NA	-26.581827	0.96
Further expansion	-0.101782	-0.037763	NA	205.119082	0.97
Corpus-based					
keesu	0.023830	-0.010205	NA	-49.121709	0.26
sapooto-suru	0.167374	-0.045745	NA	-334.947153	0.72
shinpuru	0.065205	-0.028231	NA	-130.244988	0.53
the LW stratum	0.016820	-0.017879	NA	-35.852201	0.85

Table 8.6: Regression coefficients of (i) Year of Survey and (ii) Age

8.4 Examining the variability of the individual speakers

Speakers' critical period is dependent on their year of birth. The variability of the individual speakers (after their critical period) can thus be observed by examining the effect of year of survey when the speaker's year of birth is controlled.

First, it appears that there is no systematic shift in the individual speakers across years of survey for *keesu*, *shinpuru*, and the LW stratum (the distribution of *keesu* is shown in Figure 8.8 as an example). Second, the curves for *wain* and those for *sapooto-suru* show upward shifts in the individuals over time. For example, Figure 8.9 demonstrates a jump in the level of preference for *wain* between 1979 and 1996/2000. It is then implied that people moved toward an increase in the use of these loanwords over their lifetimes. Third, the curves for the present use of LWs show downward shifts over the 35 years. In Figure 8.10, there is a clear drop between 1977 and 2000/2002 followed by a drop between 2000/2002 and 2008/2013 among those born in the 1960s and after, but such a tendency is not immediately clear for the older generations. This implies that the receptiveness of the individual speakers to loanwords in general dropped between 1977 and 2013.

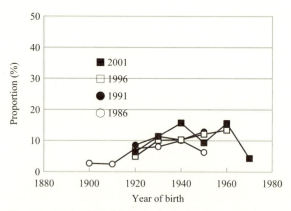

Figure 8.8: Variability of the individuals: *keesu* (< *case*)

CHAPTER 8 LOANWORD DIFFUSION IN REAL TIME 149

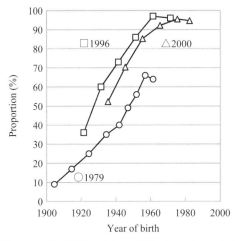

Figure 8.9: Variability of the individuals: *wain* (< *wine*)

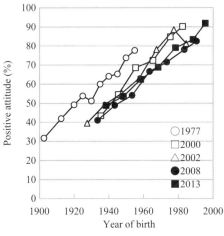

Figure 8.10: Variability of the individuals: the present use of LWs

A logistic regression analysis was conducted (stepwise, at a significance level of 0.05) to confirm the statistical significance of the effect of (i) Year of Survey (Year of Publication) and (ii) Year of Birth on the adoption of loanwords. (The model takes the form of [Formula 1] in Section 3.5.) Note that the disruptive factor (iii) Context is included into the analysis of *oopun-suru* this time too. The results (Table 8.7) confirm that the speakers born more recently show greater receptiveness to loanwords, which we have already seen as the age-effect in Table 8.6. The variable Year of Survey, however, affects the phenomenon in various ways. Positive and negative coefficients indicate that individuals are unstable over time, while "o" indicates that they are stable over time. Each case will be explained by a diagram in the following section.

	Year of Survey	Year of Birth	Context	Constant	R^2
Interview-based					
wain	0.060602	0.058587	NA	-233.957192	0.96
oopun-suru	o	0.014613	1.110060	-29.289641	0.88
Present use	-0.023899	0.038376	NA	-26.581827	0.96
Further expansion	-0.139545	0.037763	NA	205.119082	0.97
Corpus-based					
keesu	o	0.012669	NA	-26.716283	0.23
sapooto-suru	0.121629	0.045745	NA	-334.947153	0.72
shinpuru	o	0.033220	NA	-66.158917	0.47
the LW stratum	o	0.017735	NA	-37.685165	0.85

Table 8.7: Regression coefficients of (i) Year of Survey and (ii) Year of Birth

8.5 Patterns of loanword diffusion in real time

8.5.1 Change with no acceleration/deceleration

The statistical analysis shows that Year of Survey is not significant for the occurrence of the following individual loanwords: (i) *oopun-suru* (R^2 = 0.88); (ii) *keesu* (R^2 = 0.23); (iii) *shinpuru* (R^2 = 0.47), and also (iv) the LW stratum as a whole (R^2 = 0.85).

The curves in Figure 8.11 show predicted probabilities of speakers' preference for the loanword *oopun-suru* (over *kaiten-suru*) in 1979, 1996, 2000 and also the near future, 2020 and 2040. (See Section 4.7 for the detailed explanation of how predictions are made with [Formula 1].) The empty dots ($\bigcirc$, $\square$, etc.) show the observed values in 1979, 1996 and 2000. The upper curve predicts the case where the context is provided, whereas the lower curve predicts the case where the context is not provided. As the coefficient of Context is positive, we can see that the presence of the context in question promotes preference for the loanword to a high degree (0.2–0.3). The five curves overlap each other and form one curve, which indicates that there is neither upward nor downward shift over time.

The curves in Figures 8.12 show predicted probabilities of the occurrence of the LW stratum in the corpus across birth-year groups. The empty dots show the observed values in 1986, 1991, 1996 and 2001. It is evident that there are neither upward nor downward shifts across year of survey.

These two linguistic variables show the cases where the individuals remain stable over time as the apparent-time hypothesis presupposes.

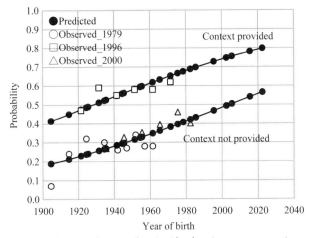

Figure 8.11: Change with no acceleration/deceleration: *oopun-suru* (< *open*)

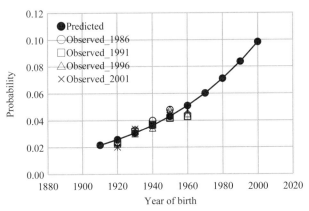

Figure 8.12: Change with no acceleration/deceleration: the LW stratum

8.5.2 Accelerated change

The statistical analysis shows that Year of Survey has a positive effect on the occurrence of the loanwords (i) *wain* (R^2 = 0.96) and (ii) *sapooto-suru* (R^2 = 0.72).

The curves in Figure 8.13 shows predicted probabilities of people's preference for the loanword *wain* (over *budooshu*) in 1979, 1996, 2000 and, in addition, in the near future of 2020 and 2040 as a prediction of the coming 40 years. Figure 8.14 shows predicted probabilities of actual use of the loanword *sapooto-suru* in 1986, 1991, 1996, 2001 and also predictions for the following decade (2006 and 2011). The empty dots show the observed values. The observed upward shifts in these figures indicate an acceleration of the ongoing change towards an increase in the adoption of the loanword in question. This means that the individuals change over their lifespan in the direction of the change taking place in the community. Both examples show the cases where the apparent-time approach underestimates the actual rate of change.

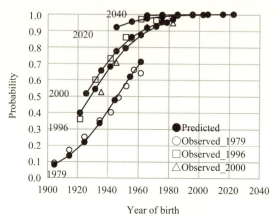

Figure 8.13: Accelerated change: *wain* (< *wine*)

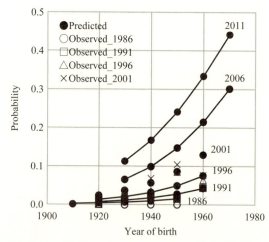

Figure 8.14: Accelerated change: *sapooto-suru* (< *support*)

8.5.3 Decelerated change

The statistical analysis shows that Year of Survey has a negative effect on (i) people's receptiveness to the present use of loanwords ($R^2 = 0.96$) and (ii) people's receptiveness to a further expansion of loanwords ($R^2 = 0.97$).

Predicted probabilities of people's receptiveness to the present loanword use are shown in Figure 8.15. The prediction is made for the years 1977, 2000, 2013 and also the near future 2030 and 2045. The empty dots correspond to the observed values in 1977, 2000 and 2003 with observed and predicted values for the years 2002 and 2008 excluded to make the figure simpler. The figure shows a downward shift of the curves over time, which demonstrates a deceleration of the ongoing change towards an increase in the adoption of loanwords. This means that the individual speakers change over their lifespan in the direction opposite to change taking place in the community. This example shows the case where the apparent-time approach overestimates the actual rate of change.

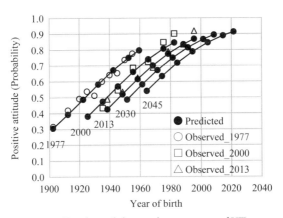

Figure 8.15: Decelerated change: the present use of LWs

8.5.4 Reversed change

Figure 8.16 shows predicted probabilities of people's receptiveness to further loanword expansion. The prediction is made for the years 1995, 2003 and also the near future 2011 and 2019. The empty dots correspond to the observed values in 1995 and 2003. We notice that the figure shows a downward shift of the curves over time in spite of the fact that a further expansion of loanwords is preferred by younger generations. This demonstrates that speakers change at a rate faster than the age gradients suggest, but in the direction opposite to change taking place in the community. This results in a reversed change.

Therefore this example shows the case where the apparent-time approach fails to predict the direction of change.

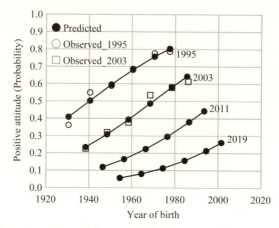

Figure 8.16: Reversed change: a further expansion of LWs in future

8.6 Towards more precise predictions of change

On the one hand, the apparent-time hypothesis predicts correctly the (i) rate and (ii) direction of change in half of the cases under investigation, but on the other hand, it fails to make accurate predictions of the rate and/or direction of change in the remaining half of the cases. Consequently, the present data revealed the presence of *lifespan change* and, at the same time, provided descriptions of its subtypes. Table 8.8 is the revision of Table 8.1, in which lifespan change is subdivided into three groups: (i) accelerated, (ii) decelerated and (iii) reversed change. The original definition of lifespan change by Sankoff, G. (2005: 1011) only mentions "change, in which individual speakers change over their lifespan in the direction of a change in progress in the rest of the community," which corresponds to *accelerated* change in Table 8.8. The present study, however, revealed that, in some cases, individual speakers change in the direction opposite to change taking place in the community overall. When individual speakers change at a rate slower than that of generational change, the rate of change will be *decelerated* over time. On the contrary, if individual speakers change at a rate faster than that of generational change, the change is *reversed* and hence the community moves in the direction opposite to what the age gradient suggests.

	Age differentiation	Variability: Community	Variability: Individuals	Rate/Direction of change	Example	
					Attitude	Behavior
1 Stability	−	−	−			
2 Age-grading	+	−	+			
3 Lifespan change	+ ↑	↑ + ↑ ↓	↑ + ↓ ↓	Accelerated Decelerated Reversed	*wain* Present use Further spread	*sapooto-suru*
4 Generational change	+	+	−		*oopun-suru*	*keesu* *shinpuru* LW stratum
5 Communal change	−	+	+			

↑: in the direction of change that the observed age gradient suggests,
↓: in the direction opposite to it

Table 8.8: Types of language change (Revised from Table 8.1)

A valid explanation for the mechanism of accelerated change would be the Mere Exposure Effect (Zajonc 1968) in psycholinguistics, in which a repeated exposure to a given stimulus is responsible for an increased preference for the stimulus. Yokoyama (2006: 200) points out, based on this hypothesis, that an increased "exposure frequency" of a given form affects one's mental lexicon, including familiarity, preference and utility of the form, and in turn promotes increased reproduction of it (see also Yokoyama et al. 2008: 73). This implies that, as the level of one's exposure to a given loanword, e.g., *wain* or *sapooto-suru*, becomes higher, one's preference or familiarity of the form becomes greater and in turn promotes further use of it.

In contrast, Labov (1994: 91) points out that decelerated change is attributed to age-grading. Provided that the observed age gradient is a reflection of a pure age-grading, the case of the deceleration of generational change toward an increase in the adoption of loanwords is explainable by the fact that people potentially becomes less open to loanword use as they grow older. Moreover, an increased use of loanwords could increase people's negative impressions of loanwords as a whole (such as "a flood of loanwords") and consequently lead to regression to native forms over time, following the norm in which the native variants are considered to be more traditional or indigenous to Japanese than loan variants. This kind of change in linguistic behavior occurs usually, as Sankoff (2006: 113) says, "as the effect of stigmatization from above."

It is worth mentioning that, in Table 8.8, the interview-based data showed that people become more likely to reject a further spread or the present use of loanwords overall as they age. The corpus-based data, however, confirmed that there is no deceleration of ongoing change in their actual adoption of the LW stratum in real time. This shows that the lifespan change on the level of people's attitude and that of their actual behavior are different things: People's attitude to a certain linguistic variable may be more susceptible to change than their actual use of it.

To conclude, the present trend study has made the best use of the existing apparent-time data in order to elucidate a change in the diffusion of loanwords in real time, leading to more accurate predictions of the phenomenon.

Notes

1 We have already witnessed a more complicated case in Section 4.5, where a change in progress involves age-grading.

2 The Okazaki survey was conducted in 1953, 1972 and 2008 (see NINJAL 1957, 1983 and 2010a–d).

3 Their report shows that the year of the first survey is "1951" (instead of "1950") in order to make the survey intervals equal (ISM & NINJAL 2014: 22). The author modified it to "1950" since the first survey, as they report, was actually conducted in 1950.

4 Particles and auxiliaries are excluded from the count.

5 Correlations between the independent variables were evaluated for each data set. It showed that the highest VIF remains below 2 in each case. The same holds true for the independent variables examined in Section 8.4.

CHAPTER 9

General Summary and Discussion

9.1 Identyfying variation on a lexical level

The current research has attempted to describe different aspects of lexical variations between the loanword forms (that are attested to some extent) and their existing native alternatives. The empirical findings gained in the previous chapters answer the four research questions (QUESTIONS I–IV) set out in Chapter 1.

The first question (QUESTION I) concerns how one can identify environments where variation occurs on a lexical level. We have witnessed that the study of lexical variation, especially a corpus-based one as opposed to an interview-based one, yields several theoretical and methodological difficulties. This comes directly from the difficulty in applying the notion of *semantic equivalence* to the study of variation beyond phonological level (Section 3.6). Some researchers suggest that the criteria should be replaced by *functional/discourse equivalence* in identifying the variable context of non-phonological variation (Lavandera 1978, Sankoff, D. 1982).

Following this discussion, in Chapter 6, I carefully located environments where lexical variants are used interchangeably on a functional level, based on an in-depth observation of the function, grammatical structure and collocational pattern of *keesu* (< *case*) and its native variants. Chapter 5, in contrast, based on synonymy determined by the dictionary-based examination, considered all environments in which the identified variants occur. The former approach gives a more fine-grained analysis with a small amount of data on the one hand, whereas the latter approach gives an analysis of a larger amount of data that is useful for generalization of the phenomenon; however, it is less in-depth than the former approach. To conclude, both approaches contributed to investigations of the structured nature of lexical variation under discussion. More specific findings are summarized in the following sections.

9.2 Socially structured nature of lexical variation

The second question (QUESTION II) asks in what manner the lexical variation in consideration is socially structured. Four language-external factors, including (i) *age/year of birth*, (ii) *register*, (iii) *style* and (iv) *education*, have proved to be significant in the preference for, or occurrence of, loanword variants throughout the volume.

First, both interview-based studies and corpus-based ones were generally able to capture *age gradients* in the adoption or use of loanwords, with this level getting higher as one becomes younger (Chapters 4, 5, 6, 7 and 8). The repeatedly-observed generational difference indicates that there are changes in progress in favor of loanwords as opposed to their native equivalents. There was an exception in which those in their teens show a delay in acquisition of some loanwords, but it has been shown that they catch up with the other generations in the course of time. This demonstrates that *age-grading* occurs in younger generations (Chapter 4).

Second, corpus-based investigations (Chapters 5 and 6) revealed that *register* and several *stylistic* factors have an impact on the occurrence of loanwords. I have pointed out the possibility that the register difference in the written corpus (BCCWJ) such as books (PB) vs. magazines (PM) is associated with the difference in the formality of a text. The register difference between public speech (SPS) and academic presentation speech (APS) in the spoken corpus (CSJ) was also found to arise from factors such as spontaneity, formality and audience size, which characterize the sociolinguistic style of the speech settings in the registers in question. In both written and spoken corpora, there was a general tendency that loan variants are disfavored in settings with more formal or less spontaneous speech style.

Third, *education* was also found to be a significant variable in the occurrence of loanwords, but this variable showed a complex picture of its relation to the phenomenon. In the written corpus, some loanwords were disfavored by the most educated group (GRAD) (Chapters 5 and 6). In contrast, the interview-based survey in Chapter 7 revealed that the occurrence of the loanword *sapooto* (< *support*) in conversation among friends increases as one becomes more educated (JH<HS<UNIV). Such an apparent discrepancy between the results of two studies would be explained by the interaction between educational and stylistic variables, i.e., the fact that only the most educated group showed style shifting between the two different settings: conversation with friends and public speech (Chapter 7). This suggests the possibility that those with higher educational backgrounds use loanwords more selectively depending on settings. In other words, the effect of an educational variable is modified by a stylistic variable. In a very casual setting such as the context of talking to one's friends, more

CHAPTER 9 GENERAL SUMMARY AND DISCUSSION 159

educated people use loanwords more frequently than less educated people.[1] Meanwhile, a more formal setting such as public speaking or writing for publication would inhibit their use of loanwords to a degree lower than that of less educated groups.[2]

In conclusion, the socially asymmetric distribution of so-called well-attested loanwords examined in this book, e.g., *keesu*, *sapooto*, and so on, suggests that they still remain peripheral bound by various social contexts such as register, style, education and the interaction between these variables.

The import of Sino-Japanese words is usually characterized as change from *above* as they were originally brought and used as learned vocabulary by intellectuals. Besides, until today SJ words have shown association with writing and formal registers in the Japanese language. Likewise, the naturalization of early Western loanwords can be described as linguistic change from above the level of consciousness; it started in the wake of the influx of Western cultures and knowledge including religion, medicine and science, much of which was at the beginning of being imported and used by those in the upper class, symbolizing the Westernization or modernization of society (Section 2.2).

The increasing influx of English donor loanwords observed in Chapter 8 suggests that the English language has been acquiring more prestige than ever before, and exerted a constant influence on the Japanese language especially since WWII. However, findings in Chapters 5–7 repeatedly show that loanwords are disfavored in socially formal contexts. An in-depth analysis of style shifting in the choice between the loan variant (*sapooto*) and its non-loan variants (*shien* and *tedasuke*) in Chapter 7 revealed that people switch to the non-loan variants (especially the SJ variant *shien*) in order to add a sense of intelligence and dignity to their speech when their speech style shifts to a more formal setting such as public speaking. The most educated people in particular regarded the SJ equivalent *shien* as more appropriate to use when speaking to the general public than the loanword *sapooto*.[3] This strongly suggests the nonstandard nature of loanwords as opposed to their native equivalents in the Japanese language. In other words, we can see that Western loanwords, especially recent borrowings for words which have corresponding native words, have not acquired the standard or prestigious status that SJ words have.[4]

9.3 Language attitudes and linguistic behavior

The third question (QUESTION III) inquires about whether or not corpus-based studies provide additional support for the result of previous surveys on attitudes towards loanwords. We have seen that sociolinguistic asymmetry in adoption of loanwords in terms of generation and style is attested to by both public *attitudes* (including their "reported behavior") (Chapters 4 and 7) and their actual *behavior* (Chapters 5 and 6). An educational variable, at a glance, shows a discrepancy between attitude and behavior, but it is apparently attributable to the fact that the variable is in interaction with stylistic variable as just mentioned above.

Chapter 8 showed that there is a discrepancy between people's stated attitudes towards the adoption of loanwords and their actual adoption of them. *Self-reports* in previous surveys revealed that the individuals become less receptive to the adoption of loanwords as they age; that is, the ongoing linguistic change towards an increase in the adoption of loanwords is decelerated. However, the *actual* adoption of loanwords in the written corpus (BCCWJ) does not prove that the speed of the ongoing change is reduced. This suggests that the longitudinal process of the adoption of loanwords should be evaluated and predicted with meticulous care by means of examinations of people's attitudes towards, and their actual use of, loanwords.

9.4 Demonstration of change in real time

The fourth question (QUESTION IV) aims to provide a picture of the process of loanword diffusion in *real time*. In order to discuss the problems of the apparent-time approach, I have made use of existing interview-based data and the diachronic component of BCCWJ (the Library Book sub-corpus) in Chapter 8. There were two problems to be tackled: (i) whether or not the observed age gradients are bona-fide examples of a change in progress; (ii) whether or not the individuals remain stable throughout their lifetime with respect to their language attitudes or behavior.

With regard to the first problem, all the cases under consideration verified the variability of the community as a whole over time, which confirms that the change is in progress in real time. With respect to the second problem, the apparent-time hypothesis, i.e., the presupposition that individuals are invariable during their lifespan, was supported by the half of the data under discussion, but, at the same time, it was also challenged by the rest of the data. It has been shown that people change their attitude toward, or behavior on, the phenomenon, either (i) in the direction consistent with that of the community as a whole moves (*accelerated* change) or (ii) in the direction opposite to it (*decelerated* or *reversed* change). In the present study, a decelerated change was attested to by people's attitude toward the present use of loanwords in general, and a reversed change was attested to by people's attitude toward a further expansion of loanwords in future. These findings put emphasis on the importance of a real-time approach to variation, especially on a lexical level, which is said to be

CHAPTER 9 GENERAL SUMMARY AND DISCUSSION 161

less stable compared with those on other linguistic levels such as phonology or syntax.

9.5 Actuation problem of loanword diffusion

As Weinreich et al. (1968: 186) points out, "the overall process of linguistic change may involve stimuli and constraints both from society and from the structure of language." Labov (2001a: 466) says that the beginnings of change are as mysterious as ever. We can, however, at least conclude something from our findings on the continuing change.

Now we turn to the actuation problem (Weinreich et al. 1968) of Western loanwords, i.e., a general question of why a certain change occurred at a certain point of time in a certain language. Ultimately, it is difficult to find a single universal reason that applies to all the loanwords brought into Japanese, since, at the very micro level, every loanword seems to have been borrowed for different, case-by-case, multiplex reasons. The loanwords examined in the current research, however, point to several possible reasons why Western loanwords are borrowed and spread when the recipient language already has corresponding or synonymous native expressions.

First, we have seen in Chapter 4 that there are cases in which a borrowed item conveys a meaning slightly different from what is meant by its native equivalent (e.g., *getto-suru* (< *get*) vs. *kakutoku-suru*). The reason why loanwords of this type spread is that they can deliver *specific* concepts or delicate shades of meaning that cannot be conveyed by the existing words.

Second, we have also found in Chapter 4 that a loanword often covers a broader area of meaning than its native equivalent (e.g., *suutsu* (< *suit*) vs. *sebiro*; *oopunn-suru* (< *to open*) vs. *kaiten-suru*). Similar arguments are also found in Kim (2011: Ch4) and Miyata (2007). It can thus be inferred that the spread of a loan variant in these cases is activated by its broad function as a *general* term compared to its corresponding native variants.

Third, direct borrowing from Western languages can reduce the problem of homonyms caused by the import of a large number of Sino-Japanese words (Arakawa 1943: 196–202). On the one hand, SJ words are specific and concise in meaning and short (space-saving) in terms of word length, and therefore are highly favorable for formal writing. These SJ words, on the other hand, also usually form massive groups of homonyms, which often lead to miscommunication in speaking. For example, according to *Kojien* 6th, the SJ word 支援 (*shien* 'support') has 10 SJ homonyms while the SJ words 機会 (*kikai*) and 好機 (*kooki*) (both refer to 'chance') have 10 and 31 SJ homonyms, respectively. Their LW equivalents サポート (*sapooto* < *support*) and チャンス (*chansu* <

chance), in contrast, do not pose such a problem; by using a Western loanword, we can avoid the difficulty in *disambiguating* the meaning of SJ homonyms.

Fourth, we have seen in Chapter 7 that NJ, SJ and LW are differentiated in terms of *stylistic* functions. The LW *sapooto* (< *support*) usually appears to express novelty or stylishness as opposed to the equivalent NJ and SJ words (*tedasuke, shien*). In contrast, NJ is regarded as more colloquial while, SJ is regarded as more intelligent or dignified, than LW. It is then not difficult to imagine that the spread of the LW *sapooto* is attributed to its stylistic functions that are differentiated from those of its NJ or SJ equivalents.

Finally, linguistic orientation towards English after WWII has increased *social* pressure for using loanwords. NINJAL (2004: 139–141) shows that 73.1% of people surveyed in Japan think that English is a predominant or influential language. Of this 73.1%, 32.1% express simply positive atitudes, while 60.2% express feelings of having no choice but to accept the situation. The change in the attitude toward the present use of loanwords shown in Chapter 8 also implies that society as a whole moves toward the increased use of loanwords.

To sum up, the continuing spread of Western loanwords is *actuated* by multiple factors. They can be (i) linguistic (e.g., specification, generalization or disambiguation of meaning), (ii) stylistic and/or (iii) social. Word choice hangs in the balance of these multiple factors. This point would explain to a certain extent why the Japanese language has multiple lexical strata.

9.6 Prospects for further research

The current research contributes to the field of variationist study by opening up the possibility of analyzing lexical variation in Japanese. In spite of its overall success in offering a general sociolinguistic profile of the alternation between loan variants and non-loan variants, the present investigation produces several suggestions for further research.

First, investigations should be extended to a broader range of lexical variables. I have conducted severeal case studies of linguistic variables (e.g., *keesu* and its native variants) that could arguably be considered representatives of loanwords that are attested in Japanese to a certain degree. However, the findings from these case studies will need further support by empirical evidence from studies of other loanwords. In order to achieve this goal, a sufficient foundation will have to be established regarding the functions, usages and collocational patterns of a wider range of loanwords and their near-synonyms. As Mogi (2011) and Kim (2011) pointed out, the present situation is far from that phase. The further accumulation of in-depth studies of individual loanwords

CHAPTER 9 GENERAL SUMMARY AND DISCUSSION 163

like Kim (2011) would promote an application of the variationist approach to lexical variation, and, in turn, the pursuit of a more comprehensive elucidation of the phenomenon.

Second, research into additional language-internal factors is required. Chapter 6 successfully investigated the use of the LW *keesu* (< *case*) in terms of quantitatively measurable language-internal factors such as syntactic structure and co-occurring predicates since *keesu* and the other three variants examined are used in noun phrases (NPs) in various linguistic environments. Nevertheless, the above factors give only an ad hoc explanation applicable only to a limited case and may not be useful for every loanword and its variants. We should therefore consider more universal language-internal factors in order to explain a broader range of lexical items, including concrete nouns, abstract nouns, verbs, adjectives, and so on.

Loveday (1996: 81) points out "the existence of many pairs in semantic opposition where a word referring to a Western phenomenon is English-based and 'complementary' with a word deriving from (Sino-) Japanese and referring to a related version of the phenomenon belonging to native culture." According to Loveday, the loanword *kusshon* (< *cushion*), for example, is semantically marked by the feature [– Japanese], as opposed to its native equivalent *zabuton* ('thin cushion') (being marked by the feature [+ Japanese]). His argument holds true for many pairs of concrete nouns such as *supuun* (< *spoon*) and *saji*, *hoteru* (< *hotel*) and *ryokan*, *kitchin* (< *kitchen*) and *daidokoro*, and so on. Here, we extend Loveday's argument to the context in which a loanword is used in order to explain its occurrence. We can hypothesize that loanwords are used more frequently as the proceeding/following context becomes more westernized; in other words, the occurrence of a loanword is affected by the presence of other loanwords occurring in the surrounding context.[5] We call this "the effect of surrounding context."

To test this hypothesis, I have looked at the context surrounding the loanwords listed in Table 4.2.[6] Table 9.1 compares the average number of loanwords contained in the context surrounding the loanword variants under investigation (LW) and that in the context surrounding their non-loanword variants (non-LW). Two types of the surrounging context were examined: (i) the 10 words preceeding and following each variant; (ii) the 100 words proceeding and following each variant. The table suggests that all the loanwords listed except for *meritto* (< *merit*) and *akauntabiriti* (< *accountability*) have more loanwords in their surrounding context than their native equivalents do, supporting the above hypothesis. This is one of the possible language-internal factors that can be applied to a wider range of loanwords.

	Variants		No. of collected tokens		(i) Average no. of LWs in 10 words before and after:		(ii) Average no. of LWs in 100 words before and after:	
ID	LW variant	non-LW variant(s)	LW	non-LW	LW	non-LW	LW	non-LW
1	*niizu*	*hitsuyoosei*	579	756	0.60	0.31	7.60	3.69
2	*ibento*	*moyooshi*	416	58	1.35	0.62	13.78	5.21
3	*meritto*	*riten*	546	368	0.69	0.79	9.00	8.70
4	*konsensasu*	*gooi*	65	366	0.28	0.19	4.12	2.43
5	*sukiimu*	*keikaku*	36	1260	0.33	0.32	4.47	3.77
6	*risuku*	*kikensei*	888	487	0.65	0.39	8.48	5.02
7	*bijon*	*tenboo*	171	160	0.47	0.30	6.23	4.14
8	*akauntabiriti*	*setsumei-sekinin*	7	31	0.14	0.48	5.14	5.48
9	*wain*	*budooshu*	445	63	1.10	0.56	11.15	3.19
10	*suutsu*	*sebiro*	251	47	1.35	0.55	9.38	3.47
11	*kitchin*	*daidokoro*	297	268	1.05	0.44	11.04	4.53
12	*oopun-suru*	*kaiten-suru*	196	51	1.48	1.20	13.10	8.96
13	*getto-suru*	*kakutoku-suru*	81	942	1.81	0.65	17.04	6.23
14	*tootaru-de*	*gookei-de*	24	26	1.88	0.46	14.29	7.50
15	*kyanseru*	*kaiyaku/ torikeshi*	28	40/ 141	0.75	0.15/ 0.13	8.11	2.43/ 1.65
16	*happii*	*shiawase/ koofuku*	46	694/ 194	1.11	0.21/ 0.18	11.37	3.31/ 2.12
17	*sapooto*	*shien/ tedasuke*	120	668/ 105	0.96	0.34/ 0.32	10.49	4.01/ 4.65

Table 9.1: Average number of loanwords in the context surrounding each variant

Third, language in a more casual setting should be examined. This book consulted written text (BCCWJ) and recordings of public speaking (CSJ), both of which are characterized as language that is relatively formal in style (and produced by those with relatively high educational backgrounds). In light of the non-standard nature of loanwords in Japanese (as shown in Chapter 7), it can be expected that one will witness heavier use of loanwords when observing language that is more casual in style, such as chatting with friends or family.

Meanwhile, since 2016, NINJAL has been building the Corpus of Everyday Japanese Conversation (CEJC), which will be a collection of 200 hours of recordings of daily conversation between 100–250 ordinary speakers (Koiso et al. 2016a, 2016b). This corpus is designed to collect speech produced by people in a wider range of registers that are associated with everyday life, e.g., conversations observed in one's home, community, workplace, school, and so on. The informants record themselves, so that the effect of an observer (the problem of

CHAPTER 9 GENERAL SUMMARY AND DISCUSSION

the observer's paradox) can be minimized.

In addition, in 2017, NINJAL released the NINJAL Web Japanese Corpus (NWJC), which is a collection of large amounts of text from the Internet (Asahara et al. 2014). One of the advantages of using such an immense sum of data is that it enables us to investigate linguistic phenomena that are relatively rare in frequency, such as lexical variation, more easily. Moreover, it is a good opportunity for us to incorporate a new type of register into the current analysis, as we are more likely to obtain more tokens of loanwords in such a register than in formal text like books. However, attention needs to be paid to the question of whether we can characterize a register like online conversation within the framework of the traditional definition of style: Can it simply said to be something between formal and casual? The most characteristic feature of online text is that addressees are not known or unpredictable to the author. Such unpredictability can lead the author either to pay more or, on the contrary, less attention to speech. The investigation of a register with unspecified addressees would help us to understand a new and unavoidable type of communication in the current age.

Although the two corpora investigated in this book are among the best corpora in terms of the volume (reasonable for the quantitative analysis) and quality (rich annotation for sociolinguistic study), an additional investigation into speech closer to vernacular or speech on the Web would add a new insight to the present research into the sociolinguistic picture of the phenomenon.

Fourth, there is room for improvement in the analytical method. Since the investigations of *keesu* (and its native variants *jirei*, *baai* and *rei*) in Chapter 6 and *sapooto* (and its native variants *shien* and *tedasuke*) in Chapter 7 deal with four- or three-way distinction, a multinominal logistic regression analysis (see Maeda 2005, for example) could be used instead of binary one in order to understand the competition among the non-LW variants. The question, however, arises as to which variant should be a reference category. One of the possibilities is that we use the most unmarked variant as a reference category. We can choose the stylistically most neutral lexical variant as a reference—that is, the variant that occurs most frequently in natural speech settings. We can expect that a NJ word would be that variant in most cases, e.g., *baai* ('case') in the case of Chapter 6 and *tedasuke* ('support') in the case of Chapter 7. In this way we can examine the possibility of the occurrence of stylistically (more) marked variants including LW and SJ as opposed to a stylistically unmarked variant. That will make our understanding of the stylistic difference between LW and SJ clearer. Another possibility is that we choose LW as a reference category so that we can see the probability of the occurrence of a certain loanword in contrast to every other variant. These points need to be considered well before the analyst conducts a multinominal logistic regression analysis. In addition, we should make sure that the sample size of each lexical item does not become too small when we create a multi-way distinction for a dependent variable in order to make the results more reliable.

Lastly, the methodology employed in this research could be extended to other languages to verify the universality of the findings gained here. For example, a language like Korean also exhibits lexical strata that are very similar to Japanese. People recognize the differentiation among *ko-yu-e* ('native Korean words'), *han-ca-e* ('Sino-Korean words,' lit. 'Chinese character words') and *oy-lay-e* ('loanwords,' lit. 'words from abroad') (Sohn 1999: 87–88). Some *oy-lay-e* are said to function as innovative alternatives to existing native Korean words or Sino-Korean words in a given context (Yang 2007); however, Korean speakers exhibit a stronger resistance to adoption of such loanwords than Japanese speakers do, probably due to the national language policy to promote linguistic purism (醇化運動) by the Korean government since the latter half of the 20th century (Yang 2005, 2012: 150).[7] Furthermore, since the Korean language does not distinguish each lexical stratum in their writing system as the Japanese language does, people may be less aware of the distinction among loanwords, native Korean words and Sino-Korean words. Such social and linguistic differences between the two languages may then exhibit different sociolinguistic patterns of the phenomenon. A contrastive study of the two would encourage us to pursue study of the universality and diversity of lexical variation and change with respect to the diffusion of Western loanwords.

CHAPTER 9 GENERAL SUMMARY AND DISCUSSION 167

Notes

1 We should note that more educated people show higher rates of recognition or acceptance of the loanwords under investigation (Ishiwata 1965, Loveday 1996). Therefore it seems that people's self-reports tend to lead to a conclusion that those with higher educational backgrounds adopt loanwords more if no stylistic context is attached to the interview question.

2 Recall that style-shifting is more prominent among MC than WC groups when speech style switches between Formal and Casual in Trudgill (1974: 93, see also Figure 7.1).

3 However, the alternation between these variants is not merely the question of prestige/non-prestige. Speakers switch to the non-loan variants in order to make their addresses easier to understand, that is, for a communicative purpose (Section 7.6).

4 However, this may not apply to all the loanwords. For example, the use of technical, academic, or specialized terms that are borrowed to introduce new concepts, e.g., *aidentiti* (< *identity*), *akauntabiriti* (< *accountability*), *konpuraiansu* (< *compliance*), and so on, convey a relatively strong sense of sophistication or forwardness.

5 We have seen in Chapter 8 that the context that contains the loanword *suupaa* (< *super market*) enhances the preference for the loan verb *oopun-suru* (< *open*) (see Section 8.3).

6 Tokens are counted if the variant in question occurs in the following context in the Publication sub-corpus, BCCWJ (PB and PM, the variable-length components only).
  · Nouns: A word ends in *hiragana* writing + Key word + Particle/Auxiliary
  · Verbs: A word ends in *hiragana* writing + Key word + *suru* ('do')/*dekiru* ('be able to')
  · *tootaru-de/gookei-de*: A word ends in *hiragana* writing + Key word + *de* (COP)

7 It should be noted that the primary interest of this movement has been removing the influence of Japanese loanwords. The emphasis on native Korean words does, however, seem to have an effect on the adoption of Western loanwords to a certain extent.

Appendices

Appendix A. Distribution of LWs by gender and age (Ch. 4)

ID	LW Variant	Year of Survey	Gender		Age	Year of Birth (median)	Acquisition	Diffusion of LW (%)	No. of Informants
1		1999	M	0	16–19	1981.5	2	29.0	62
1		1999	M	0	20–29	1974.5	1	47.2	144
1		1999	M	0	30–39	1964.5	0	51.3	154
1		1999	M	0	40–49	1954.5	0	45.7	173
1		1999	M	0	50–59	1944.5	0	42.5	193
1		1999	M	0	60–69	1934.5	0	22.2	189
1	*niizu*	1999	M	0	70+	1924.5	0	17.8	107
1		1999	F	1	16–19	1981.5	2	32.3	62
1		1999	F	1	20–29	1974.5	1	46.8	158
1		1999	F	1	30–39	1964.5	0	48.0	223
1		1999	F	1	40–49	1954.5	0	44.3	221
1		1999	F	1	50–59	1944.5	0	31.9	210
1		1999	F	1	60–69	1934.5	0	21.3	183
1		1999	F	1	70+	1924.5	0	6.6	121
2		1999	M	0	16–19	1981.5	1	71.0	62
2		1999	M	0	20–29	1974.5	0	79.2	144
2		1999	M	0	30–39	1964.5	0	78.6	154
2		1999	M	0	40–49	1954.5	0	65.9	173
2		1999	M	0	50–59	1944.5	0	58.0	193
2		1999	M	0	60–69	1934.5	0	35.4	189
2	*ibento*	1999	M	0	70+	1924.5	0	22.4	107
2		1999	F	1	16–19	1981.5	0	90.3	62
2		1999	F	1	20–29	1974.5	0	81.0	158
2		1999	F	1	30–39	1964.5	0	72.2	223
2		1999	F	1	40–49	1954.5	0	67.4	221
2		1999	F	1	50–59	1944.5	0	54.8	210
2		1999	F	1	60–69	1934.5	0	31.7	183
2		1999	F	1	70+	1924.5	0	14.0	121
3		1999	M	0	16–19	1981.5	2	62.9	62
3		1999	M	0	20–29	1974.5	1	68.1	144
3		1999	M	0	30–39	1964.5	0	72.1	154
3		1999	M	0	40–49	1954.5	0	68.2	173
3		1999	M	0	50–59	1944.5	0	64.8	193
3		1999	M	0	60–69	1934.5	0	42.3	189
3	*meritto*	1999	M	0	70+	1924.5	0	22.4	107
3		1999	F	1	16–19	1981.5	1	69.4	62
3		1999	F	1	20–29	1974.5	0	75.9	158
3		1999	F	1	30–39	1964.5	0	69.5	223
3		1999	F	1	40–49	1954.5	0	67.0	221
3		1999	F	1	50–59	1944.5	0	57.1	210
3		1999	F	1	60–69	1934.5	0	37.2	183
3		1999	F	1	70+	1924.5	0	19.8	121

ID	LW Variant	Year of Survey	Gender		Age	Year of Birth (median)	Acquisition	Diffusion of LW (%)	No. of Informants
4		1999	M	o	16–19	1981.5	o	3.2	62
4		1999	M	o	20–29	1974.5	o	6.3	144
4		1999	M	o	30–39	1964.5	o	11.7	154
4		1999	M	o	40–49	1954.5	o	17.3	173
4		1999	M	o	50–59	1944.5	o	17.6	193
4		1999	M	o	60–69	1934.5	o	13.8	189
4	*konsensasu*	1999	M	o	70+	1924.5	o	12.1	107
4		1999	F	I	16–19	1981.5	o	3.2	62
4		1999	F	I	20–29	1974.5	o	8.2	158
4		1999	F	I	30–39	1964.5	o	4.9	223
4		1999	F	I	40–49	1954.5	o	9.5	221
4		1999	F	I	50–59	1944.5	o	4.3	210
4		1999	F	I	60–69	1934.5	o	3.8	183
4		1999	F	I	70+	1924.5	o	2.5	121
5		1999	M	o	16–19	1981.5	o	0.0	62
5		1999	M	o	20–29	1974.5	o	3.5	144
5		1999	M	o	30–39	1964.5	o	4.5	154
5		1999	M	o	40–49	1954.5	o	4.0	173
5		1999	M	o	50–59	1944.5	o	6.2	193
5		1999	M	o	60–69	1934.5	o	5.3	189
5	*sukiimu*	1999	M	o	70+	1924.5	o	1.9	107
5		1999	F	I	16–19	1981.5	o	0.0	62
5		1999	F	I	20–29	1974.5	o	4.4	158
5		1999	F	I	30–39	1964.5	o	2.2	223
5		1999	F	I	40–49	1954.5	o	2.3	221
5		1999	F	I	50–59	1944.5	o	1.9	210
5		1999	F	I	60–69	1934.5	o	4.4	183
5		1999	F	I	70+	1924.5	o	3.3	121
6		1999	M	o	16–19	1981.5	I	43.5	62
6		1999	M	o	20–29	1974.5	o	52.8	144
6		1999	M	o	30–39	1964.5	o	49.4	154
6		1999	M	o	40–49	1954.5	o	49.7	173
6		1999	M	o	50–59	1944.5	o	37.8	193
6		1999	M	o	60–69	1934.5	o	21.2	189
6	*risuku*	1999	M	o	70+	1924.5	o	12.1	107
6		1999	F	I	16–19	1981.5	I	45.2	62
6		1999	F	I	20–29	1974.5	o	51.9	158
6		1999	F	I	30–39	1964.5	o	43.9	223
6		1999	F	I	40–49	1954.5	o	39.4	221
6		1999	F	I	50–59	1944.5	o	28.1	210
6		1999	F	I	60–69	1934.5	o	16.4	183
6		1999	F	I	70+	1924.5	o	5.8	121

APPENDICES

ID LW Variant	Year of Survey	Gender		Age	Year of Birth (median)	Acquisition	Diffusion of LW (%)	No. of Informants
7	1999	M	o	16–19	1981.5	I	38.7	62
7	1999	M	o	20–29	1974.5	o	45.8	144
7	1999	M	o	30–39	1964.5	o	44.8	154
7	1999	M	o	40–49	1954.5	o	42.2	173
7	1999	M	o	50–59	1944.5	o	31.1	193
7	1999	M	o	60–69	1934.5	o	23.8	189
7 *bijon*	1999	M	o	70+	1924.5	o	14.0	107
7	1999	F	I	16–19	1981.5	o	46.8	62
7	1999	F	I	20–29	1974.5	o	42.4	158
7	1999	F	I	30–39	1964.5	o	32.7	223
7	1999	F	I	40–49	1954.5	o	29.9	221
7	1999	F	I	50–59	1944.5	o	25.2	210
7	1999	F	I	60–69	1934.5	o	13.7	183
7	1999	F	I	70+	1924.5	o	8.3	121
8	1999	M	o	16–19	1981.5	o	3.2	62
8	1999	M	o	20–29	1974.5	o	4.2	144
8	1999	M	o	30–39	1964.5	o	4.5	154
8	1999	M	o	40–49	1954.5	o	7.5	173
8	1999	M	o	50–59	1944.5	o	2.6	193
8	1999	M	o	60–69	1934.5	o	5.8	189
8 *akauntabiriti*	1999	M	o	70+	1924.5	o	0.0	107
8	1999	F	I	16–19	1981.5	o	0.0	62
8	1999	F	I	20–29	1974.5	o	5.7	158
8	1999	F	I	30–39	1964.5	o	4.5	223
8	1999	F	I	40–49	1954.5	o	3.2	221
8	1999	F	I	50–59	1944.5	o	0.5	210
8	1999	F	I	60–69	1934.5	o	2.7	183
8	1999	F	I	70+	1924.5	o	2.5	121
9	2000	M	o	16–19	1982.5	o	95.9	49
9	2000	M	o	20–29	1975.5	o	94.4	108
9	2000	M	o	30–39	1965.5	o	91.7	144
9	2000	M	o	40–49	1955.5	o	83.7	178
9	2000	M	o	50–59	1945.5	o	69.9	193
9 *wain*	2000	M	o	60+	1935.5	o	52.8	309
9	2000	F	I	16–19	1982.5	I	93.7	63
9	2000	F	I	20–29	1975.5	o	96.3	161
9	2000	F	I	30–39	1965.5	o	92.6	203
9	2000	F	I	40–49	1955.5	o	86.7	210
9	2000	F	I	50–59	1945.5	o	70.7	256
9	2000	F	I	60+	1935.5	o	51.9	322

ID LW Variant	Year of Survey	Gender		Age	Year of Birth (median)	Acquisition	Diffusion of LW (%)	No. of Informants
10	2000	M	o	16–19	1982.5	o	85.7	49
10	2000	M	o	20–29	1975.5	o	80.6	108
10	2000	M	o	30–39	1965.5	o	70.8	144
10	2000	M	o	40–49	1955.5	o	53.4	178
10	2000	M	o	50–59	1945.5	o	31.6	193
10 *suutsu*	2000	M	o	60+	1935.5	o	21.7	309
10	2000	F	I	16–19	1982.5	I	87.3	63
10	2000	F	I	20–29	1975.5	o	88.2	161
10	2000	F	I	30–39	1965.5	o	71.4	203
10	2000	F	I	40–49	1955.5	o	61.9	210
10	2000	F	I	50–59	1945.5	o	44.1	256
10	2000	F	I	60+	1935.5	o	37.6	322
11	2000	M	o	16–19	1982.5	o	12.2	49
11	2000	M	o	20–29	1975.5	o	10.2	108
11	2000	M	o	30–39	1965.5	o	11.1	144
11	2000	M	o	40–49	1955.5	o	6.2	178
11	2000	M	o	50–59	1945.5	o	6.2	193
11 *kitchin*	2000	M	o	60+	1935.5	o	8.4	309
11	2000	F	I	16–19	1982.5	o	15.9	63
11	2000	F	I	20–29	1975.5	o	19.3	161
11	2000	F	I	30–39	1965.5	o	13.8	203
11	2000	F	I	40–49	1955.5	o	12.9	210
11	2000	F	I	50–59	1945.5	o	16.4	256
11	2000	F	I	60+	1935.5	o	14.3	322
12	2000	M	o	16–19	1982.5	I	34.7	49
12	2000	M	o	20–29	1975.5	o	42.6	108
12	2000	M	o	30–39	1965.5	o	35.4	144
12	2000	M	o	40–49	1955.5	o	28.7	178
12	2000	M	o	50–59	1945.5	o	25.4	193
12 *oopun-suru*	2000	M	o	60+	1935.5	o	22.0	309
12	2000	F	I	16–19	1982.5	I	44.4	63
12	2000	F	I	20–29	1975.5	o	48.4	161
12	2000	F	I	30–39	1965.5	o	42.4	203
12	2000	F	I	40–49	1955.5	o	41.0	210
12	2000	F	I	50–59	1945.5	o	38.3	256
12	2000	F	I	60+	1935.5	o	31.4	322
13	2000	M	o	16–19	1982.5	o	44.9	49
13	2000	M	o	20–29	1975.5	o	36.1	108
13	2000	M	o	30–39	1965.5	o	22.2	144
13	2000	M	o	40–49	1955.5	o	6.2	178
13	2000	M	o	50–59	1945.5	o	3.6	193
13 *getto-suru*	2000	M	o	60+	1935.5	o	1.3	309
13	2000	F	I	16–19	1982.5	o	46.0	63
13	2000	F	I	20–29	1975.5	o	41.0	161
13	2000	F	I	30–39	1965.5	o	25.1	203
13	2000	F	I	40–49	1955.5	o	11.0	210
13	2000	F	I	50–59	1945.5	o	4.7	256
13	2000	F	I	60+	1935.5	o	3.4	322

ID	LW Variant	Year of Survey	Gender		Age	Year of Birth (median)	Acquisition	Diffusion of LW (%)	No. of Informants
14		2000	M	o	16–19	1982.5	I	18.4	49
14		2000	M	o	20–29	1975.5	o	24.1	108
14		2000	M	o	30–39	1965.5	o	21.5	144
14		2000	M	o	40–49	1955.5	o	10.7	178
14		2000	M	o	50–59	1945.5	o	13.0	193
14	tootaru-de	2000	M	o	60+	1935.5	o	8.7	309
14		2000	F	I	16–19	1982.5	I	17.5	63
14		2000	F	I	20–29	1975.5	o	18.6	161
14		2000	F	I	30–39	1965.5	o	13.3	203
14		2000	F	I	40–49	1955.5	o	13.3	210
14		2000	F	I	50–59	1945.5	o	11.3	256
14		2000	F	I	60+	1935.5	o	9.0	322
15		2003	M	o	15–19	1986.0	I	60.2	88
15		2003	M	o	20–29	1978.5	o	70.4	135
15		2003	M	o	30–39	1968.5	o	65.9	176
15		2003	M	o	40–49	1958.5	o	65.8	184
15		2003	M	o	50–59	1948.5	o	57.9	259
15	kyanseru	2003	M	o	60+	1938.5	o	42.9	545
15		2003	F	I	15–19	1986.0	I	67.3	101
15		2003	F	I	20–29	1978.5	o	78.7	183
15		2003	F	I	30–39	1968.5	o	72.0	271
15		2003	F	I	40–49	1958.5	o	63.3	237
15		2003	F	I	50–59	1948.5	o	55.7	368
15		2003	F	I	60+	1938.5	o	45.0	540
16		2003	M	o	15–19	1986.0	I	20.5	88
16		2003	M	o	20–29	1978.5	o	23.0	135
16		2003	M	o	30–39	1968.5	o	22.7	176
16		2003	M	o	40–49	1958.5	o	14.7	184
16		2003	M	o	50–59	1948.5	o	16.6	259
16	happii	2003	M	o	60+	1938.5	o	13.6	545
16		2003	F	I	15–19	1986.0	o	41.6	101
16		2003	F	I	20–29	1978.5	o	23.0	183
16		2003	F	I	30–39	1968.5	o	19.2	271
16		2003	F	I	40–49	1958.5	o	19.0	237
16		2003	F	I	50–59	1948.5	o	17.9	368
16		2003	F	I	60+	1938.5	o	12.0	540

ID	LW Variant	Year of Survey	Gender		Age	Year of Birth (median)	Acquisition	Diffusion of LW (%)	No. of Informants
17		2004	M	o	15–19	1987.0	I	37.0	73
17		2004	M	o	20–29	1979.5	o	49.2	128
17		2004	M	o	30–39	1969.5	o	47.8	205
17		2004	M	o	40–49	1959.5	o	42.4	210
17		2004	M	o	50–59	1949.5	o	29.5	258
17		2004	M	o	60–69	1939.5	o	23.5	311
17	sapooto	2004	M	o	70+	1929.5	o	15.3	236
17		2004	F	I	15–19	1987.0	I	45.3	64
17		2004	F	I	20–29	1979.5	o	58.9	146
17		2004	F	I	30–39	1969.5	o	50.8	303
17		2004	F	I	40–49	1959.5	o	39.1	266
17		2004	F	I	50–59	1949.5	o	32.1	361
17		2004	F	I	60–69	1939.5	o	20.7	314
17		2004	F	I	70+	1929.5	o	7.9	215

Age-specific proportions sorted by gender for *sapooto* are not available in NINJAL (2005a: 19). The proportions shown in this Appendix were thus calculated by the author based on the raw data provided by NINJAL.

Appendix B. Frequency lists of LWs from BCCWJ (Ch. 5)

B1. LWs used as nouns (N), BCCWJ

Rank	LemmaID	Lemma_JP	Lemma	Etymology	Frequency
1	25819	データ	*deeta*	data	557
2	2503	イメージ	*imeeji*	image	519
3	11462	ケース	*keesu**	case	493
4	21906	タイプ	*taipu**	type	407
5	35287	ポイント	*pointo*	point	368
6	3965	エネルギー	*enerugii*	energy	339
7	25641	デザイン	*dezain*	design	330
8	14744	サービス	*saabisu*	service	328
9	26951	ドア	*doa*	door	325
10	15342	システム	*sisutemu*	system	313
11	25515	テーマ	*teema**	theme	308
12	32308	ファイル	*fairu*	file	288
13	37817	モデル	*moderu*	model	267
14	30757	バランス	*baransu**	balance	261
15	40734	レベル	*reberu**	level	250
16	34179	ベッド	*beddo*	bed	247
17	25512	テーブル	*teeburu*	table	243
18	39979	リスク	*risuku**	risk	239
19	25317	テレビ	*terebi*	television	234
20	30953	パソコン	*pasokon*	personal computer	233
21	23722	チャンス	*chansu**	chance	223
22	10796	グループ	*guruupu*	group	222
23	35281	ボール	*booru*	ball	218
24	24311	チーム	*chiimu*	team	210
25	19209	スタイル	*sutairu*	style	209
26	34761	ホテル	*hoteru*	hotel	204
27	37444	メッセージ	*messeeji*	message	199
28	37544	メンバー	*menbaa*	member	197
29	33767	プログラム	*puroguramu*	program	195
30	34353	ページ	*peeji*	page	190
31	189	アイディア	*aidia*	idea	186
32	13014	コミュニケーション	*komyunikeeshon*	communication	184
33	22590	タバコ	*tabako*	tabaco	177
34	19384	スピード	*supiido***	speed	176
35	26733	トラブル	*toraburu*	trouble	169
36	19214	スタッフ	*sutaffu*	staff	163
37	40548	ルール	*ruuru**	rule	163
38	30956	パターン	*pataan*	pattern	161
39	39646	ライン	*rain*	line	159
40	4216	エンジン	*enjin*	engine	158

Rank	LemmaID	Lemma_JP	Lemma	Etymology	Frequency
41	12723	コスト	*kosuto**	cost	158
42	28860	ネットワーク	*nettowaaku*	network	157
43	40836	レース	*reesu*	race	155
44	7169	カメラ	*kamera*	camera	154
45	17670	シーン	*shiin*	scene	153
46	19308	ストレス	*sutoresu*	stress	152
47	33774	プロセス	*purosesu**	process	152
48	34288	ベース	*beesu*	base	152
49	13259	コンピューター	*konpyuutaa*	computer	151
50	35173	ボタン	*botan*	button	151
51	37486	メリット	*meritto**	merit	149
52	11778	ゲーム	*geemu*	game	147
53	28673	ニーズ	*niizu**	needs	147
54	37556	メール	*meeru*	mail	146
55	10431	クラス	*kurasu*	class	140
56	21876	タイトル	*taitoru*	title	139
57	37464	メニュー	*menyuu*	menu	137
58	38965	ユーザー	*yuuzaa*	user	137
59	83696	バス	*basu*	bus	134
60	32332	ファン	*fan*	fan (enthusiast)	133
61	2776	インターネット	*intaanetto*	internet	132
62	13299	コース	*koosu*	course	130
63	103238	プロ	*puro*	pro	130
64	2451	イベント	*ibento**	event	129
65	31044	パワー	*pawaa*	power	129
66	13746	サイズ	*saizu**	size	126
67	32011	ビジネス	*bijinesu*	business	124
68	36149	マンション	*manshon*	mansion	124
69	13315	コーヒー	*koohii*	coffee	123
70	26491	トップ	*toppu*	top	120
71	41132	ワイン	*wain**	wine	118
72	7871	カード	*kaado*	card	113
73	31046	パン	*pan*	pao	113
74	32164	ビール	*biiru*	beer	113
75	10449	クラブ	*kurabu*	club	111
76	17025	ショック	*shokku*	shock	111
77	19421	スペース	*supeesu*	space	111
78	40684	レストラン	*resutoran*	restaurant	111
79	20229	セット	*setto*	set	110
80	187	アイテム	*aitemu*	item	109

Rank	LemmaID	Lemma_JP	Lemma	Etymology	Frequency
81	21928	タイミング	*taimingu*	timing	109
82	33772	プロジェクト	*purojekuto*	project	109
83	281548	グラス	*gurasu*	glass	109
84	17657	シート	*shiito*	sheet	108
85	32120	ビル	*biru*	building	108
86	32229	ピンク	*pinku*	pink	108
87	21416	ソフト	*sofuto*	soft	107
88	2931	ウインドー	*uindoo*	window	106
89	28590	ニュース	*nyuusu*	news	104
90	39990	リズム	*rizumu*	rhythm	103
91	31081	パーティー	*paatii*	party	102
92	30678	バッグ	*baggu*	bag	100

B2. LWs used as verbs (V), BCCWJ

Rank	LemmaID	Lemma_JP	Lemma	Etymology	Frequency
1	10494	クリック	*kurikku*	click	898
2	23405	チェック	*chekku*	check	267
3	19233	スタート	*sutaato**	start	145
4	2503	イメージ	*imeeji**	image	130
5	13232	コントロール	*kontorooru*	control	114
6	6986	カバー	*kabaa*	cover	92
7	116693	ドラッグ	*doraggu*	drag	89
8	795	アップ	*appu*	up	85
9	458	アクセス	*akusesu*	access	84
10	20229	セット	*setto*	set	80
11	25641	デザイン	*dezain*	design	73
12	939	アピール	*apiiru*	appeal	71
13	14371	サポート	*sapooto**	support	69
14	6756	カット	*katto*	cut	66
15	5554	オープン	*oopun**	open	62
16	10471	クリア	*kuria*	clear	58
17	40345	リラックス	*rirakkusu**	relax	58
18	2758	インストール	*insutooru*	install	57
19	33702	プラス	*purasu*	plus	55
20	40443	リード	*riido*	lead	48
21	12939	コピー	*kopii*	copy	47
22	23716	チャレンジ	*charenji**	challenge	47
23	33749	プレゼント	*purezento*	present	47
24	33757	プレー	*puree*	play	44
25	35712	マスター	*masutaa**	master	44
26	23101	ダウンロード	*daunroodo*	download	42
27	9743	キープ	*kiipu**	keep	40
28	15683	シフト	*shifuto**	shift	40
29	8884	キャッチ	*kyatchi*	catch	39
30	40352	リリース	*ririisu*	release	39
31	35818	マッチ	*matchi*	match	36
32	1284	アレンジ	*arenji*	arrange	35
33	878	アドバイス	*adobaisu**	advice	30

APPENDICES 179

B3. LWs used as adjectives (A), BCCWJ

Rank	LemmaID	Lemma_JP	Lemma	Etymology	Frequency
1	17538	シンプル	*shinpuru**	simple	125
2	19482	スムーズ	*sumuuzu**	smooth	108
3	38878	ユニーク	*yuniiku**	unique	59
4	15484	シック	*shikku*	chic	47
5	37739	モダン	*modan*	modern	46
6	39877	リアル	*riaru*	real	46
7	10683	クール	*kuuru*	cool	44
8	9114	キュート	*kyuuto*	cute	38
9	21416	ソフト	*sofuto*	soft	35
10	34141	ベスト	*besuto*	best	34
11	41022	ロマンチック	*romanchikku*	romantic	34
12	17025	ショック	*shokku*	shock	31

Appendix C. Social factors and LW distribution in BCCWJ (Ch. 5)

C1. Frequency of LWs/non-LWs by year of birth, BCCWJ

No.	Variable	Variants	1830–90	1900	1910	1920	1930	1940	1950	1960	1970	1980	1990	Total
1	advice	LW				2	9	6	17	5	1			40
		non-LW		2	1	8	24	25	21	5	3	1		90
2	balance	LW	1		19	35	47	120	146	110	18			496
		non-LW	3		1	11	17	25	56	14	4			131
3	case	LW	3		11	68	176	277	309	236	33	1		1114
		non-LW	77	52	235	838	2110	3191	3266	2459	628	7		12863
4	challenge	LW		1	3	3	17	34	15	19	2			94
		non-LW	1		1	22	40	61	64	33	17	1		240
5	chance	LW		3	2	19	72	98	95	62	21	2	1	375
		non-LW	12	11	15	114	217	304	222	172	46	6		1119
6	event	LW				2	16	39	41	52	10		3	163
		non-LW	10	7	14	54	135	196	239	130	30	3	1	819
7	image	LW				9	20	42	57	53	13	1		195
		non-LW	1	5	5	27	56	57	67	42	19	2		281
8	keep	LW			1	1	3	2	10	23	5			45
		non-LW	12	1	19	94	236	427	411	296	42	1		1539
9	level	LW				29	84	188	157	123	44	1		626
		non-LW	7		1	17	34	128	115	79	23			404
10	master	LW			1	5	4	12	23	17	11	1		74
		non-LW				2	3	4	4					13
11	merit	LW			1	8	16	60	77	78	12	1		253
		non-LW			8	43	81	106	96	75	14	1		424
12	needs	LW			2	3	51	92	101	53	4			306
		non-LW	8	5	24	73	144	188	216	99	16			773
13	open	LW			1	1	5	18	23	17	3	1		69
		non-LW	70	40	79	394	767	1079	1107	957	388	47	3	4931
14	process	LW		1	2	21	48	105	107	73	30	1		388
		non-LW	27	13	94	419	723	1179	1250	753	200	17	1	4676
15	relax	LW			3	23	6	8	28	24	4			96
		non-LW	3		1	9	13	20	20	21	5			92
16	risk	LW				15	26	97	119	118	18			393
		non-LW	5	6	15	84	172	194	257	128	57	9		927
17	rule	LW			1	16	43	81	98	78	13		1	331
		non-LW			1	23	28	58	22	22	7			161
18	shift	LW				7	7	16	30	9	3			72
		non-LW	1		2	29	51	78	85	48	7			301
19	simple	LW			1	2	15	29	45	53	19			164
		non-LW	3	1	5	32	74	124	115	95	23	2		474
20	smooth	LW			2	8	35	47	68	33	11			204
		non-LW	2		1	5	10	28	22	20	7	1		96
21	start	LW		1	2	10	40	53	89	47	10			252
		non-LW	84	85	161	816	1783	2315	2143	1602	384	48	1	9422
22	support	LW			3		6	17	28	48	10			112
		non-LW	9	9	18	152	280	474	443	300	79	6		1770
23	theme	LW		2	7	30	105	183	170	83	14	4		598
		non-LW	1	1	2	14	43	35	35	31	3			165

No.	Variable	Variants	1830–90	1900	1910	1920	1930	1940	1950	1960	1970	1980	1990	Total
24	type	LW	3	4	10	27	87	174	202	155	30	2		694
		non-LW	9	4	4	29	58	92	57	67	10			330
25	unique	LW			1	8	16	21	21	24	2			93
		non-LW	1	2	1	21	33	51	39	39	15	1		203
	Total	N	353	256	781	3682	8086	12258	12448	9080	2368	168	11	*49491
	Sample size by age group	%	0.7%	0.5%	1.6%	7.4%	16.3%	24.8%	25.2%	18.3%	4.8%	0.3%	0.0%	100.0%

*The total count is not equal to that in Table 5.6 since the author's year of birth is unknown for 25672 out of 75163 tokens.

C2. Results of the regression analyses

No. Variable	% of LW as opposed to non-LW					Regression analysis				
	1920	1930	1940	1950	1960	B	Intercept	R^2	p(t-test)	
1 advice	20.0	27.3	19.4	44.7	50.0	0.7746	-1470.5309	0.74	0.062	+
2 balance	76.1	73.4	82.8	72.3	88.7	0.2409	-388.5983	0.30	0.338	ns
3 case	7.5	7.7	8.0	8.6	8.8	0.0345	-58.7572	0.95	0.005	**
4 challenge	12.0	29.8	35.8	19.0	36.5	0.3824	-715.2223	0.31	0.325	ns
5 chance	14.3	24.9	24.4	30.0	26.5	0.2947	-547.8064	0.63	0.107	ns
6 event	3.6	10.6	16.6	14.6	28.6	0.5405	-1033.7130	0.87	0.021	*
7 image	25.0	26.3	42.4	46.0	55.8	0.8123	-1536.7800	0.94	0.006	**
8 keep	1.1	1.3	0.5	2.4	7.2	0.1343	-258.1645	0.60	0.123	ns
9 level	63.0	71.2	59.5	57.7	60.9	-0.1777	407.2173	0.29	0.353	ns
10 master	71.4	57.1	75.0	85.2	100.0	0.8519	-1574.8413	0.71	0.073	+
11 merit	15.7	16.5	36.1	44.5	51.0	0.9860	-1880.1170	0.94	0.007	**
12 needs	3.9	26.2	32.9	31.9	34.9	0.6755	-1284.5219	0.71	0.075	+
13 open	0.3	0.6	1.6	2.0	1.7	0.0437	-83.5554	0.81	0.038	*
14 process	4.8	6.2	8.2	7.9	8.8	0.0979	-182.7356	0.88	0.019	*
15 relax	71.9	31.6	28.6	58.3	53.3	-0.1033	249.1200	0.01	0.887	ns
16 risk	15.2	13.1	33.3	31.6	48.0	0.8415	-1604.2548	0.86	0.024	*
17 rule	41.0	60.6	58.3	81.7	78.0	0.9505	-1780.1031	0.84	0.030	*
18 shift	19.4	12.1	17.0	26.1	15.8	0.0671	-112.0539	0.04	0.742	ns
19 simple	5.9	16.9	19.0	28.1	35.8	0.7113	-1358.7576	0.97	0.002	**
20 smooth	61.5	77.8	62.7	75.6	62.3	-0.0077	82.9149	0.0002	0.981	ns
21 start	1.2	2.2	2.2	4.0	2.9	0.0507	-95.9082	0.62	0.115	ns
22 support	0.0	2.1	3.5	5.9	13.8	0.3143	-604.7426	0.87	0.022	*
23 theme	68.2	70.9	83.9	82.9	72.8	0.2123	-336.1256	0.22	0.429	ns
24 type	48.2	60.0	65.4	78.0	69.8	0.6120	-1123.0569	0.75	0.056	+
25 unique	27.6	32.7	29.2	35.0	38.1	0.2337	-420.7808	0.75	0.058	+

p ** < 0.01, * < 0.05, + < 0.1

C3. Frequency of LWs/non-LWs by gender, BCCWJ

No.	Variable	Variants	F	M	Total	$X^2(1)$	p-value	
1	advice	LW	6	33	39	.234	.628	ns
		non-LW	10	72	82			
2	balance	LW	102	346	448	17.503	<.001	**
		non-LW	7	113	120			
3	case	LW	106	943	1049	2.768	.096	+
		non-LW	1004	10681	11685			
4	challenge	LW	11	75	86	.071	.790	ns
		non-LW	30	185	215			
5	chance	LW	58	283	341	.019	.889	ns
		non-LW	169	844	1013			
6	event	LW	31	114	145	1.813	.178	ns
		non-LW	124	617	741			
7	image	LW	23	157	180	2.685	.101	ns
		non-LW	46	200	246			
8	keep	LW	6	32	38	3.466	.063	-
		non-LW	109	1328	1437			
9	level	LW	43	520	563	.401	.527	ns
		non-LW	24	343	367			
10	master	LW	11	49	60	.063	.801	-
		non-LW	2	11	13			
11	merit	LW	25	209	234	.054	.816	ns
		non-LW	40	356	396			
12	needs	LW	35	265	300	.113	.737	ns
		non-LW	78	635	713			
13	open	LW	14	45	59	.309	.578	ns
		non-LW	874	3334	4208			
14	process	LW	49	301	350	1.064	.302	ns
		non-LW	517	3749	4266			
15	relax	LW	16	71	87	11.549	.001	**
		non-LW	34	46	80			
16	risk	LW	29	344	373	15.636	<.001	**
		non-LW	133	686	819			
17	rule	LW	34	277	311	1.011	.315	ns
		non-LW	12	139	151			
18	shift	LW	3	64	67	.546	.460	-
		non-LW	20	268	288			
19	simple	LW	42	94	136	28.409	<.001	**
		non-LW	50	382	432			
20	smooth	LW	36	153	189	.002	.965	ns
		non-LW	16	67	83			

No.	Variable	Variants	F	M	Total	$X^2(1)$	p-value	
21	start	LW	33	204	237	1.591	.207	ns
		non-LW	1447	7044	8491			
22	support	LW	23	69	92	4.190	.041	*
		non-LW	273	1359	1632			
23	theme	LW	100	463	563	7.344	.007	**
		non-LW	14	144	158			
24	type	LW	106	527	633	3.696	.055	+
		non-LW	36	266	302			
25	unique	LW	16	73	89	.804	.370	ns
		non-LW	25	156	181			

p ** < 0.01, * < 0.05, + < 0.1

"-" indicates that 1 or more cells have expected count less than 5.

C4. Frequency of LWs/non-LWs by education, BCCWJ

No.	Variable	Variants	up to UNIV	GRAD	Total	$X^2(1)$	p-value	
1	advice	LW	17	11	28	.178	.673	ns
		non-LW	33	26	59			
2	balance	LW	168	124	292	4.385	.036	*
		non-LW	36	45	81			
3	case	LW	429	337	766	4.301	.038	*
		non-LW	4351	4001	8352			
4	challenge	LW	52	12	64	3.463	.063	+
		non-LW	92	42	134			
5	chance	LW	171	36	207	44.664	<.001	**
		non-LW	409	307	716			
6	event	LW	76	29	105	8.303	.004	**
		non-LW	320	238	558			
7	image	LW	63	48	111	8.596	.003	**
		non-LW	130	47	177			
8	keep	LW	7	2	9	3.360	.067	-
		non-LW	503	564	1067			
9	level	LW	201	211	412	10.359	.001	**
		non-LW	108	187	295			
10	master	LW	22	14	36	.334	.563	-
		non-LW	4	4	8			
11	merit	LW	97	66	163	.200	.655	ns
		non-LW	164	122	286			
12	needs	LW	106	107	213	.185	.667	ns
		non-LW	273	257	530			
13	open	LW	29	2	31	5.107	.024	*
		non-LW	2122	662	2784			
14	process	LW	121	136	257	1.454	.228	ns
		non-LW	1559	1498	3057			
15	relax	LW	39	14	53	.472	.492	ns
		non-LW	35	9	44			
16	risk	LW	127	134	261	34.000	<.001	**
		non-LW	425	187	612			
17	rule	LW	102	121	223	.589	.443	ns
		non-LW	45	64	109			
18	shift	LW	20	39	59	5.988	.014	*
		non-LW	121	113	234			
19	simple	LW	55	23	78	7.816	.005	**
		non-LW	174	154	328			
20	smooth	LW	81	35	116	.010	.921	ns
		non-LW	36	15	51			

No.	Variable	Variants	up to UNIV	GRAD	Total	$X^2(1)$	p-value	
21	start	LW	110	37	147	3.975	.046	*
		non-LW	4025	1981	6006			
22	support	LW	45	28	73	5.723	.017	*
		non-LW	543	607	1150			
23	theme	LW	218	181	399	15.790	<.001	**
		non-LW	42	81	123			
24	type	LW	253	169	422	1.925	.165	ns
		non-LW	116	98	214			
25	unique	LW	48	12	60	19.547	<.001	**
		non-LW	57	68	125			

p ** < 0.01, * < 0.05, + < 0.1

"-" indicates that 1 or more cells have expected count less than 5.

C5. Frequency of LWs/non-LWs by register (type of medium), BCCWJ

No.	Variable	Variants	PB	PM	Total	X²(1)	p-value	
1	advice	LW	33	6	39	3.936	.047	-
		non-LW	79	4	83			
2	balance	LW	397	61	458	6.771	.009	**
		non-LW	117	6	123			
3	case	LW	973	93	1066	39.938	<.001	**
		non-LW	11340	524	11864			
4	challenge	LW	83	5	88	1.466	.226	ns
		non-LW	198	22	220			
5	chance	LW	320	26	346	.601	.438	ns
		non-LW	964	65	1029			
6	event	LW	128	22	150	9.592	.002	**
		non-LW	701	53	754			
7	image	LW	159	22	181	.026	.872	ns
		non-LW	220	29	249			
8	keep	LW	23	16	39	73.248	<.001	-
		non-LW	1377	87	1464			
9	level	LW	537	44	581	.121	.728	ns
		non-LW	347	26	373			
10	master	LW	50	11	61	.052	.820	-
		non-LW	11	2	13			
11	merit	LW	207	32	239	12.106	.001	**
		non-LW	379	22	401			
12	needs	LW	289	11	300	.431	.511	ns
		non-LW	687	33	720			
13	open	LW	52	12	64	6.416	.011	*
		non-LW	3900	404	4304			
14	process	LW	345	9	354	3.152	.076	+
		non-LW	4127	197	4324			
15	relax	LW	76	13	89	.166	.684	ns
		non-LW	69	14	83			
16	risk	LW	342	33	375	.951	.330	ns
		non-LW	775	60	835			
17	rule	LW	293	23	316	5.567	.018	*
		non-LW	150	3	153			
18	shift	LW	64	5	69	.132	.716	ns
		non-LW	266	25	291			
19	simple	LW	111	33	144	24.646	<.001	**
		non-LW	406	34	440			
20	smooth	LW	169	22	191	1.272	.259	ns
		non-LW	71	14	85			

No.	Variable	Variants	PB	PM	Total	$X^2(1)$	p-value	
21	start	LW	200	39	239	17.659	<.001	**
		non-LW	7920	739	8659			
22	support	LW	90	9	99	.862	.353	ns
		non-LW	1539	110	1649			
23	theme	LW	508	63	571	7.561	.006	**
		non-LW	152	6	158			
24	type	LW	591	54	645	2.269	.132	ns
		non-LW	286	17	303			
25	unique	LW	75	15	90	3.763	.052	+
		non-LW	167	16	183			

p ** < 0.01, * < 0.05, + < 0.1

"-" indicates that 1 or more cells have expected count less than 5.

Appendix D. Frequency lists of LWs from CSJ (Ch. 5)

D1. LWs used as nouns (N), CSJ

Rank	LemmaID	Lemma_JP	Lemma	Etymology	Frequency
1	25819	データ	*deeta*	data	1879
2	37817	モデル	*moderu*	model	1348
3	15342	システム	*shisutemu*	system	1139
4	30956	パターン	*pataan*	pattern	656
5	25317	テレビ	*terebi*	television	610
6	10761	グラフ	*gurafu*	graph	567
7	21876	タイトル	*taitoru*	title	558
8	38965	ユーザー	*yuuzaa*	user	531
9	25515	テーマ	*teema**	theme	522
10	2503	イメージ	*imeeji*	image	505
11	10796	グループ	*guruupu*	group	476
12	463	アクセント	*akusento*	accent	470
13	20754	ゼロ	*zero*	zero	459
14	40548	ルール	*ruuru**	rule	458
15	31017	パラメーター	*parameetaa*	parameter	453
16	40734	レベル	*reberu**	level	446
17	25097	テキスト	*tekisuto*	text	442
18	21906	タイプ	*taipu**	type	390
19	10431	クラス	*kurasu*	class	387
20	34761	ホテル	*hoteru*	hotel	369
21	13014	コミュニケーション	*komyunikeeshon*	communication	353
22	28590	ニュース	*nyuusu*	news	342
23	13314	コーパス	*koopasu*	corpus	290
24	22299	タスク	*tasuku*	task	288
25	25820	データーベース	*deetaabeesu*	database	283
26	83696	バス	*basu*	bus	282
27	30953	パソコン	*pasokon*	personal computer	274
28	6838	カテゴリー	*kategorii*	category	266
29	32202	ピッチ	*pitchi*	pitch	263
30	4318	エージェント	*eejento*	agent	254
31	13259	コンピューター	*konpyuutaa*	computer	253
32	35287	ポイント	*pointo*	point	247
33	22590	タバコ	*tabako*	tabaco	243
34	2776	インターネット	*intaanetto*	internet	239
35	19308	ストレス	*sutoresu*	stress	234
36	10434	クラスター	*kurasutaa*	cluster	229
37	25149	テスト	*tesuto*	test	226
38	19429	スポーツ	*supootsu*	sport	224
39	1226	アルゴリズム	*arugorizumu*	algorithm	218
40	36149	マンション	*manshon*	mansion	215

Rank	LemmaID	Lemma_JP	Lemma	Etymology	Frequency
41	37556	メール	meeru	mail	215
42	32172	ピアノ	piano	piano	210
43	19147	スコア	sukoa	score	209
44	35281	ボール	booru	ball	207
45	29314	ノード	noodo	node	205
46	11462	ケース	keesu*	case	185
47	973	アプローチ	apuroochi	approach	184
48	32370	フィラー	firaa	filler	182
49	24311	チーム	chiimu	team	180
50	19413	スペクトル	supekutoru	spectre	177
51	31046	パン	pan	pao	170
52	38078	モーラ	moora	mora	166
53	19084	スキー	sukii	ski	164
54	25844	トイレ	toire	toilet	161
55	27505	ナイフ	naifu	knife	161
56	33767	プログラム	puroguramu	program	161
57	35360	ポーズ	poozu	pause	161
58	39827	ランダム	randamu	random	161
59	37544	メンバー	menbaa	member	160
60	2451	イベント	ibento*	event	159
61	32258	ピーク	piiku	peak	158
62	19581	スーパー	suupaa	super	156
63	34288	ベース	beesu	base	155
64	37486	メリット	meritto*	merit	152
65	33206	フレーム	fureemu	frame	150
66	190045	ベクトル	bekutoru	vector	145
67	33772	プロジェクト	purojekuto	project	143
68	41132	ワイン	wain	wine	141
69	1245	アルバイト	arubaito	Arbeit	140
70	33774	プロセス	purosesu*	process	139
71	39982	リスト	risuto	list	136
72	19380	スピーカー	supiikaa	speaker	135
73	103238	プロ	puro	pro	135
74	32042	ビデオ	bideo	video	133
75	120760	バイト	baito	Arbeit	131
76	11778	ゲーム	geemu	game	129
77	17025	ショック	shokku	shock	129
78	15768	シミュレーション	shimureeshon	simulation	125
79	13746	サイズ	saizu	size	124
80	39710	ラジオ	rajio	radio	123

Rank	LemmaID	Lemma_JP	Lemma	Etymology	Frequency
81	41016	ロボット	*robotto*	robot	122
82	2817	イントネーション	*intoneeshon*	intonation	121
83	27357	ドラマ	*dorama*	drama	119
84	14744	サービス	*saabisu*	service	118
85	25231	テニス	*tenisu*	tennis	118
86	21416	ソフト	*sofuto*	soft	117
87	24325	ツアー	*tsuaa*	tour	117
88	39990	リズム	*rizumu*	rhythm	117
89	3965	エネルギー	*enerugii*	energy	115
90	7169	カメラ	*kamera*	camera	112
91	34296	ペア	*pea*	pair	112
92	7871	カード	*kaado*	card	111
93	30860	バンド	*bando*	band (group)	111
94	37453	メディア	*media*	media	111
95	40684	レストラン	*resutoran*	restaurant	111
96	30757	バランス	*baransu**	balance	110
97	22900	ターゲット	*taagetto*	target	109
98	37558	メーン	*meen*	main	109
99	13315	コーヒー	*koohii*	coffee	108
100	19384	スピード	*supiido*	speed	108
101	20138	セグメント	*segumento*	segment	108
102	30534	バイク	*baiku*	bike	107
103	888	アナウンス	*anaunsu*	announce	106
104	14741	サークル	*saakuru*	circle	106
105	39960	リサイクル	*risaikuru*	recycle	105
106	14689	サンプル	*sanpuru*	sample	104
107	34316	ペット	*petto*	pet	104
108	19382	スピーチ	*supiichi*	speech	103
109	2949	ウェブ	*uebu*	web	102
110	26882	トレーニング	*toreeningu*	training	102
111	25683	デパート	*depaato*	department	101
112	33702	プラス	*purasu*	plus	101
113	26951	ドア	*doa*	door	100

D2. LWs used as verbs (V), CSJ

Rank	LemmaID	Lemma_JP	Lemma	Etymology	Frequency
1	23405	チェック	*chekku*	check	141
2	33783	プロット	*purotto*	plot	91
3	19233	スタート	*sutaato**	start	82
4	2503	イメージ	*imeeji**	image	68
5	458	アクセス	*akusesu*	access	65
6	10433	クラスタリング	*kurasutaringu*	clustering	61
7	40345	リラックス	*rirakkusu**	relax	61
8	6986	カバー	*kabaa*	cover	58
9	13232	コントロール	*kontorooru*	control	55
10	36202	マーク	*maaku*	mark	53
11	6756	カット	*katto*	cut	50

D3. LWs used as adjectives (A), CSJ

Rank	LemmaID	Lemma_JP	Lemma	Etymology	Frequency
1	39827	ランダム	*randamu*	random	154
2	17025	ショック	*shokku*	shock	66
3	19482	スムーズ	*sumuuzu**	smooth	54
4	17538	シンプル	*shinpuru**	simple	52

Appendix E. Social factors and LW distribution in CSJ (Ch. 5)

E1. Frequency of LWs/non-LWs by year of birth, CSJ

No.	Variable	Variants	1910	1920	1930	1940	1950	1960	1970	1980	Total
1	balance	LW			9	15	24	26	34	1	109
		non-LW						1			1
2	case	LW			12	16	44	57	56		185
		non-LW	20	11	267	807	990	2086	3439	9	7629
3	event	LW			6	6	10	48	78	9	157
		non-LW			29	49	38	65	105	4	290
4	image	LW			5	6	10	32	15		68
		non-LW			6	7	12	11	29	4	69
5	level	LW			7	58	84	141	154	2	446
		non-LW	1		4	11	8	13	21		58
6	merit	LW			8	15	16	47	64	2	152
		non-LW			8	17	16	46	98		185
7	process	LW	1		6	23	18	33	57		138
		non-LW	6	3	100	212	336	643	1102	13	2415
8	relax	LW			1	3	21	19	16	1	61
		non-LW			1		1		3		5
9	rule	LW			14	8	37	105	287	4	455
		non-LW				17	13	55	173		258
10	simple	LW			5	4	8	20	15		52
		non-LW		1	12	24	63	142	146		388
11	smooth	LW			2	6	11	14	20	1	54
		non-LW			1	3	10	7	19		40
12	start	LW			9	26	9	22	15	1	82
		non-LW	7	2	193	373	371	535	757	47	2285
13	theme	LW	3		60	61	110	146	138	4	522
		non-LW			1	10	13	27	94		145
14	type	LW	1	1	8	45	51	133	149	1	389
		non-LW	4		2	6	25	24	64		125
	Total	N	43	18	776	1828	2349	4498	7148	103	*16763
	Sample size by age group	%	0.3%	0.1%	4.6%	10.9%	14.0%	26.8%	42.6%	0.6%	100.0%

* The total count is not equal to that in Table 5.8 since the speaker's year of birth is unknown for 131 out of 16894 tokens.

E2. Results of the regression analyses, CSJ

No.	Variable	% of LW as opposed to non-LW				Regression analysis				
		1940	1950	1960	1970	B	Intercept	R^2	p (t-test)	
1	balance	100.0	100.0	96.3	100.0	-0.0370	171.4815	0.07	0.742	ns
2	case	1.9	4.3	2.7	1.6	-0.0262	53.8550	0.08	0.713	ns
3	event	10.9	20.8	42.5	42.6	1.1679	-2253.9579	0.90	0.053	+
4	image	46.2	45.5	74.4	34.1	-0.0722	191.2734	0.003	0.946	ns
5	level	84.1	91.3	91.6	88.0	0.1208	-147.4373	0.20	0.556	ns
6	merit	46.9	50.0	50.5	39.5	-0.2157	468.4007	0.30	0.452	ns
7	process	9.8	5.1	4.9	4.9	-0.1481	295.7170	0.63	0.208	ns
8	relax	100.0	95.5	100.0	84.2	-0.4282	932.1053	0.55	0.258	ns
9	rule	32.0	74.0	65.6	62.4	0.8280	-1560.2147	0.34	0.417	ns
10	simple	14.3	11.3	12.3	9.3	-0.1383	282.1562	0.74	0.140	ns
11	smooth	66.7	52.4	66.7	51.3	-0.3187	682.2711	0.23	0.520	ns
12	start	6.5	2.4	3.9	1.9	-0.1214	241.0030	0.57	0.243	ns
13	theme	85.9	89.4	84.4	59.5	-0.8434	1728.5750	0.63	0.206	ns
14	type	88.2	67.1	84.7	70.0	-0.3724	805.5167	0.21	0.543	ns

p ** < 0.01, * < 0.05, + < 0.1

E3. Frequency of LWs/non-LWs by gender/education, CSJ

No	Variable	Variants	Gender						Education					
			F	M	Total	X²(1)	p-value		UNIV	GRAD	Total	X²(1)	p-value	
1	balance	LW	52	47	99	1.094	.296	-	66	33	99	.498	.481	-
		non-LW		1	1				1		1			
2	case	LW	51	122	173	11.654	.001	**	79	94	173	3.044	.081	+
		non-LW	1399	5923	7322				2861	4454	7315			
3	event	LW	58	84	142	9.792	.002	**	110	28	138	.008	.931	ns
		non-LW	147	110	257				205	51	256			
4	image	LW	24	39	63	.449	.503	ns	47	16	63	.180	.671	ns
		non-LW	26	33	59				42	17	59			
5	level	LW	131	306	437	6.570	.0104	*	186	251	437	5.102	.024	*
		non-LW	7	46	53				14	39	53			
6	merit	LW	47	95	142	2.624	.105	ns	105	36	141	5.441	.020	*
		non-LW	44	133	177				110	67	177			
7	process	LW	12	119	131	4.684	.030	*	35	96	131	5.871	.015	*
		non-LW	373	1920	2293				852	1438	2290			
8	relax	LW	29	30	59	.001	.974	-	44	15	59	1.335	.248	-
		non-LW	2	2	4				4		4			
9	rule	LW	31	406	437	.256	.613	ns	156	281	437	.499	.480	ns
		non-LW	21	237	258				99	159	258			
10	simple	LW	16	31	47	7.213	.007	**	29	18	47	15.464	<.001	**
		non-LW	66	309	375				122	253	375			
11	smooth	LW	21	30	51	1.031	.310	ns	39	12	51	3.157	.076	+
		non-LW	12	27	39				23	16	39			
12	start	LW	26	46	72	3.679	.055	+	60	11	71	2.896	.089	+
		non-LW	969	1067	2036				1542	494	2036			
13	theme	LW	180	275	455	7.342	.007	**	322	130	452	19.299	<.001	**
		non-LW	39	105	144				74	70	144			
14	type	LW	159	219	378	.099	.753	ns	183	195	378	2.895	.089	+
		non-LW	52	67	119				47	72	119			

p ** < 0.01, * < 0.05, + < 0.1

"-" indicates that 1 or more cells have expected count less than 5.

E4. Frequency of LWs/non-LWs by register (type of speech) /spontaneity, CSJ

No	Variable	Variants	Register						Spontaneity					
			APS	SPS	Total	$X^2(1)$	p-value		Others	Sponta-neous	Total	$X^2(1)$	p-value	
1	balance	LW	33	66	99	.498	.481	-	39	59	98	.657	.418	-
		non-LW		1	1					1	1			
2	case	LW	103	70	173	106.465	<.001	**	88	85	173	4.371	.037	*
		non-LW	6361	961	7322				3122	4155	7277			
3	event	LW	32	110	142	1.039	.308	ns	22	114	136	27.548	<.001	**
		non-LW	47	210	257				109	148	257			
4	image	LW	19	44	63	.138	.711	ns	14	49	63	.064	.800	ns
		non-LW	16	43	59				12	47	59			
5	level	LW	308	129	437	4.883	.027	*	151	285	436	4.257	.039	*
		non-LW	45	8	53				26	27	53			
6	merit	LW	54	88	142	22.961	<.001	**	46	94	140	9.382	.002	**
		non-LW	115	62	177				88	88	176			
7	process	LW	120	11	131	4.000	.045	*	50	79	129	.272	.602	ns
		non-LW	1956	337	2293				935	1341	2276			
8	relax	LW	13	46	59	1.111	.292	-	21	38	59	.335	.562	-
		non-LW	4		4				2	2	4			
9	rule	LW	405	32	437	.317	.573	ns	233	199	432	3.122	.077	+
		non-LW	242	16	258				154	99	253			
10	simple	LW	28	19	47	7.625	.006	**	5	42	47	10.481	.001	**
		non-LW	292	83	375				126	246	372			
11	smooth	LW	19	32	51	5.223	.022	*	15	36	51	1.939	.164	ns
		non-LW	24	15	39				17	22	39			
12	start	LW	14	58	72	1.686	.194	ns	25	47	72	.525	.469	ns
		non-LW	535	1501	2036				624	1408	2032			
13	theme	LW	138	317	455	200.804	<.001	**	154	296	450	66.422	<.001	**
		non-LW	141	3	144				105	39	144			
14	type	LW	232	146	378	3.317	.069	+	145	232	377	15.918	<.001	**
		non-LW	84	35	119				70	48	118			

p ** < 0.01, * < 0.05, + < 0.1

"-" indicates that 1 or more cells have expected count less than 5.

E5. Frequency of LWs/non-LWs by formality/audience size, CSJ

No	Variable	Variants	Formality						Audience Size						
			Others	Formal	Total	X^2 (1)	p-value		Small	Medium	Large	Total	X^2 (2)	p-value	
1	balance	LW	67	30	97	2.184	.139	-	66	18	15	99	.498	.780	-
		non-LW		1	1				1			1			
2	case	LW	111	57	168	.302	.583	ns	70	45	54	169	108.394	<.001	**
		non-LW	4187	2354	6541				958	2598	3618	7174			
3	event	LW	118	17	135	18.014	<.001	**	110	17	14	141	5.713	.057	+
		non-LW	172	82	254				209	14	32	255			
4	image	LW	48	14	62	.400	.527	ns	44	11	8	63	.354	.838	ns
		non-LW	42	16	58				43	8	8	59			
5	level	LW	279	128	407	3.107	.078	+	129	133	162	424	4.529	.104	ns
		non-LW	25	20	45				8	19	23	50			
6	merit	LW	105	33	138	4.212	.040	*	88	33	21	142	23.608	<.001	**
		non-LW	107	57	164				62	43	61	166			
7	process	LW	69	56	125	10.165	.001	**	11	56	57	124	6.025	.049	*
		non-LW	1441	651	2092				337	801	1087	2225			
8	relax	LW	50	9	59	.712	.399	-	46	7	6	59	1.111	.574	-
		non-LW	4		4				4			4			
9	rule	LW	244	168	412	6.732	.009	**	32	233	147	412	46.022	<.001	**
		non-LW	117	123	240				16	81	160	257			
10	simple	LW	42	4	46	5.119	.024	*	19	16	9	44	11.127	.004	**
		non-LW	270	82	352				83	133	152	368			
11	smooth	LW	33	16	49	.373	.541	ns	32	11	8	51	10.044	.007	**
		non-LW	20	7	27				15	6	18	39			
12	start	LW	52	19	71	.263	.608	ns	58	5	9	72	1.992	.369	ns
		non-LW	1511	480	1991				1501	242	285	2028			
13	theme	LW	324	116	440	90.774	<.001	**	314	77	58	449	254.440	<.001	**
		non-LW	41	100	141				3	29	112	144			
14	type	LW	237	128	365	10.829	.001	**	146	91	137	374	11.101	.004	**
		non-LW	56	61	117				35	19	63	117			

p ** < 0.01, * < 0.05, + < 0.1

"-" indicates that 1 or more cells have expected count less than 5.

Appendix F. Distribution of variables by (I) year of survey/publication, (II) age, and (III) year of birth (Ch. 8)

F1. Proportion of (i) *wain* (< *wine*) and (ii) *oopun-suru* (< *open*)

Year of Survey	Age Range	Age (median)	Year of Birth (median)	No. of Informants	Proportion of *wain* (%)	Proportion of *oopun-suru* (%)
1979	16–19	17.5	1961.5	201	64.0	28.0
1979	20–24	22.0	1957.0	171	66.0	28.0
1979	25–29	27.0	1952.0	262	56.0	34.0
1979	30–34	32.0	1947.0	309	49.0	27.0
1979	35–39	37.0	1942.0	348	40.0	26.0
1979	40–49	44.5	1934.5	557	35.0	30.0
1979	50–59	54.5	1924.5	412	25.0	32.0
1979	60–69	64.5	1914.5	213	17.0	24.0
1979	70+	74.5	1904.5	166	9.0	7.0
1996	20–29	24.5	1971.5	191	96.0	62.0
1996	30–39	34.5	1961.5	212	97.0	58.0
1996	40–49	44.5	1951.5	274	86.0	58.0
1996	50–59	54.5	1941.5	237	73.0	55.0
1996	60–69	64.5	1931.5	202	60.0	59.0
1996	70+	74.5	1921.5	135	36.0	47.0
2000	16–19	17.5	1982.5	112	94.7	40.2
2000	20–29	24.5	1975.5	269	95.5	46.1
2000	30–39	34.5	1965.5	347	92.2	39.5
2000	40–49	44.5	1955.5	388	85.3	35.4
2000	50–59	54.5	1945.5	449	70.4	32.8
2000	60+	64.5	1935.5	631	52.3	26.8

"Proportion (%)" in the table refers to the proportion of those who chose the loanwords as opposed to those who chose their native equivalents and, if applicable, other choices including "Use both," "Do not use either of them," or "Not sure."

The report of the survey conducted in 2000 (BBK 2000: 18) only provides age-specific proportions sorted according to *gender*. The proportions regardless of gender shown in this Appendix were thus calculated by the author based on the original data in the report.

F2. (iii) Preference *for* or *against* the present use of loanwords

Year of Survey	Age Range	Age (median)	Year of Birth (median)	No. of Informants	Positive (%)	Like	Neither	Negative (%) Dislike
1977	20–24	22.0	1955.0	619	77.6	16.5	61.1	17.8
1977	25–29	27.0	1950.0	1069	73.7	11.8	61.9	22.0
1977	30–34	32.0	1945.0	1064	65.3	10.2	55.1	29.7
1977	35–39	37.0	1940.0	952	64.1	10.8	53.3	30.1
1977	40–44	42.0	1935.0	975	60.0	9.9	50.1	34.6
1977	45–49	47.0	1930.0	896	51.2	7.6	43.6	41.5
1977	50–54	52.0	1925.0	721	53.8	9.6	44.2	37.7
1977	55–59	57.0	1920.0	541	49.2	8.9	40.3	40.5
1977	60–69	64.5	1912.5	888	41.9	6.5	35.4	46.8
1977	70+	74.5	1902.5	445	31.7	4.5	27.2	41.1
2000	16–19	17.5	1982.5	112	90.2	33.0	57.2	8.9
2000	20–29	24.5	1975.5	269	84.8	20.8	64.0	13.8
2000	30–39	34.5	1965.5	347	72.4	13.8	58.5	25.7
2000	40–49	44.5	1955.5	388	68.6	13.4	55.2	29.9
2000	50–59	54.5	1945.5	449	54.5	9.8	44.7	43.0
2000	60+	64.5	1935.5	631	43.4	8.9	34.5	52.9
2002	16–19	17.5	1984.5	112	81.3	26.8	54.5	17.9
2002	20–29	24.5	1977.5	227	88.6	23.8	64.8	11.0
2002	30–39	34.5	1967.5	338	78.1	20.1	58.0	21.3
2002	40–49	44.5	1957.5	340	63.0	15.6	47.4	35.3
2002	50–59	54.5	1947.5	462	55.2	11.7	43.5	43.5
2002	60–69	64.5	1937.5	417	49.2	14.4	34.8	48.9
2002	70+	74.5	1927.5	304	39.5	12.5	27.0	53.9
2008	16–19	17.5	1990.5	80	82.5	20.0	62.5	17.5
2008	20–29	24.5	1983.5	177	78.0	19.2	58.8	20.9
2008	30–39	34.5	1973.5	274	71.5	15.7	55.8	28.1
2008	40–49	44.5	1963.5	306	66.6	12.4	54.2	33.3
2008	50–59	54.5	1953.5	353	54.1	14.7	39.4	44.5
2008	60–69	64.5	1943.5	417	48.9	14.6	34.3	48.2
2008	70+	74.5	1933.5	368	41.0	11.7	29.3	53.8
2013	16–19	17.5	1995.5	74	91.9	16.2	75.7	6.8
2013	20–29	24.5	1988.5	175	83.4	13.1	70.3	16.6
2013	30–39	34.5	1978.5	291	79.1	12.4	66.7	20.6
2013	40–49	44.5	1968.5	327	68.8	8.6	60.2	31.2
2013	50–59	54.5	1958.5	323	62.5	9.6	52.9	36.8
2013	60–69	64.5	1948.5	446	53.6	7.0	46.6	45.1
2013	70+	74.5	1938.5	517	48.9	7.5	41.4	47.2

Note that the proportions of those choosing "Not sure" are not shown in the table.

The report of the survey conducted in 2000 (BBK 2000: 23) only provides age-specific proportions sorted according to *gender*. The proportions regardless of gender shown in this Appendix were thus calculated by the author based on the original data in the report.

F3. (iv) Preference *for* or *against* a further expansion of loanwords in future

Year of Survey	Age Range	Age (median)	Year of Birth (median)	No. of Informants	Positive (%)	Negative (%)
1995	16–19	17.5	1977.5	131	78.6	19.1
1995	20–29	24.5	1970.5	277	77.6	19.5
1995	30–39	34.5	1960.5	382	68.6	27.8
1995	40–49	44.5	1950.5	492	58.8	37.2
1995	50–59	54.5	1940.5	410	54.9	40.5
1995	60+	64.5	1930.5	520	36.2	54.8
2003	15–19	17.0	1986.0	189	61.4	25.4
2003	20–29	24.5	1978.5	318	57.9	33.3
2003	30–39	34.5	1968.5	447	53.5	38.0
2003	40–49	44.5	1958.5	421	37.8	53.9
2003	50–59	54.5	1948.5	627	32.1	61.9
2003	60+	64.5	1938.5	1085	22.5	70.8

Note that the proportions of those choosing "Not sure" are not shown in the table.

The reports of these surveys conducted in 1995 (BBK 1995:48) and 2003 (NINJAL 2004: 16) only provide age-specific proportions sorted according to *gender*. The proportions regardless of gender shown in this Appendix were thus calculated by the author based on the original data in the report.

F4. Frequency of (v) *keesu* (< *case*), (vi) *sapooto-suru* (< *support*),
(vii) *shinpuru* (< *simple*), and (viii) the LW stratum in BCCWJ

Variable	Year of Publication (oldest)	Year of Birth (oldest)	Age (oldest)	LW (N)	non-LW (N)	Total (N)	LW/Total (%)
keesu	1986	1900	86	3	109	112	2.7
	1986	1910	76	3	120	123	2.4
	1986	1920	66	23	284	307	7.5
	1986	1930	56	31	355	386	8.0
	1986	1940	46	40	358	398	10.1
	1986	1950	36	5	75	80	6.3
	1991	1920	71	36	384	420	8.6
	1991	1930	61	71	555	626	11.3
	1991	1940	51	67	588	655	10.2
	1991	1950	41	48	324	372	12.9
	1996	1920	76	13	252	265	4.9
	1996	1930	66	65	578	643	10.1
	1996	1940	56	94	822	916	10.3
	1996	1950	46	92	669	761	12.1
	1996	1960	36	37	239	276	13.4
	2001	1920	81	10	147	157	6.4
	2001	1930	71	59	461	520	11.4
	2001	1940	61	103	552	655	15.7
	2001	1950	51	86	836	922	9.3
	2001	1960	41	86	465	551	15.6
	2001	1970	31	7	155	162	4.3
sapooto-suru	1986	1910	76		18	18	0.0
	1986	1920	66	1	57	58	1.7
	1986	1930	56		70	70	0.0
	1986	1940	46		101	101	0.0
	1986	1950	36		24	24	0.0
	1991	1920	71		66	66	0.0
	1991	1930	61	1	103	104	1.0
	1991	1940	51	3	123	126	2.4
	1991	1950	41	1	68	69	1.5
	1991	1960	31	1	22	23	4.4
	1996	1920	76		41	41	0.0
	1996	1930	66	3	128	131	2.3
	1996	1940	56	7	195	202	3.5
	1996	1950	46	10	108	118	8.5
	1996	1960	36	3	44	47	6.4
	2001	1920	81		34	34	0.0
	2001	1930	71	2	95	97	2.1
	2001	1940	61	8	110	118	6.8
	2001	1950	51	14	120	134	10.5
	2001	1960	41	6	73	79	7.6

Variable	Year of Publication (oldest)	Year of Birth (oldest)	Age (oldest)	LW (N)	non-LW (N)	Total (N)	LW/Total (%)
shinpuru	1986	1910	76		7	7	0.0
	1986	1920	66		16	16	0.0
	1986	1930	56	1	23	24	4.2
	1986	1940	46	4	17	21	19.1
	1986	1950	36	1	7	8	12.5
	1991	1920	71	2	17	19	10.5
	1991	1930	61		27	27	0.0
	1991	1940	51	9	31	40	22.5
	1991	1950	41	6	19	25	24.0
	1991	1960	31	2	12	14	14.3
	1996	1920	76	2	16	18	11.1
	1996	1930	66	3	26	29	10.3
	1996	1940	56	10	52	62	16.1
	1996	1950	46	8	36	44	18.2
	1996	1960	36	7	20	27	25.9
	2001	1930	71	6	31	37	16.2
	2001	1940	61	6	30	36	16.7
	2001	1950	51	13	29	42	31.0
	2001	1960	41	7	27	34	20.6
	2001	1970	31	2	7	9	22.2
The LW stratum	1986	1910	76	598	26151	26749	2.2
	1986	1920	66	2280	94023	96303	2.4
	1986	1930	56	3833	112546	116379	3.3
	1986	1940	46	3531	84783	88314	4.0
	1986	1950	36	1583	31289	32872	4.8
	1991	1920	71	2477	103170	105647	2.3
	1991	1930	61	5403	164798	170201	3.2
	1991	1940	51	5734	150390	156124	3.7
	1991	1950	41	4002	91963	95965	4.2
	1991	1960	31	1716	38220	39936	4.3
	1996	1920	76	1986	85840	87826	2.3
	1996	1930	66	4993	160733	165726	3.0
	1996	1940	56	6782	191057	197839	3.4
	1996	1950	46	7245	143678	150923	4.8
	1996	1960	36	3775	80239	84014	4.5
	2001	1920	81	1178	57196	58374	2.0
	2001	1930	71	4453	127389	131842	3.4
	2001	1940	61	6184	159054	165238	3.7
	2001	1950	51	7657	158972	166629	4.6
	2001	1960	41	6137	122372	128509	4.8

References

Aitchison, J. (2001). *Language Change: Progress or Decay?* (3rd ed.). Cambridge: Cambridge University Press.

Aizawa, M. (2012). Gairaigo Iikae Teian to wa Nan de Atta ka [What was the "suggestions for paraphrasing loanwords"?]. In M. Jinnouchi, M. Tanaka & M. Aizawa (Eds.), *Gairaigo Kenkyuu no Shintenkai* [*New Developments in Japanese Loanword Studies*] (pp. 133–147). Tokyo: Ohfu.

Altmann, G., von Buttlar, H., Rott, W., & Strauss, U. (1983). A Law of Change in Language. *Quantitative Linguistics, 18 (Historical Linguistics)*, 104–115.

Arakawa, S. (1943). *Gairaigo Gaisetsu* [*Outline of Loanwords*]. Tokyo: Sanseido.

Asahara, M., Maekawa, K., Imada, M., Kato, S., & Konishi, H. (2014). Archiving and Analysing Techniques of the Ultra-Large-Scale Web-Based Corpus Project in NINJAL, Japan. *Alexandria*, 25(1-2), 129–148.

Bailey, G., Wikle, T., Tillery, J., & Sand, L. (1991). The Apparent Time Construct. *Language Variation and Change*, 3(3), 241–264.

BBK. (1995). *Kokugo ni Kansuru Yoron Choosa: Heisei 7* [*Opinion Poll on the National Language: Heisei 7*]. Tokyo: BBK.

BBK. (1999). *Kokugo ni Kansuru Yoron Choosa: Heisei 10* [*Opinion Poll on the National Language: Heisei 10*]. Tokyo: BBK.

BBK. (2000). *Kokugo ni Kansuru Yoron Choosa: Heisei 11* [*Opinion Poll on the National Language: Heisei 11*]. Tokyo: BBK.

BBK. (2003). *Kokugo ni Kansuru Yoron Choosa: Heisei 14* [*Opinion Poll on the National Language: Heisei 14*]. Tokyo: BBK.

BBK. (2008). *Kokugo ni Kansuru Yoron Choosa: Heisei 19* [*Opinion Poll on the National Language: Heisei 19*]. Tokyo: BBK.

BBK. (2009). *Kokugo ni Kansuru Yoron Choosa: Heisei 20* [*Opinion Poll on the National Language: Heisei 20*]. Tokyo: BBK.

BBK. (2013). *Kokugo ni Kansuru Yoron Choosa: Heisei 24* [*Opinion Poll on the National Language: Heisei 24*]. Tokyo: BBK.

BBK. (2014). *Kokugo ni Kansuru Yoron Choosa: Heisei 25* [*Opinion Poll on the National Language: Heisei 25*]. Tokyo: BBK.

Bell, A. (1984). Language Style as Audience Design. *Language in Society*, 13(2), 145–204.

Cedergren, H. J., & Sankoff, D. (1974). Variable Rules: Performance as a Statistical Reflection of Competence. *Language*, 50(2), 333–355.

Chambers, J. K. (1990). The Canada-US Border as a Vanishing Isogloss: The Evidence of *Chesterfield*. *Journal of English Linguistics*, 23(1-2), 155–166.

Chambers, J. K., & Trudgill, P. (1980). *Dialectology*. Cambridge: Cambridge University Press.

Eckert, P. (1988). Adolescent Social Structure and the Spread of Linguistic Change. *Language in Society*, 17(2), 183–207.

Hashimoto, W. (2010). *Gendai Nihongo ni Okeru Gairaigo no Ryooteki-Suii ni Kansuru Kenkyuu [The Increasing Process of Loanwords in Modern Japanese]*. Tokyo: Hituzi Syobo.

Haspelmath, M. (2009). Lexical Borrowing: Concepts and Issues. In M. Haspelmath, & U. Tadmor (Eds.), *Loanwords in the World's Languages: A Comparative Handbook* (pp. 35–54). Berlin: De Gruyter Mouton.

Haugen, E. (1953). *The Norwegian Language in America, Vol. 2*. Philadelphia: University of Pennsylvania Press.

Hibiya, J. (1988a). A Quantitative Study of Tokyo Japanese. Doctral Dissertation, University of Pennsylvania.

Hibiya, J. (1988b). Varieeshon Riron [Variationist Theory]. *Gengo Kenkyu [Journal of the Linguistic Society of Japan]*, 93, 155–171.

Hibiya, J. (1995). The Velar Nasal in Tokyo Japanese: A Case of Diffusion from Above. *Language Variation and Change*, 7(2), 139–152.

Inoue, F. (2000). *Tohoku Hoogen no Hensen [Change of Tohoku Dialects]*. Tokyo: Akiyama Shoten.

Irie, S. (2010). *Chūo-Kōron* 101 Nen no Goi [Research on Vocabulary of *Chūo-Kōron* in the Last 101 Years]. *Dodai Goi Kenkyu [Doshisha Lexicology]*, 13, 9–14.

Irwin, M. (2011). *Loanwords in Japanese*. Amsterdam: John Benjamins Publishing.

Ishii, H. (1990). *Chūo-Kōron* 1986 Nen no Yoogo [Words Used in the Magazine *Chūo-Kōron* in 1986]. In NINJAL (Ed.), *Kenkyuu Hookoku Shuu [Occasional Papers 11]* (pp. 1–40). Tokyo: NINJAL.

Ishino, H. (1983). *Gendai Gairaigo koo [Discussions on Contemporary Loanwords]*. Tokyo: Taishukan Shoten.

Ishiwata, T. (1965). Gairaigo no Fukyuudo: Matsue-Shi de no Choosa kara [The Diffusion of Loanwords: A Survey in Matsue City]. *Gengo Seikatsu*, 161, 55–62.

Ishiwata, T. (2001). *Gairaigo no Soogooteki Kenkyuu [Comprehensive Study of Loanwords]*. Tokyo: Tokyodo Shuppan.

ISM & NINJAL. (2014). *Dai 4 Kai Tsuruoka-Shi ni Okeru Gengo Choosa Vol.1: Onsei/On'in Hen [The 4th Linguistic Survey in Tsuruoka City, Japan Vol.1: Phonetics & Phonology]*. Tokyo: ISM & NINJAL.

ISM & NINJAL. (2015). *Dai 4 Kai Tsuruoka-Shi ni Okeru Gengo Choosa Vol.2: Goi/Bunpoo Hen [The 4th Linguistic Survey in Tsuruoka City, Japan Vol.2: Vocabulary & Grammar]*. Tokyo: ISM & NINJAL.

Jinnouchi, M. (1993). *Saji to Supuun*: Gairaigoka to Meimei no Yure [*Saji or Supuun*: A Study on Variation in Denomination Caused by Loan Words]. *Gengo Bunka Ronkyu [Studies in Languages and Cultures]*, 4, 47–54.

Jinnouchi, M. (2007). *Gairaigo no Shakaigengogaku: Nihongo no Gurookaru na Kangae Kata [Sociolinguistic Studies of Japanese Foreign Words: From the Global*

Point of View]. Kyoto: Sekaishiso-sha.

Kageyama, T., & Saito, M. (2016). Vocabulary Strata and Word Formation Processes. In T. Kageyama, & H. Kishimoto (Eds.), *Handbook of Japanese Lexicon and Word Formation* (pp. 11–50). Boston: De Gruyter Mouton.

Kajiki, M., Iwaya, A., Kashiwakura, Y., & Asamatsu, A. (1995). Kokka ni Yoru Gairaigo Kisei [State Control over the Use of Words of Foreign Origin]. In NHK (Ed.), *NHK Hoosoo Bunka Choosa Kenkyuu Nenpoo 40* [*The NHK Annual Bulletin of Broadcasting Culture Research 40*] (pp. 191–249). Tokyo: NHK.

Kim, E. (2011). *Nijusseiki Koohan no Shinbun Goi ni Okeru Gairaigo no Kihongoka* [*Shift of the Loanwors to Basic Words in the Japanese Newspaper Vocabulary in the Second Half of the 20th Century*]. Osaka: Osaka University.

Kim, E. (2013). Gairaigo Doomeishi *Chekku* no Kihongoka [Shift of the Loan Verbal Nown *Chekku* to Basic Words]. In M. Aizawa (Ed.), *Gendai Nihongo no Dootai Kenkyuu* [*Study on Dinamics of Contemporary Japanese*] (pp. 29–45). Tokyo: Ohfu.

Koiso, H., Tanaka, Y., Watanabe, R., & Den, Y. (2016a). A Large-Scale Corpus of Everyday Japanese Conversation: On Methodology for Recording Naturally Occurring Conversations. *Proceedings of LREC 2016 Workshop on Casual Talk among Humans and Machines*, 10, 9–12. Retrieved from ⟨http://www.lrec-conf. org/proceedings/lrec2016/workshops/LREC2016Workshop-Just%20Talking_ Proceedings.pdf⟩ on August 10, 2016.

Koiso, H., Tsuchida, T., Watanabe, R., Yokomori, D., Aizawa, M., & Den, Y. (2016b). Kinkoo Kaiwa Koopasu Sekkei no Tame no Ichinichi no Kaiwa Koodoo ni Kansuru Kiso Choosa [Survey of Conversational Behavior: Towards the Design of a Balanced Corpus of Conversational Japanese]. *Kokuritsu Kokugo Kenkyuujo Ronshuu* [*NINJAL Research Papers*], 10, 85–106.

Kunihiro, T., Inoue, F., & Long, D. (Eds.). (1999). *Takeshi Shibata, Sociolinguistics in Japanese Contexts*. Berlin: Mouton de Gruyter.

Kuya, A. (2013a). Gendai Nihongo ni Okeru Gairaigo no Shintoodo: Gairaigo Shiyoo ni Kansuru Ishiki to Koodoo no Shakaigengogaku-Teki Koosatsu [Loanword Diffusion in Contemporary Japanese: A Sociolinguistic Discussion on Language Attitudes toward, and Behavior on, the Use of Loanwords]. *Shakaigengokagakukai Dai 32 Kai Taikai Happyoo Ronbunshuu* [*Proceedings of the 32nd Meeting of the Japanese Association of Sociolinguistic Science (JASS 32)*], 136–139.

Kuya, A. (2013b). Gendai Kakikotoba ni Okeru Gairaigo no Kyoojiteki Bunpu: *Keesu* o Jirei to Shite [Synchronic Distribution of Loanwords in Contemporary Written Japanese: A Case Study of *Keesu* ('Case')]. *Kokuritsu Kokugo Kenkyuujo Ronshuu* [*NINJAL Research Papers*], 6, 45–65.

Kuya, A. (2016a). Gairaigo Shiyoo ni Kakaru Sutairu no Seiyaku: *Sapooto* to Kisongo to no Tsukaiwake ni Miru Washanai Barieeshon [Stylistic Constraints on the Use of Loanwords in Japanese: The Alternation between *Sapooto* and Its Native

Equivalents as Intra-Speaker Variation]. *Shakai Gengo Kagaku* [*The Japanese Journal of Language in Society*], 19(1), 190–206.

Kuya, A. (2016b). Mikakejoo no Jikan o Riyoo Shita Gairaigo Shiyoo Ishiki no Tsuu-ji Henka Yosoku [Predicting the Diffusion of Western Loanwords in Japanese Based on the Apparent-Time Hypothesis]. *Nihongo no Kenkyuu* [*Studies in the Japanese Language*], 12(4), 69–85.

Labov, W. (1963). The Social Motivation of a Sound Change. *Word*, 19(3), 273–309.

Labov, W. (1966). *The Social Stratification of English in New York City*. Washington: Center for Applied Linguistics.

Labov, W. (1972). *Sociolinguistic Patterns*. Philadelphia: University of Pennsylvania Press.

Labov, W. (1978). Where Does the Linguistic Variable Stop?: A Response to Beatriz Lavandera. *Working Papers in Sociolinguistics*, 44. Austin: Southwest Educational Development Laboratory.

Labov, W. (1982). Building on Empirical Foundations. *Perspectives on Historical Linguistics*, 24, 17–92.

Labov, W. (1984). Field Methods of the Project on Linguistic Change and Variation. In J. Baugh, & J. Sherzer (Eds.), *Language in Use: Readings in Sociolinguistics* (pp. 28–53). Englewood Cliffs, NJ: Prentice-Hall.

Labov, W. (1994). *Principles of Linguistic Change (Vol.1): Internal Factors*. Oxford: Wiley-Blackwell.

Labov, W. (2001a). *Principles of Linguistic Change (Vol.2): Social Factors*. Oxford: Wiley-Blackwell.

Labov, W. (2001b). The Anatomy of Style-Shifting. In P. Eckert, & J. R. Rickford (Eds.), *Style and Sociolinguistic Variation* (pp. 85–108). Cambridge: Cambridge University Press.

Labov, W. (2004). Quantitative Analysis of Linguistic Variation. In U. Ammon, N. Dittmar & K. J. Mattheier (Eds.), *Sociolinguistics, Vol. 1: An International Handbook of the Science of Language and Society* (2nd ed.) (pp. 6–21). Berlin: De Gruyter Mouton.

Lavandera, B. (1978). Where Does the Sociolinguistic Variable Stop? *Language in Society*, 7, 171–182.

Loveday, L. J. (1996). *Language Contact in Japan: A Socio-Linguistic History*. Oxford: Clarendon Press.

Maeda, T. (2005). Yuusoo Choosa no Tokuchoo ni Kansuru Ichi Kenkyuu: Mensetsu Choosa Hoo to no Hikaku o Chuushin to Shite [A Study on the Characteristics of Mail Survey: A Comparison with Face-to-Face Interviewing], *Tookei Suuri* [*Proceedings of the Institute of Statistical Mathematics*], 53(1), 57–81.

Maekawa, K. (2003). Corpus of Spontaneous Japanese: Its Design and Evaluation. *SSPR 2003*, paper MM02.

Maekawa, K., Yamazaki, M., Ogiso, T., Maruyama, T., Ogura, H., Kashino, W.,

Koiso, H., Yamaguchi, M., Tanaka, M., & Den, Y. (2014). Balanced Corpus of Contemporary Written Japanese. *Language Resources and Evaluation*, 48(2), 345–371.

Maruyama, T. (2012). Dai-Kibo Koopasu no Riyoo to Meta-Deeta no Yakuwari [The Role of Metadata in the Analysis of Large-Scale Corpora]. *Dai 1 Kai Koopasu Nihongogaku Waakushoppu Yokooshuu [Proceedings of the 1st Workshop on Corpus-Based Japanese Linguistics]*, 203–210.

Matsuda, K. (1993). Dissecting Analogical Leveling Quantitatively: The Case of the Innovative Potential Suffix in Tokyo Japanese. *Language Variation and Change*, 5(1), 1–34.

Matsuda, K. (1995). Variable Zero-Marking of (o) in Tokyo Japanese. Doctoral Dissertation, University of Pennsylvania.

Matsuda, K. (2013). Sahen Dooshi no Godan Katsuyooka, Kamiichidan Katsuyooka no Genjoo [Changes of *Sahen* Verbs into *Godan* and *Kamiichidan* Verbs]. In M. Aizawa (Ed.), *Gendai Nihongo no Dootai Kenkyuu [Study on Dinamics of Contemporary Japanese]* (pp. 69–89). Tokyo: Ohfu.

Meyerhoff, M. (2011). *Introducing Sociolinguistics* (2nd ed.). London: Routledge.

Miyata, K. (2007). Gairaigo *Meritto* to Sono Ruigigo no Imi Hikaku [Comparison in Meaning between the Loanword *Meritto* and Its Synonyms]. In NINJAL (Ed.), *Kookyoo Baitai no Gairaigo: "Gairaigo Iikae Teian" o Sasaeru Choosa Kenkyuu [Loanwords in the Public Madia: Basic Researches for "Suggestions for Paraphrasing Loanwords"]* (pp. 402–409). Tokyo: NINJAL.

Miyata, K., & Tanaka, M. (2006). Gairaigo *Risuku* to Sono Ruigigo no Imi Hikaku [Comparison in Meaning between the Loanword *Risuku* and Its Synonyms]. *Gengo Shori Gakkai Dai 12 Kai Nenji Taikai Happyoo Ronbunshuu [Proceedings of the Twelfth Annual Meeting of the Association for Natural Language Processing]*, 600–603.

Mogi, T. (2011). Koopasu o Mochiita Gairaigo Sahen Dooshi no Bunseki: *Katto-Suru* o Rei to Shite [A Corpus-Based Study on Loanword Verbs in Japanese: A Case Study of *Katto-suru* (< *Cut*)]. *Tokutei Ryooiki Kenkyuu "Nihongo Koopasu" Heisei 22 Nendo Kookai Waakushoppu Yokooshuu*, 103–110.

Mogi, T. (2015). Koopasu o Mochiita Gairaigo Sahen Dooshi no Bunseki: *Maaku-suru* o Rei to Shite [A Corpus-Based Study on Loanword Verbs in Japanese: A Case Study of *Maaku-Suru* (< *Mark*)]. *Kumamoto Daigaku Bungakubu Ronsoo*, 106, 83–95.

Mori, H. (2013). Gendai Nihongo Kakikotoba Kinkoo Koopasu "Toshokan Shoseki" no Seinendai Betsu Bunpu wa Nani o Imi Shite Iru no ka: "*Denai*", "*Dewanai*", "*Janai*" no Shiyoo Wariai kara Mita Ichi Koosatsu [What Does the Birth Year Distribution in the Library Sub-Corpus in the BCCWJ Represent: A Study Based on the Percentage of "*Denai*", "*Dewanai*" and "*Janai*"]. *Dai 4 Kai Koopasu Nihongogaku Waakushoppu Yokooshuu [Proceedings of the 4th Workshop on Corpus-*

Based Japanese Linguistics], 275–284.

Mougeon, R., & Beniak, E. (1991). *Linguistic Consequences of Language Contact and Restriction: The Case of French in Ontario, Canada*. Oxford: Clarendon Press.

Myers-Scotton, C. (1993). *Duelling Languages: Grammatical Structure in Codeswitching*. Oxford: Clarendon Press.

Myers-Scotton, C. (2006). *Multiple Voices: An Introduction to Bilingualism*. Malden, MA: Blackwell.

Nambu, S. (2007). Teiryooteki Bunseki ni Motozuku *Ga/No* Kootai Saikoo [Reconsideration of Ga/No Conversion Based on a Quantitative Analysis]. *Gengo Kenkyu* [*Journal of the Linguistic Society of Japan*], 131, 115–149.

Nambu, S. (2014). Koopasu Gengogaku Oyobi Jikken Gengogaku ni Motozuku Kakujoshi Kootai no Bunseki [On the Use of Case Particles in Japanese: Corpus and Experimental Studies]. Doctoral Dissertation, Osaka University.

NHK. (1980). *NHK Bunken Geppoo* [*Monthly Bulletin of the Radio & Television Culture Research Institute*], No. 30-2. Tokyo: NHK.

NHK. (1986). *Hoosoo Kenkyuu to Choosa* [*The NHK Monthly Report on Broadcast Research*], No. 36-7. Tokyo: NHK.

NHK. (1991). *Hoosoo Kenkyuu to Choosa* [*The NHK Monthly Report on Broadcast Research*], No. 41-8. Tokyo: NHK.

NHK. (1995). *Hoosoo Kenkyuu to Choosa* [*The NHK Monthly Report on Broadcast Research*], No. 45-9. Tokyo: NHK.

NHK. (1996). *Hoosoo Kenkyuu to Choosa* [*The NHK Monthly Report on Broadcast Research*], No. 46-9. Tokyo: NHK.

NINJAL. (1957). *Keigo to Keigo Ishiki* [*Socio-Psychological Survey on Japanese Polite Expression*]. Tokyo: Shuei Shuppan.

NINJAL. (1962). *Gendai Zasshi 90 Shu no Yoogo Yooji I* [*Vocabulary and Chinese Characters in Ninety Magazines of Today I*]. Tokyo: NINJAL.

NINJAL. (1963). *Gendai Zasshi 90 Shu no Yoogo Yooji II* [*Vocabulary and Chinese Characters in Ninety Magazines of Today II*]. Tokyo: NINJAL.

NINJAL. (1964). *Gendai Zasshi 90 Shu no Yoogo Yooji III* [*Vocabulary and Chinese Characters in Ninety Magazines of Today III*]. Tokyo: NINJAL.

NINJAL. (1983). *Keigo to Keigo Ishiki: Okazaki ni Okeru 20 Nen Mae to no Hikaku* [*Socio-Psychological Survey on Japanese Polite Expression: After 20 Years from the Preceding Survey in Okazaki City, Aichi Pref.*]. Tokyo: Sanseido.

NINJAL. (1987). *Zasshi Yoogo no Hensen* [*Changes in the Language of a Magazine*]. Tokyo: NINJAL.

NINJAL. (1995). *Terebi Hoosoo no Goi Choosa 1* [*Vocabulary Survey of Television Broadcasts Vol. 1*]. Tokyo: Shuei Shuppan.

NINJAL. (1997). *Terebi Hoosoo no Goi Choosa 2* [*Vocabulary Survey of Television Broadcasts Vol. 2*]. Tokyo: Dainippon Tosho.

NINJAL. (1999). *Terebi Hoosoo no Goi Choosa 3* [*Vocabulary Survey of Television*

Broadcasts Vol. 3]. Tokyo: Dainippon Tosho.

NINJAL. (2004). *Gairaigo ni Kansuru Ishiki Choosa: Zenkoku Choosa [The National Survey on Attitudes to Loanwords].* Tokyo: NINJAL.

NINJAL. (2005a). *Gairaigo ni Kansuru Zenkoku Ishiki Choosa II [The National Survey on Attitudes to Loanwords II].* Tokyo: NINJAL.

NINJAL. (2005b). *Gendai Zasshi no Goi Choosa: 1994 Nen Hakkoo 70 Shi [A Survey of Vocabulary in Contemporary Magazines (1994)].* Tokyo: NINJAL.

NINJAL (2006). *Nihongo Hanashikotoba Koopasu no Koochikuhoo [Construction of the Corpus of Spontaneous Japanese].* Tokyo: NINJAL.

NINJAL. (2007a). *Chiiki Shakai no Gengo Seikatsu [Social Aspects of Language in a Local Community].* Tokyo: NINJAL.

NINJAL. (2007b). *Kookyoo Baitai no Gairaigo: "Gairaigo Iikae Teian" o Sasaeru Choosa Kenkyuu [Loanwords in the Public Madia: Basic Researches for "Suggestions for Paraphrasing Loanwords"].* Tokyo: NINJAL.

NINJAL. (2010a). *Keigo to Keigo Ishiki: Aicihken Okazaki-shi ni Okeru dai 3 ji Choosa [Socio-Psychological Survey on Japanese Polite Expression: The 3rd Survey in Okazaki City, Aichi Pref.] No. 1.* Tokyo: NINJAL.

NINJAL. (2010b). *Keigo to Keigo Ishiki: Aicihken Okazaki-shi ni Okeru dai 3 ji Choosa [Socio-Psychological Survey on Japanese Polite Expression: The 3rd Survey in Okazaki City, Aichi Pref.] No. 2.* Tokyo: NINJAL.

NINJAL. (2010c). *Keigo to Keigo Ishiki: Aicihken Okazaki-shi ni Okeru dai 3 ji Choosa [Socio-Psychological Survey on Japanese Polite Expression: The 3rd Survey in Okazaki City, Aichi Pref.] No. 3.* Tokyo: NINJAL.

NINJAL. (2010d). *Keigo to Keigo Ishiki: Aicihken Okazaki-shi ni Okeru dai 3 ji Choosa [Socio-Psychological Survey on Japanese Polite Expression: The 3rd Survey in Okazaki City, Aichi Pref.] No. 4.* Tokyo: NINJAL.

NINJAL. (2011b). *BCCWJ Riyoo no Tebiki 1.0 [BCCWJ User's Manual: Version 1.0].* Tokyo: NINJAL. (See the *Dictionaries & Corpora* section for NINJAL (2011a).)

NSDKK. (1977). *Kokugo ni Kansuru Yoron Choosa: Showa 52 [Opinion Poll on the National Language: Showa 52].* Tokyo: NSDKK.

Pope, J., Meyerhoff, M., & Ladd, D. R. (2007). Forty Years of Language Change on Martha's Vineyard. *Language, 83*(3), 615–627.

Rickford, J. R., & McNair-Knox, F. (1994). Addressee- and Topic-Influenced Style Shift: A Quantitative Sociolinguistic Study. In D. Biber, & E. Finegan (Eds.), *Sociolinguistic Perspectives on Register* (pp. 235–276). Oxford: Oxford University Press.

Rogers, E. M. (2003). *Diffusion of Innovations* (5th ed.). New York: Free Press.

Sanada, H. (2002). *Kindai Nihongo ni Okeru Gakujutsu Yoogo no Seiritsu to Teichaku [A Quantitative Study of the Popularization of Meiji Era Scholarly Terms].* Tokyo: Junbunsha.

Sanada, H. (2008). Gengo Henka no S-Ji Kaabu: Kaiseki Shuhoo no Hikaku to Sono

Tekiyoo Jirei [S-Curve Model of Language Change: Methods and Examples]. *Saitama Gakuen Daigaku Kiyoo: Ningen Gakubu-Hen [Bulletin of Saitama Gakuen University: Faculty of Humanities]*, 8, 1–11.

Sankoff, D. (1982). Sociolinguistic Method and Linguistic theory. *Logic, Methodology and Philosophy of Science VI: Proceedings of the Sixth International Congress of Logic, Methodology and Philosophy of Science*, 677–689.

Sankoff, D., & Laberge, S. (1978). The Linguistic Market and the Statistical Explanation of Variability. In D. Sankoff (Ed.), *Linguistic Variation: Models and Methods* (pp. 239–250). New York: Academic Press.

Sankoff, G. (1973). Above and Beyond Phonology in Variable Rules. In C. N. Bailey, & R. W. Shuy (Eds.), *New Ways of Analyzing Variation in English* (pp. 44–61). Washington: Georgetown University Press.

Sankoff, G. (2005). Cross-Sectional and Longitudinal Studies in Sociolinguistics. In N. Dittmar, K. J. Mattheier & U. Ammon (Eds.), *Sociolinguistics, Vol. 2: An International Handbook of the Science of Language and Society* (2nd ed.) (pp. 1003–1013). Berlin: Mouton de Gruyter.

Sankoff, G. (2006). Age: Apparent Time and Real Time. In K. Brown (Ed.), *Encyclopedia of Language and Linguistics Vol.1* (2nd ed.) (pp. 110–116). Amsterdam: Elsevier.

Sankoff, G., & Thibault, P. (1980). The Alternation between the Auxiliaries *Avoir* and *Etre* in Montreal French. In G. Sankoff (Ed.), *The Social Life of Language* (pp. 311–345). Philadelphia: University of Pennsylvania Press.

Sano, S. (2008). Nihongo Hanashikotoba Koopasu ni Arawareru *Sa-Ire Kotoba* ni Kansuru Suuryooteki Bunseki [A Quantitative Analysis of *Sa*-Insertion in Corpus of Spontaneous Japanese]. *Gengo Kenkyu [Journal of the Linguistic Society of Japan]*, 133, 77–106.

Sano, S. (2009). The Roles of Internal and External Factors and the Mechanism of Analogical Leveling: Variationist and Probabilistic OT Approach to Ongoing Language Change in Japanese Voice System. Doctoral Dissertation, Sophia University.

Sano, S. (2011). Real-Time Demonstration of the Interaction among Internal and External Factors in Language Change: A Corpus Study. *Gengo Kenkyu [Journal of the Linguistic Society of Japan]*, 139, 1–27.

Sano, S., & Kawahara, S. (2013). A Corpus-Based Study of Geminate Devoicing in Japanese: The Role of the OCP and External Factors. *Gengo Kenkyu [Journal of the Linguistic Society of Japan]*, 144, 103–118.

Schilling-Estes, N. (2002). Investigating Stylistic Variation. In J. K. Chambers, P. Trudgill & N. Schilling-Estes (Eds.), *The Handbook of Language Variation and Change* (pp. 375–401). Oxford: Blackwell.

Shibata, T. (1978). *Shakai Gengogaku no Kadai [Topics for Sociolinguistics]*. Tokyo: Sanseido.

Shimooka, K. (2013). *Kutsurogu* to *Rirakkusu-Suru* [The Native Japanese "Relax" and the Loanword "Relax"]. *Nihon Gengo Bunka Kenkyuu*, 17, 10–24.

Sohn, H. (1999). *The Korean Language*. Cambridge: Cambridge University Press.

Soomushoo Tookeikyoku (Statistics Bureau, Ministry of Internal Affairs and Communications, Japan). *Heisei 12 Nen Kokusei Choosa no Shuyoo Kekka [Results of the Concencsus in Heisei 12]*. Soomushoo Tookeikyoku. Retrieved from ⟨http://www.e-stat.go.jp/SG1/estat/GL08020103.do?_toGL08020103_&tclassID=000000030587&cycleCode=0&requestSender=search⟩ on March 29, 2016.

Tagliamonte, S. (2006). *Analysing Sociolinguistic Variation*. Cambridge: Cambridge University Press.

Takano, S. (2012). Kotoba no Sutairu o Rikai Shi Ooyoo Suru [Understanding and Making Use of Language Style]. In J. Hibiya (Ed.), *Hajimete Manabu Shakai Gengogaku [Introduction to Sociolinguistics]* (pp. 248–269). Kyoto: Minerva Shobo.

Tanaka, M. (2007). Kango, Wago to Hikaku Shita Gairaigo ni Taisuru Ishiki [The Public Attitude to Loanwords Compared with That to Sino-Japanese Words and Native-Japanese Words]. In NINJAL (Ed.), *Kookyoo Baitai no Gairaigo: "Gairaigo Iikae Teian" o Sasaeru Choosa Kenkyuu [Loanwords in the Public Madia: Basic Researches for "Suggestions for Paraphrasing Loanwords"]* (pp. 302–310). Tokyo: NINJAL.

Tanaka, M. (2012). Kokugo Kyooiku ni Okeru Gairaigo: Koopasu ni Yoru Ruikeika o Tooshite [Loanwords in Japanese Language Teaching: A Corpus-Based Typological Approach]. In M. Jinnouchi, M. Tanaka & M. Aizawa (Eds.), *Gairaigo Kenkyuu no Shintenkai [New Developments in Japanese Loanword Studies]* (pp. 224–242). Tokyo: Ohfu.

Trudgill, P. (1974). *The Social Differentiation of English in Norwich*. Cambridge: Cambrigde University Press.

Trudgill, P. (2000). *Sociolinguistics* (4th ed.). London: Penguin.

Watanabe, R., Tanaka, Y., & Koiso, H. (2015). Nihongo Hanashikotoba Koopasu UniDic Ban Keitairon Joohoo no Koochiku [Constructing the UniDic Version of the Morphological Information of *Corpus of Spontaneous Japanese*]. *Dai 8 Kai Koopasu Nihongogaku Waakushoppu Yokooshuu [Proceedings of the 8th Workshop on Corpus-Based Japanese Linguistics]*, 279–288.

Weiner, E. J., & Labov, W. (1983). Constraints on the Agentless Passive. *Journal of Linguistics*, 19(1), 29–58.

Weinreich, U. (1968). *Languages in Contact: Findings and Problems*. The Hague: Mouton.

Weinreich, U., Labov, W., & Herzog, M. I. (1968). Empirical Foundations for a Theory of Language Change. In W. P. Lehmann, & Y. Malkiel (Eds.), *Directions for Historical Linguistics* (pp. 95–195). Austin: University of Texas Press.

Xiao, R., & McEnery, T. (2006). Collocation, Semantic Prosody, and Near Synonymy: A Cross-Linguistic Perspective. *Applied Linguistics*, 27(1), 103–129.

Yamaguchi, M., Takada, T., Kitamura, M., Mabuchi, Y., Oshima, H., Kobayashi,

M., & Nishibe, M. (2011). *"Gendai Nihongo Kakikotoba Kinkoo Koopasu" ni Okeru Denshika Foomatto Ver. 2.2 [Electronization of Data in BCCWJ Ver. 2.2]* (No. JC-D-10-04). Tokyo: NINJAL.

Yang, M. (2005). Nikkan Daigakusei no Ankeeto kara Mita Keiyooshi-Kei Gairaigo no Juyoo Ishiki [A Study on the Awareness of Foreign Origin Adjectives through the Survey on Japanese and Korean University Students]. *Gengo Kagaku Ronshuu [Journal of Linguistic Science, Tohoko University]*, 9, 83–93.

Yang, M. (2007). Gairaigo o Meguru Ishiki ni Kansuru Nikkan Taishoo Kenkyuu [A Contrastive Study between Japanese and Korean concerning Consciousness of Loan Words]. *Kokugogaku Kenkyuu [The Japanese Language Review]*, 46, 73–85.

Yang, M. (2012). Nihongo to Kankokugo no Gairaigo no Juyoo Ishiki: Imeeji Choosa no Bunseki [Receptiveness to Loanwords in Japanese and Korean: An Analysis of an Impression Survey on Loanwords]. In M. Jinnouchi, M. Tanaka & M. Aizawa (Eds.), *Gairaigo Kenkyuu no Shintenkai [New Developments in Japanese Loanword Studies]* (pp. 148–167). Tokyo: Ohfu.

Yokoyama, S. (2006). Itaiji Senkoo ni Okeru Tanjun Sesshoku Kooka to Ippan Taioo Hoosoku no Kankei [Mere Exposure Effect and Generalized Matching Law for Preference of *Kanji* Form]. *Keiryoo Kokugogaku [Mathematical Linguistics]*, 25(5), 199–214.

Yokoyama, S., Asahi, Y., & Sanada, H. (2008). Kioku Moderu ni Yoru Keigo Ishiki no Henka Yosoku [New Method of Statistical Analysis for Longitudinal Survey Data on Honorifics Use by Psychological Model]. *Shakai Gengo Kagaku [The Japanese Journal of Language in Society]*, 11(1), 64–75.

Yokoyama, S., & Sanada, H. (2007). Tahenryoo S-Ji Kaabu ni Yoru Gengo Henka no Kaiseki [Multiple Logistic Regression Analysis for Formulating a Change in Language]. *Keiryoo Kokugogaku [Mathematical Linguistics]*, 26(3), 79–93.

Yokoyama, S., & Sanada, H. (2010). Gengo no Shoogai Shuutoku Moderu ni Yoru Kyootsuugoka Yosoku [Predictions of Dialect Standardization by the "Life-Long Assimilation of Language Change" Model]. *Nihongo no Kenkyuu [Studies in the Japanese Language]*, 6(2), 31–45.

Yokoyama, S., & Wada, Y. (2006). A Logistic Regression Model of Variant Preference in Japanese *Kanji*: An Integration of Mere Exposure Effect and the Generalized Matching Law. *Glottometrics*, 12, 63–74.

Zajonc, R. B. (1968). Attitudinal Effects of Mere Exposure. *Journal of Personality and Social Psychology*, 9(2-2), 1–27.

Dictionaries & Corpora

Horiuchi, K. (Ed.). (2011). *Gendai Yoogo-no Kisochishiki Katakana Gairaigo/Ruigo Jiten* (4th ed.). Tokyo: Jiyu Kokumin Sha.

Kenbo, H., Ichikawa, T., Hida, Y., Yamazaki, M., Iima, H., & Shioda, T. (Eds.). (2014). *Sanseido Kokugo Jiten* (7th ed.). Tokyo: Sanseido.

Masuda, K. (Ed.). (1974). *Kenkyusha's New Japanese-English Dictionary* (4th ed.). Tokyo: Kenkyusha.

Nihon Kokugo Daijiten dai 2 han henshuu iinkai, & Shogakukan kokugo jiten henshubu (Eds.). (2000-2002). *Nihon Kokugo Daijiten* (2nd ed.). Tokyo: Shogakukan.

NINJAL. (2011a). *Balanced Corpus of Contemporary Written Japanese (BCCWJ).* Tokyo: NINJAL.

NINJAL & NICT. (2004). *Corpus of Spontaneous Japnese (CSJ).* NINJAL; NICT.

Nishio, M., Iwabuchi, E., & Mizutani, S. (Eds.). (2009). *Iwanami Kokugo Jiten* (7th ed.). Tokyo: Iwanami Shoten.

Sanseido Henshuujo (Ed.). (2010). *Concise Katakanago Jiten* [*Sanseido's Concise Dictionary of Katakana Words*] (web) (4th ed.). Tokyo: Sanseido. Retrieved from ⟨http://www.sanseido.net/⟩ on May 4–16, 2015, and June 7–17, 2016.

Shinmura, I. (Ed.). (2008). *Kojien* (6th ed.). Tokyo: Iwanami Shoten.

Shinozaki, K., Aizawa, M., Oshima, M., & Hayashi, S. (Eds.). (2012). *Reikai Shin Kokugo Jiten* (8th ed.). Tokyo: Sanseido.

Yamada, T., Shibata, T., Sakai, K., Kuramochi, Y., Yamada, A., Uwano, Z., Ijima, M., & Sasahara, H. (Eds.). (2011). *Shinmeikai Kokugo Jiten* (web) (7th ed.). Tokyo: Sanseido. Retrieved from ⟨http://www.sanseido.net/⟩ on May 4–16, 2015, and June 7–17, 2016.

Summary in Japanese

現代日本語語彙の「カタカナ語化」を
めぐる変異理論的考察[1]

1 既存語彙の新たな変異形としてのカタカナ語

8世紀（奈良時代）以降の中国語からの語彙借入（lexical borrowing）とその土着化（すなわち「漢語」の定着）を借用語による日本語語彙の第一次変容とすれば、16世紀後半のポルトガル語に端を発する西欧諸語からの語彙借入は、借用語による日本語語彙の第二次変容と考えることができる。中でも20世紀後半以降の英語語彙の流入は、現代日本語語彙体系に量・質共に多大な影響を及ぼしていると推論される。

語彙借用には、（1）受け入れ言語側のレキシコンの不足を埋めるためのcultural borrowingと、（2）意味的に対応する語彙が受け入れ言語側にすでに存在するにもかかわらず生じるcore borrowingの2つがある（Myers-Scotton 2006）。西欧諸語（特に英語）からの借用語（Western loanwords / LW、以下「カタカナ語[2]」）のうち（2）のタイプが日本語に定着した結果、現代日本語においては、例文（1a・1b）に示すようにカタカナ語が既存語彙[3]と意味的に競合し交替可能となるケースが少なくない。変異理論（バリエーション理論）の枠組み（variationist framework）では、このような文脈において、カタカナ語を、既存語にとっての新たな変異形（variant）と捉えることが可能である。

(1) a. 持ち家 = "家を所有" することのメリットとは、　　　　　(PB13_00092)
　　 b. このプログラミングモデルの利点は、　　　　　　　　　(PB13_00440)
　　　 『現代日本語書き言葉均衡コーパス（BCCWJ）』（NINJAL 2011a）より

Cultural borrowingとは異なり、言語内的（language-internal）に「いわれのない」（"gratuitous"）借用（Myers-Scotton 2006: 215）ともいえるcore borrowingの増加は、事実上の「世界の共通語」として拡大を続ける英語の、他言語に対する社会的・経済的優位性を反映しているようにも思われる。文化庁文化部国語課（BBK 2000・2003・2008・2013）や国立国語研究所（NINJAL 2004・2005a）による意識調査の結果では、一般に若年層ほど外来語[4]の受容に寛容であることが明らかにされている。通時コーパスからは、カタカナ語の使

用頻度が、類義の既存語の使用頻度を上回る事例が指摘されている（Kim 2011）。これらの先行研究から、現代日本語語彙において既存語からカタカナ語への置き換えが進んでいると予測できる。本書ではこれを日本語語彙の「カタカナ語化」（diffusion of loanwords）と呼ぶ。

その一方で、日本語におけるカタカナ語の歴史は既存語彙ほど長くなく、「カタカナ語の氾濫」という言葉が示すようにカタカナ語が日本語の「純粋性」を脅かす存在として語られることも少なくない。このことは、日本語がカタカナ語の流入に完全なる無抵抗ではないことを示しており、その普及（diffusion）過程において何らかの社会的要因が作用しているという仮説を立てられる。本書の目的は、こうした日本語語彙の「カタカナ語化」をめぐる言語変化のプロセスを変異理論に基づいて解明することである。この目標を達成するために、以下の問いを設定した。

QUESTIONS
I. 既存語／カタカナ語の語彙交替（lexical alternation）が起こる環境をどう特定するか（語彙交替を変異理論の枠組みでどう扱うかという理論的・方法論的議論を含む）。
II. 既存語／カタカナ語の語彙交替は「言語外的（社会的）」(language-external / social) 要因により制約されているか。制約されているとすればその要因とは何か。
III. カタカナ語使用に対する人々の「意識」（attitude/reported behavior）と「使用実態」（actual behavior）は一致するか。
IV. 「カタカナ語化」は実時間（real time）においてどのように進行しているか。

2 カタカナ語研究の概要と問題点

これまでのカタカナ語研究の主な流れとして挙げておきたいのが、（1）計量的語彙調査、（2）コーパスに基づく個別語彙の研究、（3）社会言語学的意識調査、の3つである。

計量的語彙調査の功績は、主に20世紀の書き言葉において外来語[5]の占める割合が他語種に比べて通時的に増加していること（NINJAL 1987、Hashimoto 2010）、つまり本書でいうところの日本語語彙の「カタカナ語化」が進んでいることを実証的に示したことである（Table 2.4）。

このようなマクロなアプローチに対して、コーパス言語学の分野では、個々のカタカナ語が意味的に対応する既存語と競合しながら日本語に定着していくプロセスを、意味・用法の観点から詳細に記述する試みが続けられている（Miyata 2007、Kim 2011、ほか）。これにより計量的語彙研究が数量的に明らかにした「カタカナ語化」のプロセスを「言語内的」側面から質的に解明することに成功している。しかしながら、このような意味・用法研究においては、カタカナ語と

既存語の「違い」に焦点が当てられることが多いため、「両者がどちらも使える場合になぜ既存語ではなくカタカナ語が選ばれるのか」についての分析・考察は十分とはいえない。この問いに答えるには「言語外的」要因に目を向ける必要がある。

この点を明らかにするのが社会言語学の役割である。20世紀後半になると、文化庁・NHK・国立国語研究所などによりカタカナ語の受容や使用に関する全国意識調査が頻繁に行われた。その結果、調査協力者（informant）のカタカナ語の受容度・理解度に世代・使用場面・職業などによる違いがみられることがわかってきた（Loveday 1996、NINJAL 2004、BBK 2013）。これらの結果は、カタカナ語普及のプロセスには言語外的要因が確かに介在しており、これを勘案することで、「カタカナ語化」をより包括的に解明できることを示唆している。

社会言語学のさらなる課題は、言語変化プロセスを「言語内的」と「言語外的」の両方を含む多変量の（multivariate）要因から説明することである。また、現象と要因の関連を示すだけではなく、統計的手法に基づいて、カタカナ語普及を予測するモデルを提示することも求められている。さらにデータについても、これまで主流であった意識調査にとどまらず、コーパスを援用するなどして「意識」と「使用実態」が一致しているかどうかを検証することも重要である。本書が目指すのは、上述した異なる分野の研究手法を取り入れた領域横断的なアプローチに基づいてこうした課題に取り組むことである。

日本語におけるカタカナ語は、Table 2.3に示すとおり、(I)「インターネット」のように意味の対応する既存語がないもの、(II)「サポート」のように対応する既存語（例えば「支援」・「手助け」）があるもの、(III)「スプーン」のように対応する既存語（例えば「さじ」）はあるが両者の使用範囲にある程度明確な棲み分けが成立している（Jinnouchi 1993）もの、の3種類に分類できる。このうち、本書の主眼となるのは、理論的には、意味が既存語と競合する（II）に属するカタカナ語である。

3 データと分析方法：
変異理論からみる既存語／カタカナ語の交替

意識調査とコーパスの併用

本書で利用するデータは、文化庁・国立国語研究所・NHKなどが過去に実施したカタカナ語に関する複数の全国調査に加え、国立国語研究所が公開している『現代日本語書き言葉均衡コーパス（BCCWJ）』（NINJAL 2011a）と『日本語話し言葉コーパス（CSJ）』（NINJAL & NICT 2004）である。これらのデータを相補的に利用することで、「意識」と「使用実態」の両方をバランスよく観察するとともに、各種データの欠点を補いながら全体としてバランスのとれた分析を目指す。

S字カーブモデルによる言語変化の分析

言語変化はS字カーブの形をとって進行するといわれる（Weinreich, Labov & Herzog 1968、Aitchison 2001）。本書では、ある事象の起こる確率（probability）がS字カーブを描きながら0から1までの値をとる、以下（[Formula 1]）に示す多重ロジスティック回帰モデル（multiple logistic regression model）で分析を進める。

$$\log[p/(1-p)] = a_1x_1 + a_2x_2 + \cdots + a_nx_n + b \qquad \text{[Formula 1]}$$

ここでは、目的変数（dependent variable）を2値（binary）とし、pはカタカナ語変異形が生起する確率、$(1-p)$はそれ以外の変異形（既存語）が生起する確率を示す。このモデルでは複数の要因がカタカナ語の生起（occurrence）に関わることが想定されており、pの値は介在する複数の説明変数x_n（independent variable）の値により変化する。回帰係数a_n（regression coefficient）は説明変数x_nの重み、bは重回帰式の切片（intercept）である。このようなモデル式を利用することにより、目的変数に影響を及ぼす統計的に有意な説明変数を特定するだけでなく、算出した数理モデルを言語変化の予測（prediction）にも活用することができる（Yokoyama & Sanada 2007、Sanada 2008）。

方法論的課題

語彙バリエーション（lexical variation）を変異理論の枠組みで扱う際問題となるのは、異なる語彙間の「等価性」をどう定義するかという点である。Labov（1972）に代表されるように、もともと音韻の分野から発展を遂げてきた変異研究においては、変異形の交替には意味の変化を伴わないこと、すなわち「意味の等価性」（semantic equivalence）が前提とされてきた。このことは、文法などの音韻以外の変異項目を扱う際の問題として度々論じられてきた（Sankoff, G. 1973、Lavandera 1978、Weiner & Labov 1983）が、こと語彙に関してはこれがより深刻な問題となることは想像に難くない。Labov（1978: 8）による、"there are no true synonyms in an absolute sense" ということばから予測できるように、意味的に全く等価な（identical in referential/truth value）（Labov 1972）語群を特定することは理論的に不可能であるし、語彙の多義性を考えると異なる語彙が意味的に等価である範囲を厳密に特定することさえも実際には難しい。しかし、発話スタイル等の制約によって、ある語彙ではなく別の語彙を選択する場面は確かに存在し（Labov 1978）、このような語彙バリエーションの解明が変異研究の領域内にあることは間違いない。そこで、本書では、非音韻系の変異項目を扱う際に「等価性」の定義を「意味的」レベルから「機能的・談話的」（functional/discourse）レベルへと見直した上で適応すべきであるとの立場（Lavandera 1978、Sankoff, D. 1982）から分析を行っている。

　以上を考慮して、第6章では、カタカナ語「ケース」とその既存語「事例」・

「場合」・「例」を取りあげ、コーパスにおける用例をひとつひとつ詳細に吟味した上で、各語彙が一定の等価性を保って使用されるコンテクストを厳密に定義しようと試みている。しかしながら、この手法ではごく限られた数のカタカナ語しか分析できず、一般的傾向を見出すには限界がある。あまりに少ない事例研究から一般的傾向を導くリスクを回避するため、第5章・第8章では、辞書の語義から「同義・類義」と認められる変異形を選び、それぞれが出現する用例の全てを、全変異形が出現しうる「最大限の」("the widest possible")コンテクストとして捉えて分析対象に含めることで、より多くの語彙項目を概観した。この手法は、変異形間の「等価性」が第6章よりも緩やかに定義される点において議論の余地があるものの、第5章ではカタカナ語の生起に影響を及ぼす言語外的要因について一定の傾向をつかむことにある程度成功している。

4 年齢差:
見かけ時間上のカタカナ語分布(意識調査)

本章では、「見かけ時間」(apparent time)の概念に基づき、年齢(生年)(age / year of birth)という言語外的要因からカタカナ語の普及プロセスを概観した。さらに、変化はS字カーブを描いて進行していくという仮定に基づき、日本語話者の意識上の「カタカナ語化」がどのように進んでいくかを年齢(生年)から予測するS字カーブモデルを構築した。

「見かけ時間」という概念が有用なのは、年齢差を「見かけ上の」時間の差とみなすことによって一度の調査で観察される世代分布から変化の有無・方向(direction)・速度(rate)を予測できるからである。このとき、「言語形成期までに習得された言語記憶は、生涯にわたってあまり変わらない」という「言語形成期仮説」(Apparent-Time Hypothesis)に基づき、年齢による分布の傾き(age gradient)を変化の速度とみなすことができる。

分析に利用したのは、文化庁(BBK 1999・2000)と国立国語研究所(NINJAL 2004・2005a)がいずれも2000年前後に実施した4つの全国意識調査である。これらの調査から、同じ意味を表すカタカナ語と既存語からなる語彙群があるときに、どちらをよく使うか・どちらに慣れ親しんでいるかを問う項目を集めた。分析対象となったカタカナ語は Table 4.2 に掲げた17語である。

分析の結果、見かけ時間上の「カタカナ語化」のパターンは、(1)「スーツ」や「ワイン」などのように、年齢が下がるにつれてカタカナ語の選択率が単純増加のS字カーブを描くタイプ(Figure 4.2・Figure 4.3)と、(2)「リスク」や「ニーズ」などのように、一定までS字増加した後、最若年層である10代・20代で若干減少するタイプ(Figure 4.4・Figure 4.5)があった。(2)の語彙グループにおいて観察された最若年層における「カタカナ語化」の遅れは、言語共同体が将来的に「脱カタカナ語化」に向かうことを意味するものではなく、この世代における言語習得上の要因に起因するものと考えられる。よって、この遅れを「習得上の要因」(acquisition)という撹乱要因(disruptive factor)として変数

化し、予測の際に排除することで年齢（生年）のみの効果を抽出できるようにした。この手続きにより、(2) の語彙グループの変化速度の過小評価を防ぎ、より正確な変化予測が行えることを示した（Figure 4.13）。

5 年齢以外の言語外的要因：
性別・学歴・レジスター・発話スタイル（コーパス調査）

本章では、BCCWJ（NINJAL 2011a）と CSJ（NINJAL & NICT 2004）の 2 種類のコーパスを利用して、年齢やそれ以外の言語外的諸要因と、カタカナ語の生起との関連を要因ごとに検定した（Table 5.10）。調査対象となったのは、Table 5.5 に掲げる、BCCWJ から選出した 25 の高頻度カタカナ語とその既存語である。

　まず、年齢とカタカナ語使用の関連は半数近くの語彙項目に認められ、若年層ほどカタカナ語生起率が高い傾向にあった（BCCWJ のみ）。この結果から、これまで主に意識調査の範囲内で明らかにされてきた年齢による差（age differentiation）が、使用実態の側面においても存在することが確認された。

　さらに年齢以外の言語外的要因についても検討を行った結果、概観ではあるものの、一定程度の関連と傾向が認められた。性差（gender）については顕著な傾向がみられなかったものの、学歴（education）との関連を示した語彙項目は少なくなく、大学院修了グループ（GRAD）は大学卒グループ（up to UNIV）よりもカタカナ語使用を抑制する傾向にあることが判明した（BCCWJ・CSJ）。さらに、レジスター（register）については、BCCWJ では雑誌（PM）よりも書籍（PB）においてカタカナ語使用率が低い傾向がみられ、この差が（例えば「では」に対する縮約形「じゃ」の多少に反映されるような）両媒体のテキストの改まり度に起因する可能性を指摘した。一方、CSJ では模擬講演（SPS）よりも学会講演（APS）においてカタカナ語使用率が低い傾向にあった。その他、(1) 発話の自発性（spontaneity）が低いほど、(2) 発話スタイル（formality）が高いほど、(3) 聴衆の規模（audience size）が大きいほど、カタカナ語が生起しにくい傾向にあった。ただし CSJ のレジスター（SPS/APS）は他のいくつかの説明変数（学歴、聴衆の規模）とやや高い相関があることから、解釈に注意が必要である。

6 言語内的・外的要因を含む多変量モデルの構築：
「ケース」の場合（コーパス調査）

本章では、「ケース」とその既存語「事例」・「場合」・「例」を語彙交替の代表事例として取り上げ、そのしくみを言語内的要因と言語外的要因の両方から予測する多変量モデルを構築した（引き続き BCCWJ と CSJ を利用）。このカタカナ語を選んだ理由は、(1) 先行研究において使用頻度の経年増加が確認されている

こと（Hashimoto 2010: 52、Kim 2011）、（2）前章で分析対象となったカタカナ語の中で最も用例数が多いこと（Table 5.6）、（3）前章でみたカタカナ語の生起率と言語外的要因との関連性において、他の調査対象語の示す一般的傾向とこの語の示す傾向がおおむね一致していること、（4）この語と既存語の「等価性」を判断するにあたり参照できる詳細な意味研究（Kim 2011）が存在すること、である。

　前章よりも厳密な分析を行うため、まずは「ケース」に関する先行研究（Kim 2011）に基づき、語彙交替が可能なコンテクスト（envelope of variation / variable context）を限定した。その上で、語彙交替に寄与しうる言語内的要因を選択し、前章で検討した言語外的要因と併せて多変量解析（multivariate analysis）を行った（Table 6.12・Table 6.24）。

　その結果、言語内的要因として、当該変異形の出現する統語構造（structure）（BCCWJのみ）と共起述語（co-occurring predicate）（BCCWJ・CSJ）の2つが寄与することが判明した。「ケース」が生起しやすい環境は、（1）「超過債務でも認められたケースがある」のように「連体修飾節構造における同格名詞」[6]（Kim 2011）として機能する場合と、（2）「多い・少ない」、「増える・減る」、「起きる」のような、「多少」・「増減」・「生起」を表す述語と共起する場合[7]であった。

　言語外的要因としては、生年（年齢）・学歴・レジスター・発話の自発性などがカタカナ語の生起に寄与することが判明した。BCCWJでは、若年層（1960–70年代生まれ）において「ケース」の生起率が有意に高いことから、既存語からカタカナ語への語彙の置き換えが進行していることが示唆された。また、カタカナ語の生起率は大学院修了グループ（GRAD）において、また第5章で指摘したとおり雑誌（PM）よりも文体の改まった媒体として特徴づけられる書籍（PB）において有意に低いことがわかった。CSJにおいては、模擬講演（SPS）よりも高い発話スタイルの学会講演（APS）でカタカナ語の生起率が低かった。さらに、学会講演の中では発話の自発性による生起率の違いがみられ、自発性の低い発話（Low Spontaneity）においてカタカナ語の生起率が下がることも確認された（Figure 6.8）。

　以上から、「ケース」のように定着度が高く「基本語化」（Kim 2011）したとみなされるカタカナ語も、言語使用者の属性、レジスター、発話スタイルといった複数の言語外的要因に制約を受けて選択的に使用されていると結論付けた。

7 語彙選択に係るスタイルの制約：
「サポート」の場合（意識調査）

世代などの社会的属性間の差異に注目した「話者間バリエーション」（inter-speaker variation）に対して、「話者内バリエーション」（intra-speaker variation）は「スタイル」（style）に起因する個人内におけることばの使い分けに着目する。Inoue（2000）は、地域社会の言語的構成が複雑で使い分けが行われて

いる場合は、場面によって変化の進行速度が異なることを指摘し、変異形の普及度を時間と場面差から3次元（水槽型）のグラフで捉える「水槽モデル」を提案している。

　そこで、本章では、前章で概観したスタイルの影響をさらに深く掘り下げるため、「サポート」とその既存語である「支援」・「手助け」を事例として取り上げ、カタカナ語が生起するメカニズムを主にスタイルの観点から明らかにした。使用したデータは、NINJAL（2005a）の場面による語種の使い分けに関する項目である。調査協力者には、「新しく農業を始めるには、地域の（　　　）が必要です。」という文脈を提示した上で、「友達同士で話すとき」（Friends）、「大勢の人の前で話すとき」（Public）においてどの語彙を選択するかを尋ねたものである。

　多変量解析の結果、カタカナ語の生起は生年・学歴・スタイルという3つの説明変数から予測できることが判明した（Table 7.8）。ただし、スタイルは学歴と交互作用（interaction）をなして複雑な形でカタカナ語の生起に影響を与えていることがわかった。すなわち中卒（JHS）・高卒（HS）グループとは異なり、大学卒（UNIV）グループのみがスタイルに応じてカタカナ語を選択的に使用しており、「友達同士で話すとき」よりも「大勢の人の前で話すとき」にカタカナ語使用を抑制する傾向があった（Figure 7.9）。以上のようなスタイル差を取り入れた言語変化の「水槽モデル」がFigure 7.10に示す3次元グラフである。このような数理モデルを用いることの利点は、「確率予測の道具立て」（Yokoyama & Sanada 2007）としてデータ不足により分析対象から除外された世代のデータや、未来の世代についても予測値を算出できるところにある（Figure 7.8）。

　続いて、スタイル差を生じさせるメカニズムのうち、数理モデルでは捉えきれない部分について質的分析を行った。発話場面が「友達同士で話すとき」から「大勢の人の前で話すとき」へシフトするときに語彙の切り替え（word-switching）が生じた場合、「カタカナ語から既存語へ」（from LW to non-LW）の切り替えが「既存語からカタカナ語へ」（from non-LW to LW）の切り替えよりも多かった。そこで、「友達同士で話すとき」にカタカナ語を選択したグループのうち、場面がシフトした結果既存語への切り替えを行ったグループの「大勢の人の前で話すとき」における語彙選択の理由を、行わなかったグループのそれと比較した。その結果、調査協力者は主に（1）「知的」（intelligent）・「格調高い」（dignified）といった評価に象徴される漢語のもつ社会的威信（prestige）の高さに着目している場合と、（2）「分かりやすい」（easy）・「正確」（precise）といった漢語への評価や「分かりやすい」・「やわらかい」（colloquial）といった和語への評価に象徴される、既存語のもつ聞き手への伝わりやすさに着目している場合のあることが明らかになった。このことは、言い換えれば、カタカナ語が漢語に比べて社会的威信の高さにおいて、あるいは和語・漢語に比べて伝わりやすさにおいて、「大勢の人の前で話すとき」に使う語として評価が低かったことのあらわれである。

　「知的」や「格調高い」といった評価がことばの社会的威信と結びつくとの前提に立てば、不特定多数の人々に向き合う発話場面の相対的な改まり度の高さが、社会的威信の高い漢語への切り替えを生じさせたと考えられ、スタイル差が発話

に対する注意の度合いにより生じたことを示している（発話意識モデル/
Attention to Speech Model）（Labov 1972）。一方で、この切り替えは、不特定
多数の面前で自分をそのように見せたいという話者自身の意識のあらわれとも考
えられるため、同時に「話者デザインモデル」（Speaker Design Model）
（Schilling-Estes 2002）からの解釈も可能になる。また、不特定多数の人々の前
では「分かりやすい」・「やわらかい」といった聞き手への伝わりやすさを重視し
て既存語を選択した人がいたことは、スタイル差が聞き手への反応により生じた
ことを示唆している（聴衆デザインモデル/ Audience Design Model）（Bell
1984）。これらのことから、一見改まり度によって対比されがちな両発話スタイ
ルの差が、複数のモデルから多面的かつ複合的に解釈できることを示した。
　以上、バリエーション分析にスタイルを組み入れ、量的かつ質的に吟味するこ
とが、カタカナ語生起の細かなプロセスを解明・予測する上で有益であることを
示した。

8　実時間に基づくカタカナ語分布の変化予測：
「言語形成期仮説」再考

第4章でみたとおり、「見かけ時間」の概念は、一度の調査データから言語変化
の存在を突き止めるのに有用である（Sankoff, G. 2006）。しかしながら、この
方法論に限界のあることもしばしば議論されている。1つ目の論点は、世代差と
いうものが、加齢による個人内の言語体系の変化（age-grading）のあらわれに
過ぎない可能性があるため、言語共同体全体が変化していることを決定づける絶
対的根拠とはならないことである。2つ目の論点は、個人の言語記憶が（「言語
形成期仮説」に反して）言語形成期以降にも変わりうるため、見かけ時間に基づ
く変化速度の予測が正確でない場合[8]があるということである。中でも、個人の
語彙体系は音韻などの言語形式に比べて言語形成期以降も影響を受けやすいと考
えられるため、特に留意が必要である。以上を考慮するに、言語変化の方向や速
度をより正確に予測するためには「実時間」研究が不可欠である。
　そこで、本章では、意識調査とコーパスの実時間データから、（1）見かけ時
間上で確認された「カタカナ語化」が共同体全体の変化を伴っているかどうか
（variability of the community）、（2）「カタカナ語化」に関わる人々の意識や語
の使用実態に経年による個人内変化が認められるかどうか（variability of the
individual speakers）、の2点について検証を行った。調査項目は8項目で、（1）
個別語彙5項目[9]の受容度・使用度に加え、（2）コーパス全体（BCCWJ）に占
める外来語[10]の割合、（3）カタカナ語使用全般について問う2つの意識調査項
目[11]を扱った。その結果、全ての項目で若年層ほどカタカナ語を受容・使用し
ていることがわかり、「カタカナ語化」が進行している「可能性」を示した。

経年による共同体全体の変化の有無

続いて、年齢を固定して調査年（year of survey）の効果を調べたところ、8項目のうち7項目において、各年齢層におけるカタカナ語の受容度・使用度が、調査年が新しくなるにつれて高まっていることが確認されたため、共同体全体として「カタカナ語化」は確かに進行中（in progress）であると結論付けた（Table 8.6）。ところが残り1項目は、調査年が新しくなるにつれて共同体全体が「脱カタカナ語化」に向かっており、年齢差から予測されたものとは逆の方向に共同体が変化していることが明らかになった。

経年による個人内変化の有無

さらに、生年を固定して調査年の効果を調べたところ、8項目中4項目において効果が認められなかった（Table 8.7）。これはつまり、経年（加齢や調査年）による個人内変化が起きていないことを示しており、「言語形成期仮説」の有用性を裏付ける結果となった。しかし残り4項目については、（1）調査年が新しくなるにつれて個人が言語共同体の向かう変化と同じ方向に変化した結果、見かけ時間に基づく予測よりも「カタカナ語化」が加速される場合（accelerated change）と、（2）調査年が新しくなるにつれて個人が言語共同体の向かう変化とは逆の方向に変化した結果、見かけ時間に基づく予測よりも「カタカナ語化」が減速される場合（decelerated change）、さらには（3）見かけ時間に基づく予測とは逆方向に変化が進む場合（reversed change）が確認された（Table 8.8）。

　つまり、「言語形成期仮説」に基づく予測は、変化の「速度」や「方向」を見誤る危険性を孕んでおり、変化予測の精度向上を目指すには経年（加齢や調査年）による個人内変化を勘案できる実時間データの検証が不可欠であると結論付けた。

9　まとめと今後の展望

本書は、同じ意味を表すカタカナ語と既存語の交替を語彙バリエーションの現象と捉え、意識調査とコーパスを利用してそのプロセスの実証的な解明を試みたものである。年齢（第4章）に加え、学歴・レジスター・スタイルなどの複数の言語外的（社会的）要因がカタカナ語の普及に関わっていることを明らかにした（第5章・第7章）ほか、言語内的要因と併せてより包括的かつ詳細な「カタカナ語化」の予測モデルを示した（第6章）。また、見かけ時間によるアプローチの問題点に対処するべく、（限られた範囲ではあるが）実時間データを利用して変化の方向と速度に関する予測精度の改善を試みた（第8章）。

　本書は、現代日本語における語彙交替現象を変異研究の枠組みで分析する可能性を示した点で、変異理論に寄与するものとして位置づけられる。今後、より多様な言語内的・外的要因について検討することや、より自然な発話が観察できる

他のコーパスを調査すること、あるいは似たような語彙体系を有するものの社会言語学的背景が異なると想定される他の言語（韓国語など）における借用語彙の使用実態を観察することにより、理論の精緻化が可能となるだろう。

　外国語からの語彙借用は、言語接触が生じている状況においては普遍的な現象である。例えば、英語史上最もよく知られる事例として、ノーマン・コンクエスト（11世紀）以降の英語語彙の「フランス語化」が挙げられる。一般的に、語彙借用とその受容の過程では、受け入れ言語が言語内的・外的諸要因の影響を受けて多彩で重層的な様相を見せながら変容していることが予測される。本書では、カタカナ語使用に社会的属性による差や、場面に応じた使い分けがみられたことから、日本語が無制限に外国語からの借用語彙を受容しているのではなく、いくつもの社会的要因に影響を受けながら複雑な形で変化を遂げていることが明らかになった。本書で扱った、外国語からの借用語／既存語の競合と、それに伴う語彙体系の変容、あるいはその社会言語学的メカニズムは、人的交流や接触が増大していく現代において、多くの言語にとって重要な問題であり、これからも関心の高い問題でありつづけるだろう。本書がそれを解明する一助となれば幸いである。

Notes

1 第4章・第6章・第7章の日本語要約は、それぞれ Kuya（2016b）・Kuya（2013b）・Kuya（2016a）を部分的に参照している。

2 西欧諸語以外からの借用語（例「ダルマ／達磨」）や、擬音語・擬態語（例「キラキラ／きらきら」）などのカタカナ表記を除く。

3 和語（Native Japanese words / NJ words）と古くに土着化した漢語（Sino-Japanese words / SJ words）を含む。

4 ここでは「外来語」が本書における「カタカナ語」とほぼ同義で使われている。現代日本語においては「外来語」が主に（1）「西欧諸語からの借用語」を指す場合が多いが、歴史言語学的視点からはより広範囲に（2）「（1）と西欧諸語以外からの借用語」を意味したり、さらに広範囲に（3）「（2）と中国語からの借用語（漢語）」を指したりすることもできる。本書の日本語要約では、このような混乱を避けるために、（1）の意味での「外来語」を「カタカナ語」と表現することとした。本文（英文）ではこれに対応する語として（Western）loanwords / LW を使用している。

5 ここでの「外来語」は、「和語」・「漢語」に対する語種としての区分であり、西欧諸語からの借用語（本書での「カタカナ語」）に加え西欧諸語以外からの若干の借用語も含む。

6 本書では gap-less relative clause head（gap-less RCH）とした。

7 分析では「ある・ない」のような「有無」の述語をレファレンスカテゴリーとした。

8 見かけ時間を利用した予測よりも実際の言語変化の速度が速い事例（Pope, Meyerhoff & Ladd 2007）や遅い事例（Yokoyama & Sanada 2010）が報告されている。

9 「ワイン」・「オープンする」（NHK 1980・1996、BBK 2000）と、「ケース」・「サポート」・「シンプル」（BCCWJ）の5項目。

10 BCCWJにおける「外来語」は、「和語」・「漢語」に対する語種としての区分であり、西欧諸語からの借用語（本書での「カタカナ語」）に加え西欧諸語以外からの若干の借用語も含む。

11 「カタカナ語を使うことについてどう思うか」（現状）（NSDKK 1977、BBK 2000・2003・2008・2013）と、「今後、今以上にカタカナ語が増加することについてどう思うか」（将来）（BBK 1995、NINJAL 2004）の2項目。

Index

A
Academic Presentation Speech (APS) 26
accelerated change 154, 155, 160
acceleration 138, 139, 152
actual (linguistic) behavior(s) 6, 27, 156, 160
actuation problem 7, 161
age differentiation(s) 4, 139
age gradient 35, 137
age-grading 45, 53, 54, 137, 139, 158
apparent time 25, 30, 35, 137, 138
apparent-time approach(es) 5, 35, 36, 138
apparent-time hypothesis 35, 138, 160
Attention to Speech Model 114, 132
attitude(s) 7, 156, 160
Audience Design Model 114, 133
audience size 78

B
BCCWJ 24, 27
binary 30

C
calques 13, 15
change in progress 35, 139
coefficient of determination 31
constant 47
copula 9
core borrowing 1, 2, 3, 16
crossover pattern 115, 126
CSJ 25, 28
cultural borrowing(s) 1, 2, 16, 22, 62

D
decelerated change 138, 155, 160
deceleration 139, 153, 155

degree of freedom (df) 111
dependent variable 29, 30
diachronic corpus 25
discourse equivalence 32
disruptive factor/effect 46, 147

E
envelope of variation 4, 85
Exp(B) 111

F
fixed-length data 25
flood of Western loanwords 19
formality 114, 117
Formality (in CSJ) 26, 77
formality of a text 71
functional equivalence 32

G
gairaigo 1, 9
gap-less relative clause 86, 92
Gap-less Relative Clause Head (Gap-less RCH) 94
generational change 139, 154
goodness of fit 31

H
hiragana 9, 22, 62, 83
homophonic translations 14, 16
hybrid (HB) 22

I
independent variable 30
interaction 115, 124
interaction term 100, 106
intercept 30, 111
intra-speaker variation 114

K

kango 3, 9
kanji 9, 83
katakana 9, 22, 62, 83
katakanago 1, 9
konshugo/konseigo 22

L

language-external 3, 18, 21, 158
language-internal 18, 163
lexical borrowings 1, 3
Library Book sub-corpus (LB) 24, 28
life-long memory 138
lifespan change 138, 139, 154
light verb 9
linguistic variable 32
loan translations 13, 16
loanword(s) (LW) 7, 9, 10

M

Mere Exposure Effect 155
multicollinearity 54
multiple logistic regression model 29
multivariate analysis 100

N

native Japanese words 3, 9
native words 11
negative coefficient 30
NJ words 9, 10
non-loanwords (non-LWs) 11

O

observer's effect 27

P

PB 24
PM 24
PN 24
positive coefficient 30
prediction 29, 49

probability 29, 30
Publication sub-corpus 24

R

R^2 31
real time 25, 28, 31, 35, 138
reference category(-ries) 101, 111
registers 27, 28
regression coefficient (B) 30, 47
reported behavior 7, 160
reversed change 145, 147, 153, 160

S

s-curve 28
self-reports 7, 27
semantic equivalence 32
Simulated Public Speech (SPS) 26
Sino-Japanese words 3, 9, 159
SJ words 9, 10
Speaker Design Model 114, 133
Special-purpose sub-corpus 24
speech styles 114
Spontaneity (in CSJ) 26, 76
standardization 137
style 114, 117
stylistic variation 32, 114
synchronic corpus 25

T

token 17
type 17

V

variability of the community 31, 143
variability of the individual
  speakers 31, 148
variable-length data 25
variant(s) 3, 4, 30, 32
variationist 3, 19, 162
VIF 54

W

wago   3, 9

Wald   111

Water Tank Model   113, 133

Western loanwords   1, 11

word-switching   127

久屋愛実（くや あいみ）

略歴
松山大学人文学部英語英米文学科講師（社会言語学および英語担当）。九州大学文学部（社会学専攻）在学中に韓国ソウル大学へ交換留学したことを機に、ことばと社会との関係性に興味を持つ。卒業後は言語学を学ぶために英国オックスフォード大学大学院へ進学し、社会言語学の道へ。2011年修士号、2017年博士号取得。主な研究テーマは言語変異・言語変化。

Aimi Kuya is Lecturer in Sociolinguistics and English at Matsuyama University, Japan. She developed her interest in the relationship between language and society during a year as an exchange student at Seoul National University in South Korea, when she was studying Sociology for a B.A. at Kyushu University, Japan. She read Linguistics for her M.Phil. and D.Phil. (Ph. D.) at the University of Oxford, UK. Her current research interests include language variation and change.

主な論文
・「Belfast 英語における平叙文と平叙疑問文の文末上昇調にみられる音響的差異―コーパスを利用したイントネーション研究」『英語コーパス研究』第23号（2016）

Hituzi Linguistics in English No.30
The Diffusion
of Western Loanwords
in Contemporary Japanese
A Variationist Approach

発行	2019年2月8日 初版1刷
定価	12600円＋税
著者	©久屋愛実
発行者	松本功
ブックデザイン	白井敬尚形成事務所
印刷所	株式会社 ディグ
製本所	株式会社 星共社
発行所	株式会社 ひつじ書房

〒112-0011 東京都文京区
千石2-1-2 大和ビル2F
Tel: 03-5319-4916
Fax: 03-5319-4917
郵便振替00120-8-142852
toiawase@hituzi.co.jp
http://www.hituzi.co.jp/
ISBN978-4-89476-949-6

造本には充分注意しておりますが、
落丁・乱丁などがございましたら、
小社かお買上げ書店にて
おとりかえいたします。
ご意見、ご感想など、小社まで
お寄せ下されば幸いです。

刊行のご案内

ひつじ研究叢書（言語編）

第 127 巻　コーパスと日本語史研究
近藤泰弘・田中牧郎・小木曽智信 編　定価 6,800 円＋税

シリーズ社会言語科学

2　社会言語科学の源流を追う
横山詔一・杉戸清樹・佐藤和之・米田正人・前田忠彦・阿部貴人 編
定価 3,900 円＋税

Hituzi Language Studies

No. 1　Relational Practice in Meeting Discourse in
New Zealand and Japan
村田和代 著　定価 6,000 円＋税